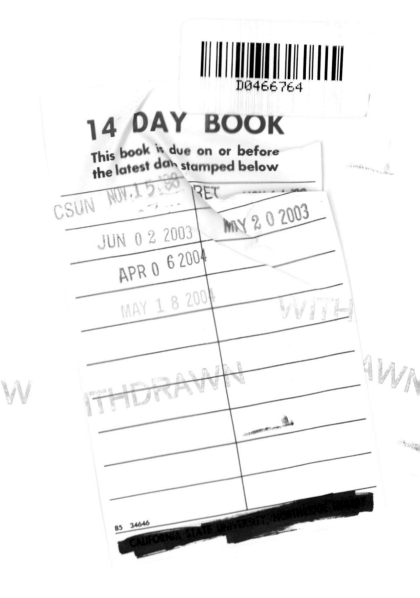

RENAISSANCE DRAMA

New Series XXV   1994

Renaissance Drama

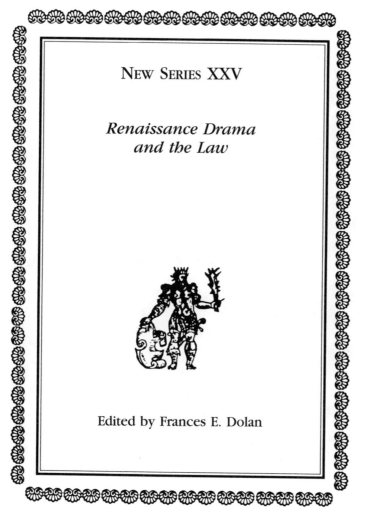

New Series XXV

Renaissance Drama and the Law

Edited by Frances E. Dolan

Northwestern University Press and

The Newberry Library Center for Renaissance Studies

Evanston 1994

Editorial Note

R*ENAISSANCE* D*RAMA*, an annual publication, is devoted to understanding the drama as a central feature of Renaissance culture. Coverage, so far as subject matter is concerned, is not restricted to any single geographical area. The chronological limits of the Renaissance are interpreted broadly. Essays are encouraged that explore the relationship of Renaissance dramatic traditions to their precursors and successors; have an interdisciplinary orientation; explore the relationship of the drama to society and history; and examine the impact of new forms of interpretation on the study of Renaissance plays.

The essays in Volume XXV (1994), "Renaissance Drama and the Law," explore a range of relationships among Renaissance drama and legal texts, controversies, and trials in sixteenth- and seventeenth-century England. This volume has been guest edited with thoughtfulness and imagination by Frances E. Dolan. She is grateful to members of the Editorial Committee. Editorial Assistant Emily Detmer contributed organizational skill and scholarly advice. Special thanks are due to Manuscript Editor Alma A. MacDougall for her diligence and care.

For Volume XXVI (1995), we are seeking essays concerned with any topic related to Renaissance drama. Submissions are due on February1, 1996.

Renaissance Drama conforms to the stylistic conventions outlined in the most recent *MLA Style Manual*. Scholars preparing manuscripts for submission should refer to this book. In order to be returned, manuscripts should be submitted with stamped, self-addressed envelopes. Submissions and inquiries regarding future volumes should be addressed to Mary Beth Rose, Editor, *Renaissance Drama*, The Newberry Library, 60 West Walton Street, Chicago, Illinois 60610.

Mary Beth Rose
Editor

Contents

RENAISSANCE DRAMA

New Series XXV   1994

Female Fidelities on Trial: Proof in the Howard Attainder and Cymbeline

KAREN CUNNINGHAM

ONVENTIONALLY, trial records claimed to be transparent conduits to a re-vealed truth isolated from the operations of fiction-making. In contrast, drama was implicitly denied claims to truth-telling in such formulations as Sidney's that the poet "nothing affirms" (155). Recent scholarship in literary and legal studies, however, has begun to explore a wide range of relationships between early modern legal events and the drama, emphasizing the ways these disciplines theatricalize legal performance, represent justice on their respective scaffolds, and criminalize members of a particular class or gender. Yet although many studies explore the cultural effects of courtroom and stage narratives and their roles in fashioning subjectivities, few have focused on the forms of persuasion operating within these texts.[1] In a series of recent essays, however, Patricia Parker has identified a pervasive early modern judicial and theatrical challenge, that of providing a credible story: "The obsessively staged desire to see or spy out secrets," writes Parker,

or in the absence of the directly ocular, to extract a narrative that might provide a vicarious substitute . . . implicates both *show* and *tell*, eye and ear, in the broader sixteenth- and early seventeenth-century problem of testimony and report, . . . a theatrical problem shared by the law courts and other contestatory sites of epistemological certainty and "evidence," of what might be reliably substituted for what could not be directly witnessed. ("*Othello*" 84)

1

Law courts and theatrical venues employ what Parker provocatively calls the "motivated rhetorics" of gender, order, and rule that are rooted in a tradition as least as ancient as Cicero and Quintilian.[2] These "motivated" verbal strategies "point not only to the new social mobility" of the early modern era—a social mobility often registered, as Barbara Correll has shown, in terms of gender anxieties (242)—but also "to rhetoric itself as an instrument of civil order, crucial to the repair of civilization after the Fall" (Parker, *Literary* 97).[3]

In this essay I would like to focus on the narrative and rhetorical strategies necessary to the provisions of proof in two distinct but related instances, the former in some detail, the latter more briefly. The first case is drawn from the annals of legal history, the second from the stages of dramatic representation: Katherine Howard's attainder for treason in 1542 and Imogen's metaphorical trial for promiscuity in Shakespeare's *Cymbeline* (c. 1608–10). Both tales turn on the sexually marked issue of female "incontinency," conjuring and containing a wayward female within the discipline of legal and legalistic rituals. Yet whereas the Howard attainder makes its truth-claims by doing what the law characteristically does, suppressing the notion that proof is something made, *Cymbeline* claims its truth through what appears to be the opposite strategy: it wears its status as a simulation on its sleeve, aggressively destabilizing the quasi-legal fictions that generate the "unfaithful woman." When a penitent Iachimo belatedly confesses to having produced only "simular proof" of Imogen's infidelity, he is not only clearing his own character but explicating one of the play's central points: proof is a feigned, mimetic version of things whose believers are, at best, victims of folly. Both the attainder and the play foreground uncertainties characteristic of early modern English struggles with the relations among epistemology, theatricality, and truth, and both formulate those uncertainties in terms of a dualism between women's apparent and secret fidelities.

I
Imagining Treason

In the Howard attainder, productions of proof take place in the context of a particular kind of crime, one of the imagination. When Edward III redefined treason in 1352 (25 Edw. III st. 5 c. 2) from behavior to thought, he extended a monarch's rule over even the "imaginings" of subjects: it became treason "to compass or imagine the death of the king, his queen or the royal heir" (Bellamy 9). As John Bellamy has shown, aside from offenses based on levying war, under the Tudors "indictments concerned with 'imagining' were dominant" (11). The instability of the category lent itself to royal manipulation, so that even wishes, words, and writings that could be construed as indirectly malicious resulted in guilty verdicts (Bellamy 10–11). By extending treason to "imaginings," Edward III had opened up the category of "constructive" or "presumptive" treason, under which most anything could become evidence of traitorous intent.[4] Further, he had created the legal space for new conceptions of patriotic or treasonous character, the former founded on an ideal of intellectual and emotional unity, the latter on a notion of subjective dualism. The true citizen of England was the loyal, integrated subject whose imaginings issued directly in "honest" and observable actions; the traitor was a dis-integrated dissembler whose behavior was not to be taken at face value but as a mask for a buried, criminal self, in which "rank corruption, mining all within / Infects unseen" (*Hamlet* 3.4.152–53). Whether cast in terms of contests between madness and reason, personal conscience and public confession, or an inward and an outer self, the errant history of treason trials is also a history of split subjectivity.[5] This perceived proliferation of selves was cause enough for legal intervention: the law claimed the territory of "imaginings" as its open field of investigation.

Defined as transgressive imagining, treason necessarily encounters the problem and affords itself the privilege of characterizing and exposing a subject's secret interior. And what a trial set out to prove it also presupposed and produced: the self-estrangement of the defendant. The task of trial participants was to overcome the obstacle of invisible action—in Edward Coke's terms, to "make [the crime] appear to the world" (Stephen 53) as self-declaring in two senses: it must appear so obvious as to seem irrefutable, and it must reveal a hidden self that was both different from the observable self and against the law. What counted as persuasive evidence in a particular trial or from one trial to another was variable and unpredictable, and was argued again and again during proceedings. In the Babington trials (1586), for example, a centerpiece of conflict was the authority of precedents and presence of witnesses; in the Queen of Scots trial (1586), it was the authenticity and authority of a packet of cryptic letters; and in the Ralegh trial (1603), it was the legitimacy of words as evidence. In every case the means of making the crime appear were rhetorical, and proof was contingent on the effective use of language in a particular situation. Yet the truth-value of speech was itself uncertain, and although some legal theorists continued to assume its authority in revealing the heart—Sir Thomas Egerton pronounced during the Babington trials that "Whoso is guiltless will speak truly and directly, but the counterfeit must speak untruths" (Cobbett 1145)—other lawyers typically assumed that there was a gap between the speech of the accused and a truth embedded in his deviant heart, and proceeded to create suspicion by emphasizing the difficulty of knowing whether one spoke truly or untruly.

Trial records deal with this epistemological uncertainty by adopting a strategy of revelation, suppressing human fabrication under the agency of divine will or unpredictable chance. The legal "truth" they represent, however, is constituted in language and rests on the sort of equivocal base formulated by Thomas Hobbes: "*True* and *False* are attributes of Speech, not of Things. And where Speech is not, there is neither *Truth* nor *Falshood*. *Errour* there may be . . ." (105). Within this thoroughly rhetoricized framework, appeals to "what really happened" are no more or less persuasive in themselves than any other linguistic maneuvers.[6]

II
Misusing Her Body

What could Katherine Howard have thought that chilly afternoon in October 1541 as she and her husband, Henry VIII, returned to Hampton Court after a progress to the north that had lasted three months? Perhaps she had hoped to console Henry, who arrived to find his son seriously ill with fever. Perhaps she had hoped to repair her relations with an anxious group of Protestant reformers, led by Archbishop Cranmer, who feared she might return the nation to papal dominance. Perhaps, worn down by the bad weather and tensions of the journey, she simply hoped to rest. Howard's own voice on these events remains elusive, lost to the historical convention of not recording women's words. Whatever her own intentions, the longed-for respite quickly culminated in the event that shaped the remainder of her short life: her attainder for treason. A brief entry in Charles Wriothesley's chronicle of 1541 reads:

This yeare, the 13th daye of November, Sir Thomas Wriothesley, knight, and Secretary to the Kinge, came to Hampton Court to the Quene, and called all the ladies and gentlewomen and her servauntes into the Great Chamber, and there openlye afore them declared certeine offences that she had done in misusing her bodye with certeine persons afore the Kinges tyme. . . . (130–31)

Initially indicted for the crime, which would have entailed a trial, Howard was ultimately attainted of treason by an act of Parliament, which evaded both the need for court appearances and the possibility of public resistance.[7]

Why did the law take an interest in Howard? The modes of explanation are less personal than national. The fourth of Henry's six wives, and a well-connected niece of the Norfolks, Howard was a pawn in a high-stakes game of political dominance between partisans of reform and revolution on one side and religious and political conservatism on the other. Representing reform and revolution, Thomas Cromwell, the king's vicar-general, had gained influence over Henry by finding the means of Henry's divorcing Catherine of Aragon and marrying Anne Boleyn, and by subsequently bringing about the Cleves marriage. On the side of the ancient prerogatives of the nobility and of Catholicism without a pope, Stephen Gardiner, bishop of Winchester, and his ally, the duke of Norfolk (Howard's uncle), were working diligently behind the scenes for a return to the old orthodoxy and the institution of a new wife to replace the Protestant Anne of Cleves; Howard was their candidate.[8] Howard first became important to the realm not as a criminal, but as a vehicle for averting political crisis and stabilizing local political alignments. Her nation, here identified with feudal leanings and conservative ancient prerogatives, had need of her.

Less than two years after her marriage in 1540, Howard found herself charged with treason. The initial claims against her depended on two issues: her having engaged in sexual activity some years earlier with Henry Mannock, who is identified in all the historical accounts as having taught her the virginals, and her having engaged in sexual activity and having contracted marriage with Francis Dereham. Relatively late in the investigations a third lover was named, Howard's distant cousin, Thomas Culpeper, for whom it was rumored she had finally cast off Dereham and to whom it was also rumored she had been affianced (Hume 375–84). It was alleged against Culpeper that he had held secret, illicit meetings with the queen, who had "incited him to have intercourse with her, and insinuated to him that she loved him better than the King and all others" (qtd. in Hume 384).

The crown contended that Howard had "offended in incontinency": under the Act of Succession used to convict Anne Boleyn in 1536, she had slandered her children and the succession by engaging in sexual activity with anyone other than the king (Thomas 43). But whereas the Boleyn treason was founded on adultery during the marriage, the Howard attainder addressed *pre*-marital behavior. There was no law—or rather, there had not yet been a construction of treason—that made female sexual activity itself traitorous. Howard was attainted, then, illegally, outside any law. Her attainder marks a distinct moment in the early modern discourses of female sexuality when a woman's premarital sexuality becomes legally identified with her marital sexuality. Ironically, after her conviction, the same Parliament that made her a traitor made the laws that criminalized her.[9]

Here is the official version of the story:

While the King's Majesty was in his Progress, one John Lassells came to the . . . Archbishop of Canterbury, and declared unto him that he had been with a sister of his married in Sussex, which sometimes had been servant with the old Duchess of Norfolk, who did also bring up the said Mistress Catherine, and being with his . . . sister chanced to fall in communication with her of the Queen, wherein he advised her, because she was of the Queen's old acquaintance, to sue to be her woman. Whereunto his sister answered that she would not so do, but that she was very sorry for the Queen. "Why?" quoth Lassells. "Marry," quoth she, "for she is light both in living and condition." "How so?" quoth Lassells. "Marry," quoth she, "there is one Francis Dereham, who was servant also in my Lady of Norfolk's house, which hath lain in bed with her in his doublet and hose an hundred nights. And there hath been such puffing and blowing between them, that once . . . a maid which lay in the house with [Catherine] said to me she would lie no longer with her because she knew not what matrimony meant." (Qtd. in Thomas 46)

What is fascinating here, above the tale itself, is the power of these rumors to elicit wonder and conjecture: when Lassells reported this family chatter to Archbishop Cranmer, Cranmer "was marvelously perplexed therewith." When Cranmer subsequently transmitted the tale to the Lord Chancellor and the earl of Hertford, and sought their advice about what to do with the rumors, they too "marvelled" at the tale. It is difficult to assess the sincerity of these reactions; one historian reports that it was a "matter for amazement that not a whisper as to the unsuitability of the new union [had] reached the king. So many people seem to have been aware that Catherine Howard was a woman with a past . . ." (Jerrold 256).[10] And *Hall's Chronicle, Containing the History of England* reports that the queen "was accused to the Kyng of dissolute liuyng, before her marriage, . . . and that was not secretly, but many knewe it" (842). Yet however widely knowledge of Howard's past had circulated, the trial represents that knowledge as a shocking revelation, a "marvel" whose rhetorical effect is to convey a sense of the uniqueness of the information and to imply a prior belief about Howard with which this tale is incompatible. Although the response to the news is naturalized in terms of emotions, the art is not nature's. Reared on Aristotle, every schoolboy knew the rhetorical force of wonder in provoking and directing speculative thinking: "[I]t is owing to their wonder that men both now begin and at first began to philosophize" (*Metaphysics* 247).[11]

Spurred to action by Lassells's perplexing tale, the counselors agreed that the king must be told, and Cranmer undertook the task. Yet in a move as multivalent as it is significant, "because . . . [he] could not find in his heart to express the same to the King's Majesty by word of mouth, he declared the information thereof to His Highness in writing" (qtd. in Thomas 46). Unable to repeat the rumors "by word of mouth," Cranmer reworks Lassells's oral saga into a document, subjecting it to the strictures of scripted narrative. And as she is written, Howard is situated in a complex historical process in which documentary evidence is gaining authority and becoming institutionalized as the most persuasive form of testimony. During the late sixteenth century, the famous court reporter Edmund Plowden pronounced that "our law says that nothing is true but what may be tried, for truth never wants trial" (Abbott 213). By the late seventeenth century, English law will suggest that nothing is true but what is in print.[12] In the interim, trials continuously include debates about what will count as evidence, sometimes taking writing as more legitimate than speaking, sometimes demanding oral validation of written claims.[13]

The effect of transforming the accusations against Howard into a document is to distance the author from the tainted behavior inscribed in the text: represented as a man distracted by heartfelt sympathy for the pain the news may bring Henry, Cranmer disappears into the report, reinforcing the sense that the tale speaks in its own, unmediated voice. Yet paradoxically, the document acquires an added aura of credibility precisely because of Cranmer's personal position: its written form is attributed to the self-negating figure of a faithful "secretorie"—"His pen in this action is not his owne"—whose task is "utterlie to relinquish anie affectation to his own doings" or admixture of his own will in bearing messages (qtd. in Parker, "*Othello*" 81).[14] The oral claims against Howard were a mélange of rumors from widely dispersed witnesses, the sort of anecdotes that might at best issue in a disjointed, multivocal work.[15] The written charges imposed material and thematic unity on the fragments and produced a univocal story with a pointed theme—Howard's moral weakness and Parliament's legal triumph—all the while making the events appear to narrate themselves. The "guilty" Howard comes to exist in writing, in the form of evidence whose truth-claims are growing increasingly persuasive, and as inscribed by one whose extra-legal status as a reliable "secretorie" lends the charges credibility.

The Howard case stakes part of its claims to truth on its status as an official document, offering the palpable reality of paper as the substantial reality of a "criminal record." How else does it generate conviction? By structuring its moralities as mutually contingent, defining, and exclusive. It discredits Howard by crediting her accusers, exempting them from the taint of personal malice in the process. Although Lassells was widely known to be a zealous anti-Catholic working on the side of the reformers, the source-story represents him as a man removed from court politics, an average citizen who heard of Katherine's behavior only by accident. The revelation of the crime appears as a spontaneous event; it is a quasi-miraculous eruption into an occasional conversation between siblings, for he only "*chanced* to fall into communication with [his sister] of the Queen" (emphasis added). Cleared by the operations of accident of any hidden self-serving motives, Lassells is here also allied with the good of the nation and shown as one whose personal and national devotion are identical: asked why he came forward, he vowed it was his duty as a citizen.[16] Mary Lassells Hall, too, is represented as free from self-interest, for she refuses to trade on her prior relationship and seek a position with such a tainted queen. In a sustained process of differentiation between the two women, Mary Lassells Hall's moral rectitude becomes the condition for Katherine Howard's moral turpitude: that Mary "feels very sorry" for Katherine distinguishes the noble country wife from the voluptuous queen along sexual and moral axes. Hall's authority is legitimated here by her recognition (or more accurately, her reproduction) of an official ideology that takes unmarried female sexual activity as "light" behavior, and her tender emotions serve as a standard of female conduct against which Howard is measured. This narrative of pity indicts the queen by constructing her morally acceptable and superior "other," a monogamous country wife.

Within three days of reading the initial charges on 2 November 1541, Henry had left Hampton Court for London; he never saw his wife again.

What replaces him in the accounts is a body of textual evidence that rhetorically generates the corroboration it needs, minting "truth" and coherence from elements unrelated to each other. The procedure reveals the unstated order of criminal investigations: it is not the "facts" that lead inquisitors to the right conclusion, but prior conclusions that bring useful "facts" to light.[17] With their purpose of expelling Howard in mind, Henry's surrogates examined Lassells, his sister Mary, Mannock, and Dereham; they found these witnesses "constant in [their] former sayings" (Cobbett 448) or congruous with each other. When Sir Thomas Wriothesley interviewed Mannock, he heard

that [Mannock] had commonly used to feel the secrets and other parts of [Katherine's] body, ere ever Derrham was so familiar with her; and Derrham confessed that he had known her carnally many times, both in his doublet and his hose between the sheets, and in naked bed, alledging such Witnesses of three sundry women one after another, that had lein in the same bed with them when he did the acts. . . . (Cobbett 448)

"Then the rest of the witnesses, eight or nine men and women, were examined, and agreed in one tale" (qtd. in Jerrold 270). Again late in the proceedings, Culpeper confirmed the depositions of his private conversations with Katherine, though probably under duress and torture in the Tower (Hume 380). What this piling on of a master narrative reveals is that in legal discourse to corroborate is not to *re*produce a fact that already exists, but to *produce* the fact. Perhaps most importantly, corroboration produces the effect of "corroboration." The weight of persuasiveness is on the congruity of the stories, on producing from ostensibly unrelated people and events a tale in which repetition serves as both narrative and subjective unity. The congruity testifies both to the truth of the stories (they match because they are all objective observations about an independent fact) and to the interior of the accused (they match because they are all accurate reflections of a specifiable, although invisible, interior). The diction of discovery masks the interventions of the interrogators: the witnesses were "found" to tell the same tale. Yet Stanley Fish has argued persuasively that

similarity is not something one finds, but something one must establish, and when one establishes it one establishes the configurations of the cited cases as well as of the case that is to be decided. Similarity . . . is not a property of texts (similarities do not announce themselves), but a property conferred by a relational argument in which the statement *A* is like *B* is a characterization (one open to challenge) of *both A* and *B*. (*Doing* 94)

Relating one tale to another is not a process of perfect matching but of continuous revision, as different details are foregrounded and others dropped. In the Howard case as elsewhere, the very process of corroboration is the process of producing narrative consistency.

In a text that repeatedly grounds its authority in its power to forge continuities, Howard's body submits to the demands of narrative signification and testifies against her. According to Lassells's sister, "one Mannock . . . knew a privy mark of [Katherine's] body" (Cobbett 447); Dereham, too, confessed to knowing the "privy mark." Through exchanges of partners, in diverse places, and across passages of time, Katherine could be identified as herself by this single material fact. These substantiating details rest uneasily amid a transition from medieval evidentiary symbolism, in which marks on the body speak in God's voice, to early modern juridical practice, in which marks on the body serve as visible, objective evidence of criminal identity. What is striking is that the privy mark is evoked as something "self-evident" in two senses: it is evidence of a guilty self and it is evidence so self-declaring it appears to need no supplemental explanation. What is equally striking is that the verbal description produces the phenomenon that it also purports merely to record: there is no perspective from which to observe this "privy mark" neutrally, before it receives an interpretation as the sign of Howard's promiscuity. To see it as "privy" is already to have assigned it an interpretation according to a context (assumed by, though not argued for, during the proceedings) that differentiates public from private parts of the body; to see it as a "mark" is already to see it as a mark *of* something (see Fish, *Doing* 77–78).

Some decades later Edward Coke will remark that of all forms of evidence, eyewitnessing is the least reliable. But here the claim to eyewitnessing is the source of Mannock and Dereham's official authority. The privy mark enters the narrative as the sort of "ocular proof" that Othello longs for, substituting a bodily detail for acts that cannot be seen. It puts the accusers in the possession of a particular kind of knowledge, persuasive because private, and it undermines the wife's credibility, for she has failed to arm herself against the penetrating gaze of any man except her husband. Described as something the alleged lovers saw, the mark proves Howard's double violation of marital conventions, her transgression of rules of property (for her body is her husband's) and of hierarchies of agency (for she acted as though she possessed the authority to dispose of her body according to her own will). A variation from "normal" skin surfaces, this bodily deviance metonymically implies Howard's sexual and subjective deviance, representing both in a material sign of fleshly excess. In each case, the mark signifies Howard's failure to conform, body and soul, to the norms of the dominant social order. In it, as though by magic, the law has made apparent an external, embodied sign of internal, moral corruption.

In the Bakhtinian sense, this marvelous detail transforms Howard into a grotesque body, a "degraded" figure whose openness and accessibility radically jeopardize patrilinear authority and social organization. The relevant historical contrast to this representation of Howard's promiscuous body is that of her immediate predecessor, Anne of Cleves. With haste only Hamlet could properly describe ("the funeral baked-meats / Did coldly furnish forth the marriage tables" [1.2.180–81]), Henry wed Katherine within three weeks of the Cleves annulment. Yet Anne remained in England, officially repositioned as "the King's adopted sister, with precedence before all other ladies but the King's wife and daughters" (Hume 355). She swore in a letter to her brother that "my body remaineth in the integrity which I brought into this realm" (Hume 356n1). An essential element in the Howard story, Anne emerges as a necessary other against whose bodily and spiritual "integrity" Katherine's promiscuity could be built.[18]

Armed with the mutually corroborating texts and the crucial bodily detail of the privy mark, Henry's representatives interrogated the queen.[19]

[A]t the first she constantly denied it, but the matter being so declared unto her that she perceived it to be wholly disclosed, the same night she disclosed the whole to the Archbishop of Canterbury [Cranmer], who took the confession of the same in writing subscribed with her hand. Then were the rest of the number, being eight or nine men and women which knew of their doings, examined, who all agreed in one tale. (Qtd. in Thomas 47–48)

Although Howard's initial position is resistance (she "constantly denied" the charges), by the account's end she has become a final instance of belated corroboration. The law, after all, ferreted out the "truth." The problem is that we have no precise record of what Cranmer "declared" to her nor what she "disclosed" to him, and we have no precise record of what the "eight or nine men and women which knew of their doings" had "agreed" on. What we have is an official version of a figure who comes to recognize herself in a story authored by her prosecutors. This section of the account closes by activating an influential and spurious logic of identity, that of self-continuity, emphasizing the truth of these memorial reconstructions: "Now may you see what was done before the marriage; God knoweth what hath been done since" (qtd. in Thomas 48). Implying a God not in evidence, who sees into the recesses of the hidden heart, and evoking the idea of a permanent, unchanging selfhood, the account refashions the queen along the outlines of a memorially reconstructed "Katherine Howard": the Katherine Howard who married Henry is continuous with (continued to be the same as) the one who was between the sheets huffing and puffing with Mannock, Dereham, and Culpeper.

At its culminating moment, the Howard story conflicts not over the issue of whether Howard is a criminal, but over the issue of what crime she acknowledges as her own. In both versions of her execution, she is represented as having embraced the decorum of formal death: on the night before she died, she had an executioner's block brought to her room, "that she might learn how to dispose her head upon it." She then "calmly and smilingly rehearsed her part in the tragedy of the morrow" (Hume 395). The official version of her scaffold speech, delivered on 13 February 1542 and recorded in the *Letters and Papers of the Reign of Henry VIII*, reports that she "spoke shortly. She died . . . in full confidence in God's goodness" (qtd. in Hume 395). As it does in numerous contemporary scaffold testimonies, Howard's speech as reported lends the attainder credibility by corroborating it; her penitent demeanor reflects the successful display of official power in overcoming traitors; and her beheading testifies to the success of the law in penetrating and punishing even the "imaginings" of its subjects.

There is, however, a competing unofficial version of the speech, recorded in the *Spanish Chronicle of Henry VIII*, in which Howard is represented as resisting the abject position of the condemned. In this text, instead of complying with the terms supplied by convention, Howard redraws the contours of her identity: although she admitted that "she had grievously sinned and deserved death," she denied having "wronged the King in the particular way that she had been accused of" (qtd. in Hume 395). Seizing authority not to proclaim her innocence but to define her guilt, Howard shifts the grounds of her criminality from the legal verdict to her own desires:

She proudly and calmly gloried in her love for her betrothed Culpeper, whom she knew she soon would join in death. . . . Even as he, with his last breath, had confessed his love for her, and had mourned that the King's passion for her had stood in the way of their honest union, so did she . . . proclaim that love was victorious over death; and that since there had been no mercy for the man she loved she asked no mercy for herself from the King. . . . If she had married the man she loved, instead of being dazzled by ambition, all would have been well; and when the headsman knelt to ask her forgiveness, she pardoned him, but exclaimed, "I die a Queen, but I would rather have died the wife of Culpeper. . . ." (Qtd. in Hume 394–95)

The moral of every confession, writes Christopher Pye, was the condemned's self-negating inscription within the law: "I see I must die, because I have not been constant to myself" (115).[20] Howard's second confession, however, raises the question of which "self" she has betrayed. It sparks an alternative logic of self-continuity, re-identifying Howard with the theme of fidelity, but tying that fidelity to her non-royal lover. The former scaffold speech imagines her as the source of Henry's personal victimization and the nation's political jeopardy; her reputed promiscuity represented the delegitimation of monarchical succession. But the latter imagines her as an individual agent clinging faithfully to her role as Culpeper's wife, despite having been led astray by the flatteries of an overly amorous king. As represented in this second scaffold speech, the king was an obstacle to her "honest union" with Culpeper. Perhaps this is Howard's more serious crime: shunning the putative privileges of royal matrimony to reclaim the supremacy of her own domestic imaginings.[21] To do so was to envision a different England, one in which a teleology of royal marriage did not govern all premarital sexuality, in which marriage might be a matter of personal consent rather than national proclamation, and in which emotional fidelity, rebellious and invisible, claimed its own authority.

Howard's attainder redefined her into a system of sexual promiscuity and concealment. Her body was remade into a repository of secret places and privy marks; her mind was reformed into a site of pure willfulness (her motto had been "No other will than hers"; Jerrold 259); and her past was rewritten as a sequence of encounters with doublets and hose between the sheets.[22] At the time she married, she was assessed as the child of a "noble and illustrious family"; a woman with "a notable appearance of honour, cleanness, and maidenly behavior"; a "jewel" of womanhood and virtue (qtd. in Thomas 45). By parliamentary decree, she became, instead (or, in the logic of self-continuity, she reverted to being), a woman who "led an abominable, base, carnal, voluptuous and vicious life, like a common harlot, with divers persons, . . . maintaining however the outward appearance of chastity and honesty" (qtd. in Jerrold 273).

III
Playing Out Belief

In Howard's history, as in the attainder itself, we see competing visions of nationhood and competing interests construed as "national." Although I asserted earlier that Howard's "nation had need of her," what the attainder makes evident is that one *version* of the nation had need of her: her marriage signified the political ascendancy of an idea of England that was conservative, Catholic, and feudal in its leanings, and it promised through the legitimating power of patriarchal succession to transmit that England to future generations. Her body became a site of competition not as "her" body, but, under the marriage contract, as the property of her royal husband. She figured in the perpetuation of the nascent Tudor dynasty at a time when social and political stability was typically anchored in representations of genealogical succession. Within the confines of this national project, any assumed act of adultery "at any point could make a mockery of the whole story" (Rackin 160).

Among Henry's widely remarked contributions to early modern social instabilities was his dissolution of English Catholicism and founding of the Church of England, which nationalized religion and thereby nationalized the right of English authority to oversee a subject's interior life. Yet what goes unremarked is that simultaneous with this religious reorganization was Henry's implementation of matrimonial high treasons. Under the Reformation Parliament of 1530–34, "of the new acts which concerned treason in general three were the result of the king's matrimonial ventures. . . . Henry had started on the path of supporting his marriages with the sanctions of treason" (Bellamy 37). Like treasons in general, the matrimonial treasons register deep anxieties about the implications of split subjectivity and the existence of a secret self whose loyalties and desires might differ from those of an observable self, threatening the cohesiveness and stability of the social order that authorizes the behaviors of that subject in the first place. Unlike other treasons, however, the matrimonial treasons formulate this fear of subjective dualism specifically in terms of women's unobservable sexuality: variously transvalued as transgressing social order, as blurring distinctions among conventional categories of mastery and subordination within marriage, and of undermining the stability of gendered categories of dominance and submission in the culture more generally, women's unseen sexuality came to signify the potential for errant self-will and personal agency.

In his study of the juridical field, Pierre Bourdieu argues, "What is at stake in [a trial] is monopoly of the power to impose a universally recognized principle of knowledge of the social world . . ." (837).[23] In bringing about that "principle of knowledge of the social world," what the law typically masks—what it must mask in order to be "law"—is the pervasiveness of social and rhetorical instabilities, and the concomitant fabrication of evidence (the production of a credible story, to return to Parker's terms) as a social and epistemological anchor. The question of providing trustworthy evidence was bound up with a broad historical shift that gradually differentiated "evidence" from "fact": understood as interpretable signs from the natural and supernatural realms, prodigies and miracles competed for authority during an extended process in which reliable evidence came to be incompatible with intention (Daston 94-95).[24] In treason trials generally, prosecutors enhance their claims to reliability by allying themselves with natural or divine evidence, discredit the defendants' credibility by allying them with intentionally crafted artifice, and produce an official document that erases the agency of human authors.

IV
Simular Proofs

Although the Henrician matrimonial treason acts were repealed, their social and discursive force continued. Displaced into "petty treason," matrimonial trials continuously reiterated and published official equivalences between an ordered, hierarchical marriage and an ordered England.[25] Put another way, the process of "knowing" the truth about women became a way of "knowing" the state of the nation as it was perceived to be reflected in traditional gender categories. And just as concerns about patrilinear succession, unified (loyal) subjectivity, and the stability of gender assignments persisted in legal venues, so, too, did the reproduction of these tensions in a range of popular genres. Throughout the century, Tudor-Stuart dramas are full of stagings of female fidelity under scrutiny, and many plays could be used to study theatrical truth-telling.[26] Shakespeare's *Cymbeline*, in particular, puts Imogen on trial when the probing of female fidelities was once more acute: early in James I's reign, the nation was undergoing a political conversion from Elizabethanism to Jacobeanism, legitimate succession was again a controversial topic, and prosecutions for treason and its sister crime, witchcraft, had risen (Paster 244, Maus 33). Both kinds of cases addressed "problems of discovering an inward truth" (Maus 33).

Although law courts claimed authority to establish officially the guilt or innocence of a subject's hidden self, the theater was leveling its own claim to telling reliable stories. Jean-Christophe Agnew has shown that during the early modern decades, "traditional social signs and symbols had metamorphosed into detached and manipulable commodities," and "professional theater offered itself, ironically, as the most credible instrument with which to visualize, so to speak, the lost transparency of these ordinary acts" (97–98). In order to assert its credibility, the theater can embrace what the law must suppress: the self-conscious display of its own processes, especially the processes of human mediation and intervention. In contrast to its position in the courtroom, evidentiary constructedness itself in the theater is neither good nor bad; its moral and thematic effects are contingent on its specific dramatic contexts.[27]

In Christopher Marlowe's *Doctor Faustus*, for example, theatricality affirms its credibility by appearing to critique the very notion of the authority of visible evidence, exposing that evidence as fictive and illusory. Foregrounding the problem of developing authoritative interpretations, the play returns to an overdetermined element of bodily evidence, a privy mark, to ground a moment of verification. It briefly focuses on a German emperor at whose request Faustus has conjured Alexander and his paramour. The persuasive, ordering force of the scene is a detail derived from an old rumor about a clandestine lover:

> EMPEROR
> But, Faustus, since I may not speak to them,
> To satisfy my longing thoughts at full,
> Let me this tell thee: I have heard it said
> That this fair lady, whilst she lived on earth,
> Had on her neck a little wart or mole;
> How may I prove that saying to be true?
> FAUSTUS
> Your majesty may boldly go and see.

EMPEROR

Faustus, I see it plain,
And in this sight thou better pleasest me
Than if I gained another monarchy.

(4.2.58–67)

What is the truth about the paramour's past and how does one know it? The emperor recalls having heard of the private mark, but he also mistrusts both his own memory and the truth of what he remembers. Perhaps it was only gossip. What, then, is the authoritative status of gossip? (In the Howard case, after all, Mary Lassells Hall was only gossiping.) In *Doctor Faustus* the paramour's corpse corroborates the emperor's memory; the memory corroborates the rumor; the rumor corroborates the historical reality of an anonymous paramour who is a staged delusion; and that delusion proves that a particular hero once lived. Marlowe's scene is deliberately equivocal in making sight the site of conflict, where a fabricated, memorial reconstruction bestows "eyewitness" validity on an absent past.

Like Marlowe's play, which derives much of its energy from mining the instabilities of theatrical illusions, Shakespeare's *Cymbeline* wears its simulation on its sleeve.[28] But what had been harmless (or more accurately, desired) within the frame of Marlovian magic turns potentially tragic within the darker frame of Shakespeare's work. The play dramatizes a range of ways that figures "know" what they know, attending self-consciously to the uncertainties of getting at the truth. In the process, it embeds the tainting of its heroine in a pattern of quasi-legal language that foregrounds problems of "knowing Imogen," ultimately linking authentic knowledge to the reestablishment of legitimate dynastic succession.[29]

As it did in the attainder, in *Cymbeline* the investigation into female fidelity gains a halo of objectivity and truth-seeking by appearing initially to surface independently of personal motives. Just as Lassells only "chances" to take up the issue of Howard's sexuality with his sister, so Posthumus, Iachimo, and their French, Dutch, and Spanish interlocutors only randomly and coincidentally revisit a conventional argument about ladies:

FRENCH

It was much like an argument that fell out last night, where each of us fell in praise of our country-mistresses; this gentleman at that time vouching—and upon warrant of bloody affirmation—his to be more fair, virtuous, wise, chaste, constant, qualified, and less attemptable than any the rarest of our ladies in France.

IACHIMO
That lady is not now living, or this gentleman's opinion by this worn out.
POSTHUMUS
She holds her virtue still, and I my mind.

(1.4.60–69)

Phrased in the familiar terms of patrilinearity that repeatedly link each lady's virtue ("more chaste") to each man's legitimacy, the wager polices national boundaries by policing female sexuality: on the assured sexual virtue of each woman rests the superior political *virtù* of each country.[30]

Like the Howard-Cleves linkage, the Imogen-ladies linkage forged here circulates a persuasive mode of thought: that the superior virtue of one woman is contingent on the inferior virtue of another. Structured as a contest between mutually exclusive moralities, the wager reiterates the trope of alternativity characteristic of trial rhetoric. In the attainder, either Howard or Mary Lassells "knows what marriage is"; again, either Howard or Anne of Cleves "retains her body in integrity." With quasi-legal precision, the "either/or" rhetoric limits the vantage points from which one might imagine the questions, narrowing the scope of conjecture. Here, similar logic aims to control the play of the imagination and constrict the ways one might think "womanhood": Posthumus "began / His mistress' picture; which by his tongue being made, / And then a mind put in't, *either* our brags / Were crack'd of kitchen-trulls, *or* his description / Prov'd us unspeaking sots" (5.5.174–78; emphasis added).

Unlike the attainder, however, the play undermines the limiting force of alternativity by shifting the ground of competition from what the ladies *are* to what the men are *doing*, interjecting into the argument what the law struggles continuously to reformulate and displace, the problematic question of intentionality. In general, legal records limit and shape the voices and perspectives they include to a unified, conclusive version of events and the criminal. They are engaged in producing a "conviction" in both the legal and intellectual sense about the condemned's hidden (criminal) character. That narrowing is helped along in the Howard attainder by the absence of Howard's voice, which might cause one to assume that the charges were not contested because they could not be contested. (In this context, Howard's absence might be taken as guilty silence, implicitly becoming additional evidence against her.) Shakespeare's play, however, displays Imogen's tainting dialogically, as a multivocal competition in which various voices, proofs, and motives contest and qualify each other. What the attainder unifies, the play multiplies, particularly the operations of personal motives in producing credible stories.

Shakespeare lays out the wager as a competition among the men to dominate the imaginative and verbal space, as they strive to avoid appearing as "unspeaking sots." In an evocative pun, Posthumus swears to hold his mind "*still*" (emphasis added), continuing in his belief and sustaining his mental calm. By the scene's end, what is under interrogation is not Imogen's fidelity but Posthumus's, Iachimo's target: "I make my wager rather against your confidence than [Imogen's] reputation" (1.5.120–21). The challenge, as Shakespeare writes it, is to belief itself, to the capacity "to sustain the imagined . . . object in one's own psyche, even when there is no sensorially available confirmation that that object has any existence independent of one's own interior mental activity" (Scarry 180).

That such interior activity is sustainable is the point of Imogen's skeptical resistance to Iachimo. Prior belief enables her to reject Iachimo's conversion of the Posthumus she knows into "the Briton reveller" (1.6.61), to refuse to be "reveng'd" on him, and to turn the tables on the teller of the tale. Her complex reaction collapses the distance between making a "true report" and being an honest man, and she specifies that the validity of the evidence rests on the purity of the evidence-giver's heart, and that honest testimony springs from a desire not for personal gain but "for virtue":

> If thou wert honourable,
> Thou wouldst have told this tale for virtue, not
> For such an end thou seek'st,—as base as strange.
> Thou wrong'st a gentleman, who is as far
> From thy report as thou from honour . . .
>
> (1.6.142–46)

Reiterating Egerton's conservative comments cited above, that the truth of the tale is guaranteed by the internal integrity of its teller ("Whoso is guiltless will speak truly and directly, but . . ."), Imogen distances the "report" from the figure it describes by identifying the intervention of intentionality: in Iachimo, interiority, staged as troublesome and elusive in its morality, slips easily into an even more elusive ulteriority, staged as insistently immoral.

Under the pressure of intentionality, evidence of infidelity in *Cymbeline* acquires a new aggressiveness. The play identifies false reports as kinds of

"assault" (1.6.150), their violence associated with Iachimo in references
to literary and legendary rapists, their particular form not a physical but
a rhetorical act: constructing a new Imogen identical with the idea of
infidelity.[31] As many scholars have noted, Iachimo's secret entry into Imogen's private bedchamber evokes an atmosphere of physical and emotional
violation and penetration, as his eye moves from a general view to the
room's tightest corners:

> I will write all down:
> Such and such pictures; there the window; such
> Th' adornment of her bed; the arras, figures,
> Why, such and such, and the contents o' th' story.
> (2.2.24–27)

Explicitly acknowledging the central importance of the "contents o' th'
story" (the one Imogen was reading and the one he is writing) in constructing his persuasive image of Imogen-incontinent, Iachimo makes visible
both the act of writing and the decorative details that will lend credibility
to his having occupied private territories, appropriating ornamental elements to the needs of corroboration. The scene self-reflexively exposes the
operations of intention in building disbelief: this accuser begins with his
conclusion ("but to my design"), collecting those "facts" that will best fit
the story he plans to tell, and he transforms his story into writing, creating
a substantial written record as a substitute for imaginary bodily acts. The
theory of substitution operating here, in which writing bestows sustained
"life" on words, is familiarly expressed in Baldesar Castiglione's *The Book
of the Courtier*: "writing is nothing other than a kind of speech which
remains in being after it has been uttered, the representation, as it were,
or rather the very life of our words" (71). Yet what is distinctive in the
theater is the body on stage, which in *Cymbeline* contradicts rather than
confirms written and oral report. What this tale of infidelity records—
Imogen's promiscuity—the staging refutes: as Iachimo writes, Imogen lies
sleeping, a body of evidence that is, to recall her words, far from report.

When, on his return to Posthumus, Iachimo claims to have found a secret
Imogen quite different from the faithful mistress Posthumus imagines, he
offers that discovery as though it were self-evident. The clearest thing
about evidence in *Cymbeline*, however, is that it is neither stable nor self-
pronouncing, its meanings open to resistance and reformulation. In her
symmetrical account of "belief and resistance," Barbara Herrnstein Smith

describes two views of knowledge: traditional, rationalist accounts "insist on the possibility of the *correction* of prior belief by present evidence," whereas constructivist accounts "stress the *participation* of the prior belief in the perception of present evidence . . ." (126-27). Shakespeare's scene is crafted of a dialogue between these stances. Each time Iachimo (the rationalist here) offers his evidence, Posthumus (the constructivist) recontextualizes it, relying on his prior belief in Imogen's character to plant the ostensible fact in another explanatory field where it does not mean what it would (promiscuity, adultery) if it were left undisturbed in the contexts Iachimo controls.

When Iachimo accuses Imogen, Posthumus challenges him to "make it apparent"; when Iachimo describes her bedchamber, Posthumus discredits the details as "things [Iachimo] might have heard of here, by me / Or by some other"; when Iachimo describes the furnishings, Posthumus grants his having seen them, but denies their status as proof of sexual activity: "Let it be granted you have seen all this— . . . / . . . the description / Of what is in her chamber nothing saves / The wager you have laid" (2.4.92-95). When the bracelet momentarily influences Posthumus, Philario reinterprets the meaning of Iachimo's possession: "It may be probable she lost it" (2.4.115). Iachimo overcomes Posthumus's resistance by expressing his knowledge as *visual* memory: as he offers the apparently irrefutable material evidence of the bracelet—"She stripp'd it from her arm. I see her yet" (2.4.101)—he represents the moment as an observed event whose meaning is as visible as the act itself.[32] Slipped from Imogen's body, the bracelet metonymically and visibly evokes the slippage of her chastity.

The bracelet enters the scene as substantial evidence designed to enable resolution; instead, its meaning becomes the source of further irresolution, as it spawns multiple alternative explanations and reveals the peculiar ambiguous status of objects in a trial.[33] Imogen prophetically identified one of the stories the bracelet might tell when she discovered its loss: "I hope it be not gone to tell my lord / That I kiss aught but he" (2.3.152-53). Iachimo's own version of the bracelet's meaning depends on adopting the view that there is only one explanation for his possessing it, one order of truth: Imogen permitted him access to her private self, signified by this personal ornament, and removed from her body (detached from herself) her fidelity to Posthumus.[34] When the witness finally swears, "By Jupiter, I had it from her arm" (2.4.121), Posthumus revises his belief to fit Iachimo's version of the story: "The cognizance of her incontinency /

Is this. She hath bought the name of whore thus dearly" (2.4.127–28).[35] Through Iachimo's interventions, the multiple meanings of this piece of evidence come to corroborate one another, as contrived proximity slips into willful promiscuity. That the rivals express this complex dynamic of legal belief and resistance as a mere *transference* of what is empirically knowable from one knower to another suppresses the mediation of the interlocutors' motives and of language itself.

One of the curiosities of Shakespeare's play is that although Posthumus had earlier demanded more material evidence—"Render to me some corporal sign about her, / More evident than this; for this was stol'n" (2.4.119–20)—it is the bracelet that wins him over. In *Cymbeline*'s sources, as in the attainder and *Doctor Faustus*, a mole proves the female's promiscuous identity, and it does so by assuming a normative virtuous body: irregular markings imply irregular desires. In Shakespeare's play, only after Posthumus believes that Iachimo "hath enjoy'd her" does additional evidence appear:

> If you seek
> For further satisfying, under her breast—
> Worthy [the] pressing—lies a mole, right proud
> Of that most delicate lodging. By my life,
> I kiss'd it; and it gave me present hunger
> To feed again, though full.
>
> (2.4.133–38)

The redirected import of this mole is less to prove the claims against Imogen than to punish Posthumus for "holding his mind" by graphically representing Iachimo's knowledge of "Imogen-incontinent" as physical knowledge. In the reference to the mole, with its associations with "her breast" and the "present hunger / To feed," Iachimo's proof crosses over into what Parker describes as a "pornographic doubleness": it both opens up and denies to the eye the "secret" part of woman ("*Othello*" 67). The potential meanings of that opening up are multiplied by the roles bodily marks play in the widespread contemporary practice of witch-hunting. Linking witchcraft trials to the ambiguous, contradictory position of women in post-Reformation culture, Christina Larner has shown that these popular legal events continuously reproduced the patriarchal practice of differentiating between women on the basis of conformity to dominant social codes (84–88). And Gail Paster has explained that these trials introduced "the witch into the category of the sexually deviant and transgressive female," subjected the woman's body to a "shameful transformation," and found "in the apparent objectivity of bodily evidence a means of occluding the ideological grounds for social division" (250, 245).[36]

In *Cymbeline*, the objectivity of that bodily evidence is never at issue; rather, its meanings shift and multiply with the contexts in which it appears. As Iachimo crafts it, Imogen can be identified as "herself" and that self can be aligned with "the name of whore" by a private mark that is offered as though it were self-interpreting. As Shakespeare crafts it, however, the self-identifying body is neither gender-specific nor uniform in its meanings, and the feature designed to cement the representation of "Imogen-incontinent" becomes the means of destabilizing her identity again and of effecting social and political transformations none of the play's characters could foresee. In the play's final scene, the mole is recast from the sign of corruption and transgression into the sign of royalty and legitimate dynastic succession: King Cymbeline's long-lost son Guiderius is revealed as a nobleman and reinserted into the royal lineage through a mole he shares with his sister: "This is he, / Who hath upon him still that natural stamp. / It was wise Nature's end in the donation, / To be his evidence now" (5.5.365–68). Repositioned by the operations of patrilinearity from potential queen—"O Imogen, / Thou hast lost by this a kingdom" (5.5.372–73)—to loving wife and sister, Imogen aligns herself with those operations by embracing domesticity and reimagining it as sovereignty: "No, my lord; / I have got two worlds by 't" (5.5.373–74).

It is here that the God-not-in-evidence who haunts treason trials, evoked in order to testify to the internal honesty and subjective integrity of the participants, appears in the form of the playwright. Throughout, Shakespeare has positioned the spectators alongside himself as possessors of divine knowledge, equally privy to the truths that Imogen is faithful, Iachimo a hypocrite, and his reports sinister falsifications of sustained chastity. In a final turn, however, Shakespeare claims still-superior knowledge by bringing to light what no character and no spectator could foresee: Nature's hand in marking the royal siblings' bodies. As they do in the Howard attainder, so here, the meanings of the "natural stamp" mutate with the interpretive contexts in which it operates *as* evidence. Yet what the law obscures, this play foregrounds: the hand of the author in providing proof.

Taken as a theatrical deliberation on the uncertainties of early modern struggles with epistemology, theatricality, and truth, *Cymbeline* makes

its claims to credibility through the strategy of an exposé, revealing the
intentions of men in the operations of persuasion: representing motivated
evidence, Iachimo confesses "my practice so prevail'd / That I return'd with
simular proof enough / To make the noble Leonatus mad, / By wounding his
belief . . ." (5.5.199–202). In formulating its claims to truth-telling, the play
raises the specter of a threatening dualism between women's apparent and
secret fidelities—"Your daughter's chastity—there it begins" (5.5.179)—
but it exposes that dualism not as the fearful truth but as a powerful fiction.

<h1 style="text-align:center">V</h1>

Both the Howard attainder and *Cymbeline* are among the clusters of
tales told in trials, plays, ballads, and pamphlets that conditioned the idea
of female fidelity in early modern English culture. Each is an instance of the
repetitious cultural activity of playing out belief, and each formally posits
a crucial moment in a woman's history when (due to the machinations of
fate, chance, or nosy neighbors) her observable character suddenly cracks
and a corrupt interior becomes visible. In both texts, female fidelity exists
within a more general theory of nationhood and identity—one organized
around ideas of the legitimacy of patrilinear purity, unified subjectivity, and
secure gender hierarchy—that was asserted, interrogated, and reasserted
again and again in law courts and theaters.

In producing its credible story, the attainder tends to minimize the effects
of human agency and intervention, whether in something so elusive as personal motive or so apparent as a material document, formulating the force
behind legal proceedings as God's hand in the lives of men and women:
"Now you may see what was done before the marriage; God knoweth what
hath been done since" (Thomas 48). The theater, on the other hand, might
draw on any notion of evidence, natural, human, or divine, to make its
claims. *Cymbeline* maximizes human intervention in Iachimo's production
of "Imogen-incontinent." In the process, it identifies evil motives with
individuals, making those motives the personal contrivances of villains:
"*my* practice" prevailed, confesses Iachimo, "*I*" produced "simular proof
enough" (emphasis added). If one effect of that displacement is to confine
the scope of "ill will" to an individual (and prototypical) Machiavel, a
concomitant effect is to obscure the operations of dominant social codes
and discourses in bringing about "convictions."

During the sixteenth and early seventeenth centuries, both law courts
and theaters are formalizing their respective disciplines as professions, in

some ways competing with each other to offer the more reliable version of things. To claim their respective credibilities, each repeatedly activates its epistemological rules for limiting what will be seen as "in the true," in Michel Foucault's useful formulation ("Discourse" 224). Yet whatever the terms of the contest, it is important to remember that the consequences for constructing credible stories of female fidelities on stage and in court were quite different: in the play, the unfaithful female is cleared of all offenses and shown to be the victim of personal malice who lives to embrace a socially and theatrically sanctioned domesticity. But even if she had not been cleared, and had gone to her death like Desdemona, the boy who played her would nonetheless have revived and survived to play another day.[37] In the attainder, the unfaithful female is convicted of all offenses and shown to be an agent of malice and national instability. We do not know Katherine Howard's precise birthdate. We do know that she had been queen of England for less than two years when she was beheaded on the Tower Green, 13 February 1542.[38]

Notes

Shorter versions of this essay were presented at the South Atlantic Modern Language Association annual convention and Shakespeare Association of America annual meeting. I am grateful to colleagues at those conferences for their suggestions, and particularly to Frances N. Teague for pointing me to *Cymbeline*. I want also to thank James R. Siemon, Constance Jordan, Karin S. Coddon, and my anonymous readers for their comments. The assistance of Frances E. Dolan has been invaluable.

1. Two studies that do attend to forms of persuasion are Greenblatt, *Sir Walter*; and Maus. The seminal work on the scaffold-theater link is, of course, Michel Foucault's *Discipline and Punish*.

2. See, for example, her *Literary Fat Ladies*, esp. chs. 5 and 6.

3. The status of proof as something made has gained attention recently. See the series of essays on "questions of evidence" in three consecutive issues of *Critical Inquiry*—17.4 (Summer 1991), 18.1 (Autumn 1991), and 18.2 (Winter 1992).

On the relations among dramatists, rhetorical training, and legal disciplines, see, in addition to Parker, Altman and Finkelpearl.

4. The Reformation Parliament of 1530–34 extended the Edwardian treason statutes (26 Henry VIII c. 13), making wishing and words the centerpiece (Bellamy 29). Although there had been fewer than ten treason statutes enacted during the years from 1352 to 1485, there were sixty-eight treason statutes enacted from 1485 to 1603 (Bellamy 12).

On the ease with which the Crown could construct "presumptive treason," and on the use of torture in the Howard case, see Lacey Baldwin Smith 162–63.

5. See Coddon, Hanson, and Maus respectively. Coddon argues that the discourse of treason "disintegrates the identity so precariously fashioned by notions of inward control and self-vigilance" (381–82).

6. This is not to suggest that there are not facts or real events, but that access to them in early modern courtrooms is radically mediated. On the forceful use of strategic language to construe and produce authoritative interpretations in legal and rhetorical studies, see Fish, *Doing* 9.

7. What I am calling "the Howard attainder" is a compilation of documents. The full text of the formal charges appears in Walter Jerrold's biography, reprinted from *Letters and Papers of the Reign of Henry VIII*, vols. 15 and 16; and in William Cobbett's collection, which relies on *Lord Herbert's Life of Henry VIII*. Other commentary is drawn from Wriothesley's chronicle; Hall; and Martin Hume's biography, which agrees with the *Letters and Papers*, vols. 15 and 16. A preliminary comparison with documents in the records office shows Cobbett to be accurate. I cite in this essay only those elements of Howard's biography and attainder that appear in two or more of the sources here identified. The notable exception is the second scaffold speech (p. 13 above), which appears in Hume and about which he says: "The accounts of Chapuys, Hall, and Ottewell Johnson say simply that she confessed her faults and made a Christian end. The *Spanish Chronicle of Henry VIII* gives an account of her speech, of which the above is a summary" (395n1).

Two useful biographies of Katherine Howard are by Lacey Baldwin Smith, esp. ch. 5, "Rival Queens"; and Jerrold.

8. Thomas Cromwell, architect of Henry's Protestant policy and supporter of the Cleves marriage, was beheaded on Tower Hill on 28 July 1540, the same day Henry married Katherine Howard at Oatlands. Howard's uncle, the duke of Norfolk, was Cromwell's arch-rival and "the likely agent of a strong Catholic reaction and even of that possible reversion to subservience to papal dominion which for ten years Cromwell had striven to make impossible" (Jerrold 256).

9. The full text of the indictment is reprinted in Jerrold 273-74. According to Hume, the disclosures about Howard's lovers all referred to conduct previous to Howard's marriage to the king. The acts constructively became treason *post facto* in new legislation that made the issue of concealment central (375):

An Act was also passed, declaring that it shall be lawful for any of the King's subjects, if themselves do perfectly know, or by vehement presumption do perceive any will, act, or condition of lightness of body in her which shall be the Queen of this realm, to disclose the same to the King or some of his Council. But they shall not openly blow it abroad or whisper it, until it be divulged by the King or his Council. If the King or any of his successors shall marry a woman which was before incontinent, if she conceal the same it shall be high treason, &c. (Thomas 52)

The act was repealed by 1 Edw. VI c. 12 and 1 Mary I (Thomas 52).

10. See also Hume, who reports that Howard "was known to have been a giddy, neglected girl before her marriage, having been brought up by her grandmother . . . without the slightest regard for her welfare or the high rank of her family" (368).

11. On the emotional and speculative effects of rhetorical strategies, see also Aristotle, *Poetics*, esp. 637; and Altman 1.

12. I am indebted here to an unpublished manuscript by Joseph Lenz.

13. Ralegh resisted the charges against him, for example, by attacking the very authority of

the testimony as evidence—"Your words cannot condemn me"; "Your phrases will not prove it" (Stephen 18, 23)—demanding a more material form of proof.

14. Compare Jonathan Goldberg's citation of Angel Day: "A Letter . . . is that wherein is expreslye conveied in writing, the intent and meaning of one man, immediately to passe and be directed to an other, and for the certaine respects thereof, is termed the messenger and familiar speeche of the absent" (251).

15. Before the case concludes, evidence against Katherine will include Mary Lassells Hall's gossip with her brother; her brother's recounting of that gossip to Cranmer and inclusion of himself in the story; Cranmer's first written version, which includes Lassells as both partic-ipant in the original conversation and as informant and good citizen, and includes Cranmer as the loyal servant of the king reporting distasteful information in writing; the individual interrogators' written fragments of testimony from the various witnesses each questioned independently; the initial written version presented to Parliament with the recommendation that Howard be invited to testify; and the second written version presented to Parliament that conflated the multiple statements of witnesses into generalizations about all agreeing to the tale.

On the reciprocal shaping of legal and fictional texts, see Davis.

16. Lacey Baldwin Smith asserts that Lassells was motivated by Protestant hatred and zeal and that the "discharge of his duty" and the "welfare of his soul" demanded that he expose Howard (158).

17. On the priority of having a purpose before one can bring the meaning of a statute to light, see Fish, "Normal" 1204.

18. Among the paradoxical elements in the Cleves-Howard history is a rumor about Anne: "there was other loose talk, also, going on to the effect that on one of the visits of Anne of Cleves to Hampton Court after Henry's marriage with Katharine, the King and his repudiated wife had made up their differences, with the consequence that Anne was pregnant by him" (Hume 368). Though the rumor proved false, it took Anne's reported pregnancy as evidence of her spousal legitimacy, despite Henry's having another wife.

19. The officials were Archbishop Cranmer, the Lord Chancellor, the duke of Norfolk, the Lord Great Chamberlain, and the bishop of Winchester.

20. Pye is citing William Camden's *The History of Princess Elizabeth*, 189. Compare Elaine Scarry's discussion of confession; she identifies the condemned as one made "to understand [her] confession . . . as an act of self-betrayal . . . in which the one annihilated shifts to being the agent of [her] own annihilation" (47).

21. On the formulaic and normative aspects of scaffold speeches, see Sharpe; and Dolan, "Gentlemen." See also Dolan's study of the construction of female subjectivity in cases of petty treason, "Home-Rebels."

22. The translation and thus the social meaning of Howard's motto remains in dispute, varying with conflicting assumptions about her role. It appears in a letter from a French ambassador: "Non autre volonté que la sienne" (*Letters and Papers of Henry VIII*, xvi, 12; qtd. in Jerrold 259). "Volonté" is feminine; "la sienne" has been variously translated "hers" or "his." Jerrold finds the feminine translation consistent with his view of Howard's character as an independent woman; in contrast, Lacey Baldwin Smith offers the masculine translation ("No other wish save his" [150]), which he finds consistent with his idea of Howard's submissiveness to Henry.

23. Similarly, Lacey Baldwin Smith argues that neither the truth of the testimony nor the question of guilt in treasons was as important as publicity: truth "had already been settled by royal will, and the prisoners were considered guilty until proved otherwise"; the role of a trial and its adjudicators was not to judge facts, but "to achieve complete publicity" of an official version of events and their perpetrators (196–97).

24. Lorraine Daston puts the question of evidence and intention thus: "How did evidence come to be incompatible with intention, and is it possible to imagine a kind of evidence that is intention-laden?" (94–95). She finds the answer in sixteenth- and seventeenth-century literature on prodigies (prototypical "scientific" facts) and miracles (prototypical "argumentative" evidence).

25. The dissolution of matrimonial high treason may have to do with the fact that after Henry VIII, no adult male served as monarch again until 1603. Succession passed from Henry in 1547 to the young Edward VI (son of Henry VIII and Jane Seymour); in 1553 to Lady Jane Grey for nine days; in 1553 to Mary I (daughter of Henry VIII and Catherine of Aragon); in 1558 to Elizabeth I (daughter of Henry VIII and Anne Boleyn); and in 1603 to James I.

Although incidents of petty treason may or may not have risen during the Jacobean era, popular representations increase significantly; see Dolan, "Home-Rebels." On the links among historical and civil order, rhetorical order, and household order, see Parker, *Literary* 125.

26. The most familiar text in such studies is *Othello*. For diverse readings of it relative to issues of evidence, see Parker, "*Othello*"; Greenblatt, "Improvisation"; and Maus.

27. Although the suppression of human intervention is a consistent aspect of legal prosecutions, its theatrical display need not characterize all dramas. My aim here is not to generalize about what theater as an institution always does, but to look closely at one play that stages its questions of proof specifically in terms of simulation.

28. Perceptive readings of *Cymbeline* in general and Posthumus's character in particular are by Douglas Peterson, who identifies the conventional humanist problem of the "the crippling inability to discern between truth and seeming" (119); Joan Hartwig, who asserts that "to a certain extent, reality depends upon the person who perceives it, and habitual attitudes tend to narrow the individual's vision" (86); and James Edward Siemon, who makes the argument for Posthumus's nobility.

For an overview of wager plots, in which a husband bets on his wife's fidelity, see J. M. Nosworthy's introduction to the Arden edition, esp. xx–xxv; and Homer Swander's discussion of the convention of the "blameless hero" and his subtle reading of the shifts in belief in the wager scenes (269).

29. For general references to law, see Leah S. Marcus's essay on Cloten's use of legalisms and legal themes (144–46), and her discussion of conflicts between Roman and common law in James's efforts to establish the union with Scotland (152).

30. On the nationalism theme, see Knight; and Marcus, who comments that the "ruptured, then revitalized marriage of Imogen and Posthumus in *Cymbeline*, like the actual marriages engineered by James, can be linked to his higher policy of creating a united Britain out of nations in discord" (142).

31. On the sexually violent images of Tarquin and Tereus, see Miola.

32. In their recent work on twentieth-century evidence, Elizabeth Loftus and Katherine Ketcham argue: "Implicit in the acceptance of this [eyewitness] testimony as solid evidence

is the assumption that the human mind is a precise recorder and storer of events" (16). According to this assumption, memories are preserved intact.

33. See Scarry: "when one encounters an object in a legal proceeding, one will be encountering it only in its aberrant condition" (296).

34. Describing a point of view she will later refute, Daston writes: "facts owe no permanent allegiance to any of the schemes into which they are impressed as evidence. They are the mercenary soldiers of argument, ready to enlist in yours or mine, wherever the evidentiary fit is best" (93).

35. For an analysis of how Shakespeare imitates and differs from his sources in his use of the evidence, see Swander 261-64.

36. This emphasis on the evidentiary force of a privy mark has a distinctly national identity: "a major difference between English and virtually all other national forms of witchcraft prosecutions was the almost obsessive attention that English authorities paid to the presence on the witch's body of a 'bigge,' or mark . . ." (Paster 247).

On the interpretation of bodily marks as signs of witchcraft, see also Newman, esp. ch. 4; and Macfarlane.

37. I am not suggesting that stage representations are without significant material consequences; this essay assumes that they are profoundly forceful. There are, however, distinctions between the kinds of consequences that issue from representations in drama and in law.

38. Howard's year of birth is variously identified between 1515 and 1523. For a detailed overview of the question, see Lacey Baldwin Smith, "Appendix: Catherine Howard's Birth," 209-11.

Works Cited

Abbott, L. W. *Law Reporting in England, 1485-1585*. London: Athlone, 1977.

Agnew, Jean-Christophe. *Worlds Apart: The Market and the Theater in Anglo-American Thought, 1550-1750*. Cambridge: Oxford UP, 1986.

Altman, Joel. *The Tudor Play of Mind: Rhetorical Inquiry and the Development of Elizabethan Drama*. Berkeley: U of California P, 1978.

Aristotle. *Metaphysics*. Trans. W. D. Ross. *Introduction to Aristotle*. Ed. Richard McKeon. New York: Modern Library, 1947. 243-96.

———. *Poetics*. Trans. Ingram Bywater. *Introduction to Aristotle*. Ed. Richard McKeon. New York: Modern Library, 1947. 624-67.

Bakhtin, Mikhail. *Rabelais and His World*. Trans. Hélène Iswolsky. Bloomington: Indiana UP, 1984.

Bellamy, John. *The Tudor Law of Treason*. London: Routledge, 1979.

Bourdieu, Pierre. "The Force of Law: Toward a Sociology of the Juridical Field." Trans. Richard Terdiman. *Hastings Law Journal* 38 (1987): 805-53.

Camden, William. *The History of Princess Elizabeth*. Ed. Wallace T. MacCaffrey. Chicago: U of Chicago P, 1970.

Castiglione, Baldesar. *The Book of the Courtier*. Trans. George Bull. London: Penguin, 1976.

Cobbett's Complete Collection of State Trials. 32 vols. London, 1809. Vol. 1.

Coddon, Karin S. " 'Suche Strange Desygns': Madness, Subjectivity, and Treason in *Hamlet* and Elizabethan Culture." *Hamlet*. Ed. Susanne L. Wofford. New York: Bedford, 1994. 380-402.

Correll, Barbara. "Malleable Material, Models of Power: Women in Erasmus's 'Marriage Group' and *Civility in Boys*." *English Literary History* 57 (1990): 241-62.

Critical Inquiry. "Questions of Evidence." 17 (1991): 741-867. 18 (1991): 79-153, 300-386.

Daston, Lorraine. "Marvelous Facts and Miraculous Evidence in Early Modern Europe." *Critical Inquiry* 18 (1991): 93-124.

Davis, Natalie Zemon. *Fiction in the Archives: Pardon Tales and Their Tellers in Sixteenth-Century France*. Stanford: Stanford UP, 1987.

Dolan, Frances E. " 'Gentlemen, I have one thing more to say': Women on Scaffolds in England, 1563-1680." *Modern Philology* 92 (1994): 157-78.

———. "Home-Rebels and House-Traitors: Murderous Wives in Early Modern England." *Yale Journal of Law and the Humanities* 4 (1992): 1-31.

Finkelpearl, Philip J. *John Marston of the Middle Temple: An Elizabethan Dramatist in His Social Setting*. Cambridge: Harvard UP, 1969.

Fish, Stanley. *Doing What Comes Naturally: Change, Rhetoric, and the Practice of Theory in Literary and Legal Studies*. Durham: Duke UP, 1989.

———. "Normal Circumstances, Literal Language, Direct Speech Acts, the Ordinary, the Everyday, the Obvious, What Goes without Saying, and Other Special Cases." 1980. *Critical Theory Since Plato*. Rev. ed. Ed. Hazard Adams. New York: Harcourt, 1992. 1200-1209.

Foucault, Michel. *Discipline and Punish: The Birth of the Prison*. Trans. Alan Sheridan. New York: Vintage, 1979.

———. "The Discourse on Language." Appendix. *The Archaeology of Knowledge*. Trans. A. M. Sheridan Smith. New York: Pantheon, 1972. 215-37.

Goldberg, Jonathan. *Writing Matter: From the Hands of the English Renaissance*. Stanford: Stanford UP, 1990.

Greenblatt, Stephen. "The Improvisation of Power." *Renaissance Self-Fashioning: From More to Shakespeare*. Chicago: U of Chicago P, 1980. 222-54.

———. *Sir Walter Ralegh: The Renaissance Man and His Roles*. New Haven: Yale UP, 1973.

Hall's Chronicle; Containing the History of England. . . . London, 1809. New York: AMS, 1965.

Hanson, Elizabeth. "Torture and Truth in Renaissance England." *Representations* 34 (1991): 53-84.

Hartwig, Joan. *Shakespeare's Tragicomic Vision*. Baton Rouge: Louisiana State UP, 1972.

Hobbes, Thomas. *Leviathan*. Ed. C. B. Macpherson. Harmondsworth: Penguin, 1968.

Hume, Martin. *The Wives of Henry the Eighth: And the Parts They Played in History*. New York: Brentano's, n.d.

Jerrold, Walter. *Henry VIII and His Wives*. New York: Doran, n.d.

Knight, G. Wilson. *The Crown of Life: Essays in Interpretation of Shakespeare's Final Plays*. 1947. New York: Barnes & Noble, 1966.

Larner, Christina. *Witchcraft and Religion: The Politics of Popular Belief*. Ed. Alan Macfarlane. Oxford: Blackwell, 1984.

Lenz, Joseph. "Articles of Faith: Making Words Matter." Unpublished manuscript. Seminar paper, "Shakespeare and Proof." Shakespeare Association of America, April 1993.

Loftus, Elizabeth, and Katherine Ketcham. *Witness for the Defense: The Accused, the Eyewitness, and the Expert Who Puts Memory on Trial*. New York: St. Martin's, 1991.

Macfarlane, Alan. *Witchcraft in Tudor and Stuart England*. London: Routledge, 1970.

Marcus, Leah S. "*Cymbeline* and the Unease of Topicality." *The Historical Renaissance: New Essays on Tudor and Stuart Literature and Culture.* Ed. Heather Dubrow and Richard Strier. Chicago: U of Chicago P, 1988. 134-68.

Marlowe, Christopher. *Doctor Faustus.* Ed. Irving Ribner. New York: Odyssey, 1966.

Maus, Katharine Eisaman. "Proof and Consequences: Inwardness and Its Exposure in the English Renaissance." *Representations* 34 (1991): 29-52.

Miola, Robert S. "*Cymbeline*: Shakespeare's Valediction to Rome." *Roman Images.* Ed. Annabel Patterson. Baltimore: Johns Hopkins UP, 1984. 51-62.

Newman, Karen. *Fashioning Femininity and English Renaissance Drama.* Chicago: U of Chicago P, 1991.

Nosworthy, J. M., ed. Introduction. *Cymbeline.* The Arden Shakespeare. Cambridge: Harvard UP, 1955.

Parker, Patricia. *Literary Fat Ladies: Rhetoric, Gender, Property.* London: Methuen, 1987.

———. "*Othello* and *Hamlet*: Dilation, Spying, and the 'Secret Place' of Woman." *Representations* 44 (1993): 60-95.

Paster, Gail Kern. *The Body Embarrassed: Drama and the Disciplines of Shame in Early Modern England.* Ithaca: Cornell UP, 1993.

Peterson, Douglas L. *Time, Tide, and Tempest: A Study of Shakespeare's Romances.* San Marino, CA: Huntington Library, 1973.

Pye, Christopher. *The Regal Phantasm: Shakespeare and the Politics of Spectacle.* London: Routledge, 1990.

Rackin, Phyllis. *Stages of History: Shakespeare's English Chronicles.* Ithaca: Cornell UP, 1990.

Scarry, Elaine. *The Body in Pain: The Making and Unmaking of the World.* New York: Oxford UP, 1985.

Shakespeare, William. *Cymbeline. The Complete Plays and Poems of William Shakespeare.* Ed. William Nielson and Charles Hill. Cambridge: Houghton, 1942. 458-99.

———. *Hamlet.* Ed. Cyrus Hoy. New York; Norton, 1963.

Sharpe, J. A. " 'Last Dying Speeches': Religion, Ideology and Public Execution in Seventeenth-Century England." *Past & Present* 107 (1985): 144-67.

Sidney, Philip. *An Apology for Poetry.* 1583, 1595. *Critical Theory Since Plato.* Rev. ed. Ed. Hazard Adams. New York: Harcourt, 1992. 142-62.

Siemon, James Edward. "Noble Virtue in *Cymbeline*." *Shakespeare Survey* 29 (1976): 51-61.

Smith, Barbara Herrnstein. "Belief and Resistance: A Symmetrical Account." *Critical Inquiry* 18 (1991): 125-39.

Smith, Lacey Baldwin. *A Tudor Tragedy: The Life and Times of Catherine Howard.* New York: Pantheon, 1961.

Stephen, H. L., ed. *State Trials: Political and Social.* 2 vols. London: Duckworth, 1899. Vol. 1.

Swander, Homer. "*Cymbeline* and the 'Blameless Hero.' " *English Literary History* 30 (1964): 259-70.

Thomas, Donald, ed. *State Trials: Treason and Libel.* London: Routledge, 1972.

Wriothesley, Charles. *A Chronicle of England during the Reigns of the Tudors, from A.D. 1485 to 1559.* Ed. William Douglas Hamilton. 1875. 2 vols. New York: Johnson Reprint, 1965. Vol. 1.

Contract and Conscience in Cymbeline

CONSTANCE JORDAN

EARLY MODERN bodies politic—of the family and of the state—were shaped by the terms of verbal contracts observed over time by the continuous consent of the parties to them. In large measure this compliance reflected the fact that what was contracted for were duties of no quantifiable value but rather in the nature of benefits. The services of love and fidelity were beyond institutional enforcement and perhaps even determination. Their very vagueness made performance an act of discrimination and more particularly of conscience. Within the family, certain kinds of material support were, of course, subject to court order; fathers were required to feed and house children up to a certain age; husbands also had to provide for wives. Within the state, parties were comparably if less ambiguously bound: monarchs and magistrates had to promote the welfare of the people; subjects were expected to obey their superiors. But even these obligations were subject to interpretation.

The obedience of subjects was limited to "things indifferent" to their spiritual salvation. Monarch and magistrate were bound to observe positive law in many respects, even when they considered that the commonwealth would benefit from action that, strictly speaking, was illicit. Difficulties became apparent in two kinds of circumstances: that is, when the monarch claimed a wider scope for the prerogative, his absolute or extraordinary power above positive law, than common law and customary practice indicated was allowable and "constitutional"; and, by contrast, when he exercised the prerogative licitly but in such a way as to violate what the subject considered a sacred or natural right. In the first instance, his over-reaching could be (and was) met with a kind of protest that invoked positive law and tradition. In the second instance, the subject who resisted was effectively an "outlaw": his future "in this life" depended on the extent to which he could summon a real and revolutionary force. In actual practice, he had to choose exile or—resisting albeit passively—martyrdom. Both sets of circumstances fostered a public and political discourse characterized by a high consciousness of the function of conscience and its justification as a determinant of action and responsibility. Here a frequent point of reference was the power of the word to bind parties to mutual obligations. The monarch's word was critically at issue when he exercised his absolute power and authority in actions sanctioned by law and custom; in this instance, the obedient subject had to rely for justice only on the monarch's promise to minister to his whole people and their common wealth.

This essay will explore some of the meanings generated by the terms of verbal contracts and their engagement with conscience as they are represented in *Cymbeline*. It will focus particularly on the marriage of Imogen and Posthumus, and on the tribute to be rendered to Augustus Caesar by Cymbeline. The first is guaranteed by the words of betrothal and entails fidelity; the second, largely symbolic, was instituted by the word of Cassibelan, Cymbeline's ancestor, as a debt the conquered British king owed (and his successors would owe) the Roman emperor. Both contracts are validated by conscience. When Posthumus loses faith in and hence is unfaithful to Imogen, he violates the promises he made at his betrothal. The meaning of Cassibelan's grant and the relations it institutes are comparatively more complex. It marks the indebtedness of a conquered and hence vassal state. In practice, however, such a contract could be and often was subject to revocation if and when the conquered state gained the power to resist its conqueror. A common fate of agreements between states, where the law of nations was strictly speaking unenforceable by any court, agreements between a social or political superior with absolute power and his subject were also susceptible to challenge. In all cases, whether between states or within a political body, the power of a word, an oath, a verbal contract to bind in conscience was in fact possible only as a paradoxical double bind: binding the superior's power conscientiously to minister to the subject is the subject's countervailing power conscientiously to resist his superior.

As words instituting obligations to be honored over time, verbal contracts in *Cymbeline* have a presumptive (if fictive) validation in salvation history. Chronicles of ancient Britain represented the reign of Cymbeline as coinciding with the rule of Augustus Caesar, a time when all the world was to be taxed, a time of universal peace and the birth of Christ.[1] Mankind was then to live under a new dispensation. Dramatizing events that occurred at a moment after which they were to become susceptible to a Christian justice and love, the play informs its sense of the power of human words by invoking the infinitely more compelling power of the Word. Its authority both supersedes whatever human words may institute and confirms the acts of conscience that bring them to expression.

The Family

The play's opening scene conveys the most important feature of a contract: its status as a promise and therefore as a matter of conscience. At immediate issue is Imogen's betrothal. As the gentlemen who know court gossip reveal, the "bloods" of courtiers neither "obey the heavens" (choosing celibacy) nor do they accept Cymbeline's decision to imprison Imogen and exile Posthumus (1.1.1–3). Cymbeline's promotion of Cloten, his own abject and venal stepson, to be Imogen's prospective consort is clearly incestuous. Although Posthumus is the foster son of Cymbeline, who "breeds" (1.1.42) him after he is orphaned, his marriage to Imogen violates no natural law. It is further justified by a moral calculus and perceptions of worth, factors made mysterious by allusions to kingship and dynasty that suggest the propriety of the match. The courtiers celebrate Imogen's "election" of Posthumus as a response to his "virtue"— "the regions of the earth" do not have his "like" (1.1.52–53, 20–21). His worth is both demonstrable by his deeds and signified by his ancestry, which, although obscured in the immemorial mists of time (it cannot be "delve[d] . . . to the root" [line 28]), is symbolically royal—his father is Leonatus and he is Posthumus Leonatus, one of the "lion's whelp." In scriptural prophecy *leonatus* is identified with Judah, the progenitor of the house of David: "The sceptre shal not depart from Iudah . . . and the people shal be gathred vnto him" (Gen. 49.9–10). By being displaced from the succession by Cymbeline's sons at the end of the play, Posthumus will be seen merely to have figured what they actually ensure: a proper dynastic succession.[2] His character as a metaphor of kingship is respected throughout the action of the play.

But specious as Cloten's suit may be, promoted by Cymbeline and his queen in defiance of natural law, Imogen's marriage to Posthumus is not valid in all respects. It was evidently not a public marriage, *per verba de praesenti*, endorsed by family and friends, expected of a woman of property, and usually preceded by a written contract, but rather clandestine and marked only by a verbal contract to be married, *per verba de futuro*, a form of marriage elected by persons who either had little property or wished to defy parental wishes. Clandestine marriages were not legally binding before consummation; in effect, the fact of consummation in a clandestine marriage served the same function as the act of agreeing to marriage before witnesses in a public marriage.[3] Exiled in Rome, Posthumus insists that Imogen is a virgin and so reveals the provisional status of their marriage. Despite the status of their marriage, however, the betrothal of Imogen and Posthumus is a valid verbal contract. The *verba de futuro* on which it is based signified not only a promise to marry (i.e., consummate their union in time) but also to accept the obligations of a married couple: to be faithful to each other. As I've suggested, the play's reference to sacred history makes its representation of betrothal and the agreement to pay tribute especially remarkable; it unifies the disparate "matters" of story (Imogen's marriage) and chronicle (British tribute) by a common concern with conscience.

In English legal practice, contracts of all kinds had been considered to have a conscientious dimension for centuries. In 1602, conscience became an explicit issue with respect to a kind of contract that relied for its power to enforce behavior entirely on the spoken word. Such contracts were verbal in contrast to written contracts, entered into without legally recognized witnesses. They were inherently weak and susceptible to challenge. The decision of Sir Edward Coke in Slade's case, an action for debt that depended on a verbal contract, made its promissory dimension particularly remarkable. Coke's reasoning underscored the power of the spoken word that even when unwitnessed or undocumented acquired a legal authority.

Actions for debt were usually based on a writ or on a verbal agreement for which witnesses could be produced. When a verbal agreement had been made in the absence of witnesses, the defendant typically resorted to a procedure known as an "action of debt," which allowed for a trial by "wager of law." In such a trial, the defendant would summon a number of oath-takers who would swear not to the facts of the case but that the defendant's claim that he owed nothing to the plaintiff was good: they would swear either that he had paid the plaintiff or that no contract existed. The problem with this procedure is obvious: oath-takers could be and were bought—their word was for hire (Simpson 137–40, 295–99; Plucknett 647–48). To remedy this abuse, Coke focussed on the salient feature of contracts entered into without writ or witnesses, namely, that their legal remedies were susceptible to perjury. He stipulated that a plaintiff in a case involving a verbal contract, a spoken word, could resort to a different procedure. He could bring an "action upon *assumpsit*." In these cases the thing assumed referred to the thoughts and intentions of the parties to the contract. Their contract, although not substantiated by evidence in the ordinary way, was nonetheless considered to be capable of substantiation because it had a place in conscience. *Assumpsit* prohibited the defendant from relying on testimony of oath-takers and required that he submit to an investigation of evidence relevant to his defense to determine what would have been clear if the contract in question had been documented or witnessed. As Coke noted, this change in procedure was necessary because the "wager of law" could no longer protect the interests of the plaintiff (assuming it ever had): "experience proves that mens consciences grow so large that the respect of their private advantage rather induces men (and chiefly those who have declining estates) to perjury" (2: fol. 95, 95v). In effect, Coke made a verbal agreement to perform an action the equivalent of a promise to perform an action: "every contract executory imports itself an *assumpsit*, for when one agrees to pay money or to deliver anything, thereby he assumes or promises to pay, or deliver it" (94). Whereas the "wager of law" had demonstrated how fragile was the moral force behind taking an oath, *assumpsit* made a contract legally binding by transforming it into a matter of conscience—in short, by imbuing the verbal expression of a contract with a moral force.

Assumpsit was no more than a second-best solution. Coke would have preferred a society more open to ideals, a society in which words, oaths, and agreements did not require an investigation to prove their validity or meaning. Remarking generally on the moral decay of the times, he states: "I am surprised that in these days so little consideration is made of an oath, as I daily observe, *Cum jurare per Deum actus religionis sit* [for to swear by God is an act of religion, i.e., of faith]" (95v). Coke's belief that an interest in private gain rather than in public justice determined the course of the law made a virtue of skeptical inquiry.

Conscience in *Cymbeline* is a factor in decisions made by many of its characters, none of whom are as affected by their outcomes as Posthumus and Imogen when they respond to the promises made at their betrothal. These include a promise to keep faith, not only by not being unfaithful but also by not losing faith in the other's fidelity. The couple sharply differ in their understanding of these promises. Neither is adulterous. But while Imogen does not doubt Posthumus's fidelity, Posthumus does doubt hers. The terms defining his doubt are contractual and suggest mercantile relations—what they lack is any reference to conscience. It is no accident that they are initially "Italian" terms and to be associated with the mentality of the merchant, the moneylender, and the trader in currency bought and sold on foreign exchanges, activities prone to actions for debt.[4] At first, Posthumus rejects Iachimo's terms; it is only after repeated insults that he adopts them in order, as he mistakenly thinks, to defend his honor.

Iachimo is all calculation: to him, Posthumus appears to be "of crescent note," like a bill of exchange that increases in value as its term nears expiration. His "endowments" can be "tabled" in a "catalogue"; at the same time, he is subject to devaluation; his "weight" by marriage, relying on a "word" not "matter," is only hypothetical (1.5.1–15). Iachimo's view of women is comparably objectifying: they are all for sale. Upon his arrival in Rome, Posthumus exhibits a different mentality, suggesting a nobleman's largess: he expects to be his friend Philario's "debtor" for "courtesies"; Philario responds in the same vein by stating that his "poor kindness" is "o'er-rate[d]" (1.5.34–36; cf. *The Winter's Tale* 1.1). Speaking of his marriage while still in Britain, Posthumus used a similar language expressing value; he had declared Imogen's "loss" to herself and therefore his gain as "infinite" (1.2.51). The language of incommensurability here is intended to convey how inadequately any reference to measure can comprehend value; it implies a difference between price that is calculable and a worth that is beyond calculation. Why Posthumus does not continue to use this language is partly anticipated by the gifts he and Imogen have exchanged in Britain. Hers to him is a diamond ring, a token of their betrothal that she sees as without any term or condition as long as she is alive (1.2.42–45); his to her is a bracelet, a "manacle of love," which is to signify the same thing but looks rather like a device to secure property and therefore seems ironic (1.2.53). Once in Rome, Posthumus is easy prey for Iachimo, who teases him from his faith by language that prices Imogen's diamond and, by association, her fidelity. Posthumus replies that she, a "gift of the gods," cannot be priced, but the little "religion" that holds him back for a moment soon gives way before an urge to equate Imogen and her virtue with a sum of money (1.5.67–73, 79–82, 133–34). The fact that his wager is for a considerable sum does not obscure the lack of faith and bad conscience that has motivated it. His wager has removed his wife from an inner world of feeling and faith and placed her in a market of items and objects. Once at stake, Imogen becomes an object of calculation, not only priced but also theoretically subject to market fluctuations.

Posthumus's situation becomes contractually contradictory as a consequence of his wager. He allows himself to become indebted to Iachimo for a honorable reputation: he seeks to prove he is not a cuckold. Iachimo, in turn, takes up the position of a witness who will provide evidence that will either support or deny Posthumus's claim. Because it is evidence that will not be questioned by a jury, Iachimo actually functions as an oath-taker—a function that, as Coke noted, was highly susceptible to perjury. In the case at hand, Iachimo's self-interest is obvious. He is in fact a party to a second contract: the wager he makes with Posthumus (in effect, charging him with being a cuckold), one that effectively breaks the terms of the earlier contract of betrothal with its promise of spousal fidelity. Its language is explicit; Iachimo and Posthumus make a "covenant," a "match," a "bargain," a "wager"; they draw up "articles" set down by "lawful counsel" (1.5.40–66). Posthumus elects to defend himself from the threat of a bankrupt marriage (the first contract) by the word of an oath-taker who stands to benefit from that bankruptcy (the second contract). The idea of a wager figures twice: as Posthumus's bet and as the procedure by which he defends himself. In the event, he is shown to be unfaithful by doubting his wife's fidelity; she, by contrast, is revealed to be faithful to all her vows. When Iachimo attempts to tease Imogen out of believing in Posthumus, he is unsuccessful; she rejects his speech as an "assault" on the honor of a gentleman (1.7.145–50). The details of the episode expose the corruption possible when, in the absence of faith, the value of a human relationship is subjected to mercantile negotiation.

Iachimo's intention is quite obviously to win the wager. As soon as he knows he cannot do so in fact (Imogen will not be seduced), he resorts to deceit. Like the oath-taker Coke objected to, his word is not to be tied to any truth but merely to a fiction that will serve his own material interests. This much is clear when, emerging from the trunk in Imogen's bedchamber in which he has hidden, he inventories her possessions: even her "mole cinque-spotted" becomes a "voucher" (2.2.38–39). His lust is not the lover's who longs for the horses of the night to run slowly but rather the merchant's who wants a quick return on his investment: "Swift, swift, you dragons of the night, that dawning / May bare the raven's eye" (48–49). The process by which Posthumus is duped into believing Iachimo's perjury reveals the extent to which he shares Iachimo's mentality.[5]

The initial reasons Posthumus gives for doubting Iachimo's word and the "evidence" he gives to prove Imogen's adultery remain good at all stages of the interrogation and not just at its outset: it could all be the result of a conspiracy. If a servant could have reported the contents of her bedchamber and stolen her bracelet, a maid could have described her "mole" (2.4.133–36). Posthumus's failure to persist in doubt reflects a more fundamental distrust of women. Like Iachimo, he sees them as merely objects; they have a price (like a diamond) but no unique worth. His state of mind is expressed as a dream of parthenogenesis, a unique and unpartnered generation in which the male is the only parent and the "woman's part" excised altogether. "Is there no way for men to be, but women / Must be half-workers?" he asks (2.4.153–54). As the answer is no, he insists that generation produces only "counterfeits" (158)—coins appearing to correspond to a price but actually of adulterated worth. By revealing that he thinks of woman as a property without generative agency, Posthumus also reveals that he could not have kept his own promise to keep faith in marriage, a revelation that in retrospect makes his parting from her all the more pathetic. Aboard his ship bound for Rome, Posthumus eventually vanishes from the horizon of sight, but clearly not from Imogen's mind as she hears Pisanio describe the scene (1.4.8–16). The perspectivism of the image establishes the difference between a perception of an entity that fluctuates circumstantially (in this case, with space) and an inner vision of a being that retains her worth despite contingency. The sense of this difference is again evident later in the play when the character of Cymbeline's lost sons is at issue. They exhibit a royalty quite independent of place. "Place," as their guardian Belarius explains, only "lessens and sets off" (3.3.13)—it has nothing to do with an inherent virtue.

Posthumus's wager obviously affects Imogen's status as heir, the British succession, and the commonwealth as a whole. Iachimo's fictionalized picture of Posthumus in Rome—he "slaver[s] with lips as common as the stairs

/ That mount the Capitol"—politicizes adultery (1.7.105-06). Although a fiction—Posthumus is not adulterous—the image hides a truth. Having priced Imogen, Posthumus engages in a kind of prostitution. Rejected by her husband and abandoned by her father, Imogen's state is metaphorically "headless." Its vulnerability is further suggested by Iachimo's "trunk." Having told her to seek revenge for Posthumus's supposed adultery or else lose her "great stock," Iachimo emerges from his trunk to compile evidence that will reduce her moral stock to nothing in Posthumus's eyes. Important to the play's imperial theme is the image of a royal "stock" figuring Cymbeline's dynastic interests—interests that the play will depict as extending to the translation of empire from Rome to Britain. Cymbeline's "trunk" is what remains after the branches of his family tree, his sons and his daughter, are lopped off, lost or abandoned; when they return at the end of the play, the king's "stock" is revived.

The language of arboriculture was current in defenses of the Union of England and Scotland in the interest of creating a British empire. In general, these texts pictured the Union as an extension of the monarchy to occur when the two branches of the kingdom, England and Scotland, were regrafted to a central trunk. A common authority is to Zechariah, who celebrates the union of Judah and Israel as their return to the "tree" of Joseph.[6] A second reference in the most prominent of these defenses, John Thornborough's *The Ioiefull and Blessed Reuniting of the two mightie & famous kingdomes, England and Scotland into their ancient name of great Brittaine* (1605), alludes to the *conditions* in which such a truncated tree can be revived. They define the nature of the monarchy itself, and particularly its kind of rule; in a context in which the tree in question is prospectively imperial, the text implies its limitation with respect to divine law and God's will. Thornborough's text, from Daniel, describes the regeneration of Nebuchadnezzar. Imagined as "tree of great height," the king is reduced to a "stump," a sign that God punishes overweening ambition. Daniel prophesies the revival of the royal "tree" "after that thou [the king, Nebuchadnezzar] shalt knowe that the heauens haue the rule." He is to "breake of [his] sinnes by righteousnes, & [his] iniquities by mercie to the poore" (Dan. 4.11-27). In short, the king must not pretend to divinity. Thornborough thought that James I had already respected Daniel's conditions: "great Britain" is "for the height of his honor, like the tall and goodly Cedar, in whom the dream of Nabudchodonorser hath beene verified . . . out of the Stumpe of the rootes . . . the tree is growne vp againe to [its] former beautie" (C4v, D). To find Cymbeline's stock revived, however, Shakespeare's audiences have to wait for the end of the play.

The move to defer resolution is, of course, characteristic of romance. In this case, the interval between Cymbeline's loss of Imogen, his heir and the last of his children, and her return and the rediscovery of his sons is marked by various trials. They conclude when, having lost his queen, he regains his headship in marriage and in his kingdom. His relations with his subjects become "gracious," predictive of the Christian era that is about to begin, and also in line with the requirement that a Christian king act for his people. The moment at which his reformation is apparent coincides with his agreement to pay Augustus Caesar. By honoring this contract, a verbal contract made in circumstances that no longer obtain, Cymbeline exhibits his willingness to respect its promissory character and its guarantee in conscience.

The State

Caius Lucius, speaking for Augustus Caesar, asks Cymbeline for tribute on the basis of an agreement made years earlier by Cassibelan, Cymbeline's uncle, to pay Rome an annual sum in recognition of Julius Caesar's conquest of Britain (3.1.5-9).[7] In theory, a victor's rights following conquest were absolute; over time, of course, they invited modification or, worse, provoked outright revolution. The conflict over tribute in *Cymbeline* ends in a negotiated settlement; although the British have won, the Romans are paid. The idea of imperial rule is reconceived to preserve the liberties of the subject. Initially, however, the British monarchy chooses resistance. The queen and Cymbeline argue two quite different cases.

The queen states that Cassibelan's word is meaningless because Rome never actually conquered Britain. Caesar's was but "a kind of conquest." In reality, "he was carried [by the British] / From off our coast, twice beaten" (3.1.23, 26-27). This protest is based on what most audiences would have recognized as a patent lie; virtually everyone in Shakespeare's London would have seen or heard of some evidence of Roman Britain. The queen's misrepresentation of fact is comparable to a tyrant's silencing of the subject. She presumes that her word will not be subject to question, even on the basis of contradictory evidence. Cymbeline denies tribute on subtler grounds. He bases his position on the prior and fundamental freedom of the British people, a freedom that permits them to cancel any contract limiting that freedom provided they have the will and the force to do it. His argument makes the word of his ancestor subject to a kind of contingency; it holds good only in certain circumstances:

> You must know,
> Till the injurious Romans did extort
> This tribute from us, we were free. Caesar's ambition,
> Which swell'd so much that it did almost stretch
> The sides o' th' world, against all colour here
> Did put the yoke upon's; which to shake off
> Becomes a warlike people, whom we reckon
> Ourselves to be. . . . Say then to Caesar,
> Our ancestor was that Mulmutius which
> Ordain'd our laws, whose use the sword of Caesar
> Hath too much mangled; whose repair, and franchise,
> Shall (by the power we hold) be our good deed,
> Though Rome be therefore angry.
>
> (3.1.47–59)

Following Caius Lucius's pronouncement of "War and confusion / In Caesar's name" (66–67), Cymbeline declares that the British will follow the example of the "Pannonians and Dalmatians [who] for / Their liberties are now in arms" (74–75). This is suggestive language. It implies that British freedom entails more than independence from the Roman "yoke," that it is provided for in British law and as much to be exercised *by* the British subject (under positive law) as in behalf *of* a subject Britain (under the *ius gentium*, the law of nations). In short, British defiance of Roman hegemony is rooted in her institution of a positive law that comparably defies an abrogation of the liberties of the British subject within Britain.

The notion of a double freedom—of the British people and the British subject—drew on a uniquely English understanding of imperialism. To promote support for the Union, James I had represented the peace that would follow it as an extension of the peace between England, Spain, and the Low Countries that was concluded in 1604. He would consequently become a second Augustus whose *pax Britannica* would supersede its Roman prototype. He had also inherited an earlier and historically Tudor imperialism whose ideological function was not to harmonize but rather to divorce English and Roman interests. Published by Henry VIII as a feature of Reformation policy, the doctrine that the English monarch was an "emperor without a superior" was a means to justify the liberties of the

English subject under Elizabeth. After 1559, the doctrine protected the vast properties—formerly of the church but confiscated by the Tudors—that belonged to English subjects.[8] By its association with property, it was seen also to guarantee English liberties. The two imperialisms, British and English, were in a sense contradictory. The imperialism James pretended to was associated with absolutism, at least in some measure. The imperialism of the Tudors was bound up with English liberty and liberties. Linking the two was the question asked by all political systems and, notably, dramatized by the action in *Cymbeline*: the limits of a subject's obedience to authority.

In general terms, the question was framed by reference to Scripture's representation of the historical Caesar and the nature of his rule after the birth of Christ. It asked under what circumstances was Caesar to be obeyed, whether in matters of tribute or other situations. The dictum in Matthew 22 proved to be enigmatic. When asked whether it was "lawful to giue tribute to Caesar," Jesus answered: "Giue . . . Cesar the things which are Cesars, and giue vnto God those which are Gods" (19-21). Interpretations of this text usually restricted Caesar's claims to those which did not impinge on the subject's obligations to God. Aquinas prefaced his discussion of obedience by stipulating the fundamental "freedom" of all Christians. In his commentary on Peter Lombard, he noted that the dicta in Matthew 22 are preceded by a declaration of Christian liberty:

It would seem that Christians are not bound to obey the secular powers, and particularly tyrants. For it is said, *Matthew* XVII, 25: "Therefore the children are free (*liberi*)." And if in all countries the children of the reigning sovereign are free, so also should the children of that sovereign be free, to whom all kings are subject. Christians have become the sons of God as we read in the *Epistle to the Romans* (VII,16); . . . Christians then are everywhere free, and are thus not bound to obey the secular powers.[9]

As Aquinas recognized, however, there is a countervailing argument in Romans 13: "Let euerie soule be subiect vnto the higher powers. For there is no power but of God: & the powers that be, are ordeined of God" (1). To mediate these claims of freedom and subjection, Aquinas went on to qualify obedience so that it was due only when it was truly "of God," and "derived from God [*a Deo descendit*]." He acknowledged that authority (*prelatio*) did not derive from God if it was falsely obtained or wrongly used. In cases in which an authority commands the performance of a sinful act, a subject "is obliged to disobey [*tenetur non obedire*]" (182-83). In cases in which an authority exceeds the scope of his office—"as, for example, when a master demands payment from a servant which the latter is not bound to make"—a subject "need not obey . . . need not disobey [*non tenetur obedir . . . (non) tenetur non obedire*]" (184-85). In all cases, the subject's conscience determines the validity of a command and of the authority making it.

Erasmus returned to Romans specifically to explain the conduct of a Christian prince. Discussing tyrannical rule in his *Institutio principis christiani* (1516), he notes that although Paul had in fact commanded Christians to obey a pagan prince (*ethnicus princeps*), he would have devised a different rule to cover a Christian polity (had such a thing existed). As Christians, both prince and people were to regard their obligations in light of divine love: "owe no one anything unless you love each other [*inter vos nemini quicquid debeatis nisi vt inuicem diligatis*]."[10] True, Paul had ordered people to tolerate bad magistrates for the sake of civil order, but he had also said that Christians were privileged to live in a new era. To Erasmus this meant that a Christian prince was not to command his people "to undertake slavish works," nor was he "to dispossess them or to seize their goods [*ad seruiles operas adigere, exigere possessionibus, expilare bonis*]" (150); in short, to make them martyrs. After the creation of a Christendom, Erasmus maintained, Paul's dicta were to be modified. As the foundations of a Christian polity, they created a Caesar whose authority was subject to question and whose power was limited. His pagan prototype had been absolutely free, even by Pauline standards; he, by contrast, was bound by principles that transformed his freedom into something like a servitude.

Arguing for a "free and absolute" monarchy, James I (and absolutists who later supported him) rejected Thomist and Erasmian interpretations of Scripture and insisted that Paul's words were to be taken literally at all times. To imagine that the "Spirit of God," having commanded the people to give their rulers "heartie obedience for conscience sake, giuing to *Caesar* that which was *Caesars*, and to God that which was Gods," would renege on this fundamental point of government was a "shamelesse presumption." It posited an "vnlawfull libertie" of the people (72). Scripture allowed them rights only in conscience; they could not disobey the monarch and remain within the law; their only recourse was to ask for grace. Constitutionalists, on the other hand, tended to adhere to traditional Christian notions of a polity, which were on the whole consistent with their idea that monarch

and people were bound together by mutual duties and obligations under
positive law. But their habit of linking the freedom of a subject in conscience to his liberties as a property holder had theoretical and practical
consequences unforeseen in literature that dealt with general principles.

Inevitably, their language of freedom of conscience, a Christian liberty,
became bound up with the language of property, the liberties of the subject. With the exception of purely doctrinal matters, in no respect did the
distinction between the monarch and God have more meaning than in
disputes over property, subsidies, impositions, and other forms of tribute
that were owed to or demanded by the monarch. Invoking Aquinas, Sir John
Fortescue had limited the monarch's authority and power over the property
of subjects and had stated that beyond what the monarch could demand
by his prerogative, his revenues were a gift from the people. Moreover, all
his revenue was to be spent in the interest of the commonwealth:

Ffor as Seynt Thomas saith, *Rex datur propter regnum, et non regnum propter
regem* (a king is given for the kingdom not the kingdom for the king). Wherfore
all that he dothe owith to be referred to his kyngdome. Ffor though his estate be
the highest estate temporall in the erthe yet it is an office, in wich he mynestrith
to his reaume defence and justice. And therfore he mey say off hym selff and off
his reaume . . . *seruus seruorum Dei* [that he is a servant of the servants of God].
(126-27).

The monarch was supported by his people not because he was absolute
but because they had "much ffredome in thair owne godis" (140)—that
is, their right to property was the guarantee that he would not want for
support.[11] Later commentators were more precise in considering the possibility that the people might resist such support—presumably acting on
their freedom—should they see it as inhibiting the growth of the commonwealth. In his *Pandectes of the Law of Nations* (1602), William Fulbecke
made the monarch's prudence a condition of his ability to get tribute: "it
behoueth euerie Monarch to haue a watchfull care of his subiects good,
and to bend the force of his minde to the preseruation and maintenance
of their safetie and good estate; so subiects should not grudge to pay vnto
them tributes & subsidies and other publike impositions" (S4). Barnabe
Barnes saw that the monarch's temperance in collecting and spending was
the chief assurance of his revenue: a prince is to be "vertuously liberall
according to strict conscience" (C2v). But such formulations also set limits
to freedom: they left the monarch's prerogative absolute. Were a subject

to exercise his Christian freedom against the prerogative, he took himself outside the protection of positive law. This point is made inferentially by George Saltern in a treatise ostensibly devoted to the thesis that English (or British) common law was at one with divine law.

Of the antient Lawes of great Britain (1605) rehearses an extract from the *leges Anglorum* which claims that after Britain became Christian, their bishop, Elutherius, empowered their kings to reject the authority of the Roman Caesar. His phrasing is, I think, deliberately ambiguous. It is not always clear whether the Caesar in question is the Roman emperor or merely a figure of any head of state. If he is Roman, then the British king stands in the position of subject and is encouraged to be as free as a Christian conscience will allow. If he is any head of state, then the British king is being instructed in the limits of his own authority and power—limits imposed by the countervailing freedom of his Christian subjects. In any case, Caesar's rule is to be circumscribed by the greater authority of God. "We may (saith he [i.e., Elutherius]) alwaies reproue the Lawes of *Rome* and *Caesar*, but not the Lawes of God," states Saltern, an assertion that implies British independence of Rome. When Saltern reports that the bishop ordered the British king, Lucius, to "rule by Gods law & not by *Caesars*," however, it looks as if he is referring to the monarch's Christian conscience (Dv). Saltern had identified the "principles" of English "Common Lawes" and the "auncient British constitutions" with "the verie Lawes of the eternal God," "written in the two immortal tables of nature & Scripture," and effectively denied the absolutist premise that the monarch, obeying divine law, could flout positive law (B2). But this formulation left the prerogative as absolute and the subject who disobeyed it without legal recourse. Resisting the prerogative, the subject became an outlaw automatically and a revolutionary potentially. By 1606, a case involving a customs duty, a form of revenue and therefore a kind of tribute from the subject to the monarch, had clearly established this point.

Sitting on the court of the Exchequer, Chief Baron Fleming decided that John Bate, an importer of currants, had to pay the king a customs duty. This was a consequence of the fact that the monarch's prerogative, absolute and above positive law, had always covered imports and exports; in any case, the tax was against an item, not a man and his labor, and it did not, therefore, impinge upon his liberties as a holder of property. On the question of liberties in general, Fleming's decision embraced issues beyond the payment of customs duties. It described the character of the prerogative and its practical consequences. As Fleming admitted, the prerogative—by conferring an authority and power beyond determination in positive law—could freely go wrong as much as right. It was, in that sense, a terrible instrument. Faced with the prerogative, a subject had only the recourse provided by petition; having no standing at law, he could only ask for grace:

> And whereas it is said that if the King may impose [i.e., by the prerogative], he may impose any quantity what he pleases, true it is that this is to be referred to the wisdom of the King, who guideth all under God by his wisdom, and this is not to be disputed by a subject; and many things are left to his wisdom for the ordering of his power, rather than his power shall be restrained. The King may pardon any felon; but it may be objected that if he pardon one felon he may pardon all, to the damage of the commonwealth, and yet none will doubt but that is left in his wisdom. . . . to restrain the King and his power because that by his power he may do ill, is no argument for a subject. (343-44)[12]

What "wisdom" a monarch might call on when empowered absolutely was therefore the question. Fleming, like all theorists of the monarchy, had stipulated that the prerogative must be used for "the general benefit of the people and is *salus populi*; as the people is the body and the King the head" (340-41). The wisdom informing its exercise must reflect a common interest. But he also pointed out that the only faculty promoting monarchic wisdom in prerogative cases would be a moral one. Such wisdom would necessarily depend on a discrimination of better and worse, good and evil—distinctions that have their basis in conscience.[13] This reasoning clearly exposed the subject's vulnerability. Were he to challenge the monarch on a matter falling within the scope of the prerogative, no positive law would protect him. Literally an "outlaw," he had to live by whatever lights his conscience could supply. *Cymbeline* represents three notable challenges to monarchic authority, each by a subordinate who acts on the basis of moral conviction.

Conspicuously unwise in his toleration of the queen's tyranny, Cymbeline's misgovernment is mended, to a degree, by Cornelius, the queen's physician, and Pisanio, Posthumus's servant, who disobey or in some way contravene the commands of their superiors. They do so deceptively and without attracting attention. A third, Belarius, Cymbeline's soldier-courtier, represents a more critical case. His abduction of Cymbeline's sons is actually an instance of treason; it makes him an "outlaw" (4.2.138). It also ends by preserving the kingdom: helped by Posthumus, who leaves the

Roman army and disguises himself as a British "peasant," Belarius and his two foster sons rescue Cymbeline in battle and defeat the Romans. There is then no political or material reason that Rome should continue to collect British tribute; that Cymbeline pays tribute is therefore a political paradox and only comprehensible on moral grounds. It indicates that the force of a word, a verbal contract, inscribed in conscience, can supersede the weight of circumstance, registered in moments of history. The play concludes by a series of acknowledgments of contracts broken and then renewed. They are all reviewed in light of the most imposing of contracts made by the Word of God for the generations to come and continuously present in *Cymbeline* by a consciousness of the "time when" the action of the play is represented as having taken place.

Having fought for Britain in disguise, Posthumus allows himself to be captured as a Roman. He has accepted Pisanio's proof of Imogen's death, a "bloody cloth," and, although he accuses Pisanio of a bad conscience (the "bond" of service requires only obedience to "just" commands [5.1.1-7]), he focuses on his own breach of faith. It justifies his imprisonment in a Roman "bondage" whose only release is in death, a "liberty" from the consciousness of sin (5.4.3-11).[14] The language of calculation is voiced again but only to be rejected, not once but twice. Posthumus wishes to render his "whole self" to satisfy a debt that he could legally discharge by the payment of a mere fraction (18-28), but Jupiter, who governs such business, is disposed to make gifts rather than engage in commerce. Posthumus's dream of the Leonati, his parents and his brothers, indicates how forcefully a moral arithmetic determines his sense of personal worth. He "sees" them plead with Jupiter to spare him: his pitiable birth, his orphanhood, his virtue in Imogen's eyes, his undeserved exile, Iachimo's treachery all speak to their claims for consideration. Posthumus experiences the god's answer in a more sensuous and palpable way.

Jupiter's descent appears anomalous in its fusion of moral decorum and visual hyperbole—the god, seated on an eagle, was presumably lowered from the rafters to the sound of thunder and the smell of sulphur (114-19). The scene makes sense, however, as the moment at which the two "matters" of wager and chronicle, marriage and empire, are brought together. Jupiter settles the matter of the wager, for which Posthumus believes he should die, by rejecting the Leonati's claims for justice but bettering their requests by displaying mercy. He answers them by a Christian logic: "Whom best I love I cross; to make my gift, / The more delay'd, delighted" (101–02). What is exchanged in the balance is the god's benefit of a human life; Posthumus will not only live but prosper. Jupiter's actions also represent the matter of chronicle by their reference to two prophetic accounts of the future British empire.

The divine eagle, actually a prop and figuratively the god's power, is a reminder that Posthumus shadows an imperial self. It is also the central figure in the Roman soothsayer's prophecy of victory. Misinterpreted at first, the true meaning of the prophecy is not apparent before the last moments of the play. Jupiter's eagle in 5.4 recalls the first of these interpretations in 4.2:

> I saw Jove's bird, the Roman eagle, wing'd
> From the spongy south to this part of the west,
> There vanish'd in the sunbeams, which portends
> (Unless my sins abuse my divination)
> Success to th' Roman host.
>
> (348–52)

As the audience can now recognize, the truth in the soothsayer's prophecy is mingled with falsehood: the British have in fact defeated the "Roman host." The eagle which has signaled success seems to have altered his Roman and traditional character to embrace a British and novel presence. Plausible in light of figurations of James's own imperial monarchy in contemporary Stuart iconography,[15] the identification of a triumphant British eagle flying west anticipates the conflation of empires, Roman and British (a version of the classic notion of *translatio imperii*), imagined in the play's concluding vision of history.

The tablet Jupiter leaves with Posthumus establishes a direct link between the marriage story and its place in the future history of empire. It tells of two fortunes, one of "a lion's whelp . . . to himself unknown," who will "without seeking find, and be embrac'd by a piece of tender air," and the other of "a stately cedar" whose "lopp'd branches . . . which, being dead many years, shall after revive, be jointed to the old stock, and freshly grow." These events will signal the end of Posthumus's "miseries," and the "peace and plenty" of Britain (5.4.138–45). Ignorant of the language of Scripture and pro-Union literature, Posthumus cannot know that "the lion's whelp" or Judah signifies the Scottish inheritance; or that embraced by "air" (or revived), it will be at one with Britain, and the two, the heirs of Scotland and Britain, will form one empire. Nor could he guess that the "old stock" of a "stately cedar" (a tree of state or royal dynasty), which is about to be revivified by the return of its branches, constructs an image favored by pro-Union apologists. His own situation gives no hint as to how Jupiter's words will be fulfilled; they are not only literally riddling but dramatically enigmatic. Posthumus is being asked to have faith in what he cannot find plausible or even quite understand.

The final scene, dazzling in its revelations, realizes the terms of the prophecy as if to dramatize the hand of providence in human history. Those who have been lost are found: Imogen, Belarius, Guiderius, Arviragus. Offenders are recognized and pardoned: Posthumus, Iachimo, Belarius, Guiderius. The courageous are praised: the four "peasants" who saved Cymbeline. Villains are named and dismissed: the queen and Cloten. And law is celebrated. It is imagined less as the natural law of mortality, registered in generation, and more as the divine law of keeping one's word, apprehended by conscience. It is not fully recognized before Posthumus recognizes Imogen; it is only realized when Cymbeline exercises his absolute power of pardon and honors Cassibelan's agreement by paying Roman tribute.

When Imogen identifies Posthumus and tries to stop his grief, he sees her merely as a page boy and knocks her down: "There lie thy part" (5.5.229). His impulsive beating of a subordinate testifies to his continuing tendency to objectify whoever is beneath him in rank or by virtue of gender. The "staggers" that then afflict him are both retribution and a lesson (233); he is put down because in victorious Britain status is to be conferred by kinds of virtue. Imogen's response is enigmatic, but it rectifies their relations:

> Why did you throw your wedded lady from you?
> Think that you are upon a rock, and now
> Throw me again.
>
> (261–63)

Her words reflect her history as faithful and Fidele; they also imply her chaste sexuality.[16] Posthumus responds appropriately by asking her, now his "soul," to be fruitful (5.5.264) and thereby recalls her complaint that Cymbeline, by exiling Posthumus, had "like the tyrannous breathing of the north, / [Shaken] all our buds from growing" (1.4.36–37). By calling Imogen his soul, Posthumus rejects the notion of her as a pricey item and renews the terms of betrothal. He also experiences a more pervasive conversion of spirit in which Cymbeline then finds inspiration.

When Cymbeline orders the execution of his Roman captives, including Lucius, in order to appease the kinfolk of slaughtered Britons, he appeals to an ancient code of retributive justice that defied the usual practice of bargaining for ransom. By refusing to negotiate with the Romans, Cymbeline exercises his absolute authority and power to refuse pardon or anything comparable to pardon. His wisdom in doing so is, however, called into question when Posthumus pardons Iachimo, who has confessed his part in promoting Posthumus's faithless wager: "my heavy conscience sinks my knee . . . [take] the bracelet of the truest princess / That ever swore her faith" (5.5.414–18). Posthumus becomes a model of prerogative rule, telling Iachimo, "Kneel not to me: / The power that I have on you, is to spare you," to which Cymbeline responds, "Nobly doom'd! / We'll learn our freeness of a son-in-law: / Pardon's the word to all" (418–23). This change in policy illustrates more than a presumptively benign exercise of the monarch's absolute power. By associating his "freeness" specifically with the prerogative power to pardon, that is, by not making the grander and more extensive claims of a "free and absolute" monarch (as, for example, they were expressed by James I), Cymbeline tacitly invokes the political relations of a constitutionalist monarchy.

His moment of self-reflection coincides with his recognition of his "son-in-law," not only as his daughter's husband but as one of the four "peasants" whose resistance to an imperial force was the occasion of his own salvation. To acknowledge Posthumus as Imogen's consort signals in a formal way what the action has already established: that Cymbeline must abandon and indeed has abandoned plans for the incestuous marriage he had earlier envisaged. To learn his son-in-law's "freeness"—in the sense of his freedom to resist even the authority and power from which he, an outlaw, has no legal recourse—also constitutes a warning. Absolute authority and power are absolute only to a point: the monarch is not a god. Beyond positive law and the "auncient constitution," the subject has a footing in Nature that makes contingent even the prerogative. Cymbeline, as Caesar's subject, benefits from this resistance, which validates, in turn, his respect for conscience and contract. Cymbeline as king of Britain and prospectively emperor of the west is therefore in a position to arrive at the "wisdom" Fleming had indicated was the only guarantee that the prerogative would be exercised to the benefit of the subject. As Fleming's decision and Saltern's treatise reveal, the common law leaves the subject vulnerable to the monarch's absolute will. *Cymbeline* dramatizes the limitation of that will by a resistance that gets its strength and inspiration from the "outlaw" in natural law.

The soothsayer's interpretation of Jupiter's tablet confirms that what has just happened on stage is the result of a divine intention; it establishes what those characters who had been made helpless by their own confusion (especially Pisanio) had hoped for: the heavens working in and through history. The soothsayer's *re*-interpretation of his own vision of the Roman eagle's flight west obviously speaks both to the fact that Rome has not won the kind of victory he had earlier foreseen but has secured the tribute she had requested in the first place. It alludes by figures of thought and of speech to the forces both personal and numinous that have resolved the conflict between Rome and Britain. Its explanatory power is the more important because Cymbeline himself gives no reason why the queen's argument for rejecting tribute, to which he did not in any case subscribe, is no longer good, nor does he explain why he is no longer convinced that his own position on very fundamental English liberties and liberty is correct. He simply "promises" to pay Caesar "our wonted tribute" (463). In effect, he repeats Cassibelan's promise—a promise that he must now regard as holding good despite the fact that the circumstances in which it was first made no longer obtain.

Cymbeline's decision to honor his ancestor's verbal contract is plausible only if he has accepted what he earlier rejected: a word given in good faith has a force in conscience. What guarantees its privilege is both in Nature and in the Word, the hidden subject of the soothsayer's new interpretation of the Roman eagle:

> For the Roman eagle,
> From south to west on wing soaring aloft,
> Lessen'd herself and in the beams o' the sun
> So vanish'd; which foreshadow'd our princely eagle,
> Th' imperial Caesar, should again unite
> His favour with the radiant Cymbeline,
> Which shines here in the west.
>
> (471-77)

British victory and Roman success coincide in a moment at which imperial rule is both enlarged and reduced—enlarged by assimilating a western people, reduced by light from a sun in the west. The eagle's fabled vision— said to be able to look into the sun—becomes one with the radiance it seeks. Literal historicism opens a figuratively contrived perspective on salvation history when the soothsayer's words are read as puns: thus the Roman eagle "lessen'd" (that is, "lessoned") herself in the "sun" (that is, the Son) and so "vanish'd." The condition of this Roman lesson—the eclipse of Caesar before God—would therefore appear to be the precondition of the *translatio imperii,* which is clearly alluded to as Caesar's "favour" to "radiant" Cymbeline. Cymbeline literally pays tribute to the Roman Caesar; figuratively, however, he pays tribute to that lessoned or instructed emblem of imperial rule by which he must now, that is, in the future the play looks forward to, agree to govern. Under the aegis of the Word, this new imperialism paradoxically guarantees the liberties and liberty on which Cymbeline had originally insisted. It leaves the Britons as "naturalized" Romans,[17] the tribute they owe to Caesar paid not from the abject position of a conquered people but granted in conscientious observance of a contract. Tribute paradoxically signals their freedom, not their servitude. It also casts Cymbeline in the self-reflexive light that according to virtually all theories of monarchy, whether absolutist or constitutional, was supposed to show him how to rule. His status as subject, by way of fictions of accident, deprivation, or sympathetic identification, provides a mirror in which he can see the effects of his authority and power. Enabling these exchanges is the contractualism effected by the human word and legitimated by divine law represented in the Word.

Notes

1. See Holinshed 1:478-79; Geoffrey of Monmouth, *De origine et Gestis Brittanorum* 1.26, qtd. in Moffet 209; John Stow, *Chronicles of England* 35, qtd. in Geller 243. See also Spenser 2.50.

2. For suggestions on topicality in *Cymbeline,* see Marcus.

3. For details on marriage law, see Stone, *Road to Divorce* 51-58; see also Stone, *The Family* 30-37. On the play's representation of sexuality in general, and some aspects of the marriage contract in particular, see Bergeron. See also Thompson.

4. On women as objects in a market, see Hutson. For the inventoried female body, see Parker. For the theater and market activity, see Agnew.

5. Posthumus's suit is later assumed, both literally and figuratively, by Cloten, who incarnates the spirit of mercantilism even more crudely than Iachimo. He buys music in order to "penetrate" her (that is, he buys an "air"), and he sees marriage as a way to get rich (2.3.7-8, 11-18, 81-82). He tells Imogen that her "contract" with Posthumus is null because he is a "base wretch," and she cannot be allowed the "enlargement" available to "meaner parties"

who "knit their souls . . . in [a] self-figur'd knot" (2.3.114–21); that is, her marriage must find its social and material correlatives.

6. John Thornborough argued that England and Scotland were "at first both but one. [But] . . . it pleased God, for sinne of people, to breake those Bands . . . *to dissolve the brotherhoode of Israell and Iuda*" and invoked Zech. 11.14: "Then brake I asunder mine other staffe, euen the Bandes, that I might dissolue the brotherhode betwene Iudah and Israel." Explaining Zechariah, Thornborough refers to Ezek. 37.19: "Thus said the Lord God, Beholde, I wil take the tre of Ioseph, which is in the hand of Ephraim, and the tribes of Israel his fellowes, and wil put them with him euen with the tre of Iudah, and make them one tre, and they shalbe one in mine hand." Later, James is represented as a single "Vine," divulged by "the inserting and fast grafting of each branch and al fruite into his owne Royal person, as into a fruitfull and flourishing vine, even into the head of the whole body" (cf. Jer. 23.5–8) (*The Ioiefull and Blessed Reuniting* A, Av, A2). In an earlier treatise Thornborough asked, "Are not diuerse boughes from one tree, and all they of one and the same substance? And may not diuers people vnder one Prince, though they are deuided in persons, yet be vnited in lawes?" (*A Discovrse Plainely Prouing* C3v). See also Barnabe Barnes's treatise, in which he notes that the "auncient tree" of Britain has been grafted with Danish, French and Saxon branches, collected in the person of James I: "these seuerall plants graciously sprout out on high, like the sweet Cedars in *Salomons* forrests: which shortly by transportation or inoculation of their sprigs into other kingdomes may beare rule and preheminence in all the goodliest gardens of the world" (L3v). For the iconography of the cedar in *Cymbeline*, see Simonds 241–43.

7. Cymbeline's refusal to pay tribute is not mentioned in Holinshed's chronicles. See Rossi.

8. To illustrate Henrician imperialism, John Guy quotes the preamble to the Act of Appeals: "Where by divers sundry old authentic histories and chronicles it is manifestly declared and expressed that this realm of England is an empire, and so hath been accepted in the world, governed by one supreme head and king having the dignity and royal estate of the imperial crown of the same, unto whom a body politic, compact of all sorts and degrees of people divided in terms and by names of spiritualty and temporalty, be bounden and owe to bear next to God a natural and humble obedience; [the king] being also institute and furnished by the goodness and sufferance of Almighty God with plenary, whole and entire power, preeminence, authority, prerogative and jurisdiction" (24 Hen. VIII c. 12; Guy 67). For an extended examination of *Cymbeline* in light of Stuart church/state relations, see Hamilton 128–62.

9. b. 2, 44.2.2; ed. D'Entrèves, 180–81.

10. This text reproduces that of the *Opera omnia* (1540). For a modern English translation, see *The Education of a Christian Prince*. The idea of Christian obligation is expressed to a different purpose by William Tyndale; see his *The Obedience of a Christian Man*.

11. Fortescue compares English with French subjects and finds the former rich, free, and taxable, and the latter poor, lacking justice, and likely to rebel: "Ffor nothyng mey make [a] people to arise but lakke of gode, or lakke of justice. But yet sertaynly when thay lakke gode thai woll aryse, sayng that thai lakke justice" (140). For the concept of revenue before the Great Contract (1610), see Holmes.

12. For Bate's case, see Oakley.

13. Bate's case therefore characterized the monarch's power as a "mystery"; to the extent that this allowed him not to give a reason for his actions, it gave rise to parliamentary resentment. See Judson 159-60.

14. This "bondage" is to what Posthumus recognizes as sin; it is to be distinguished from the obligations of parties to a contract. "Liberty" from the first comes with grace; mutual freedoms are the condition of the second. For a different view, see Lawrence.

15. For a literary representation of this iconography, see especially Barnes, who illustrates James I's monarchy by allusions to an eagle and the sun: James is "hyeroglyphically represented by the figure of the sun" and the "eagle," who looking into the "Sunne," finds "miracles within that sanctified orbe of bright vertue." The eagle is also "shadowed in Phoebus or Apollo, bearing also with him the thunderbolts of Iupiter (who mystically reueileth soveraigne Maiestie) to grinde, burne, and consume into powder the violence of his enemies" (par. iii, iiii.v, A). For the self-representation of James I, see Goldberg.

16. J. M. Nosworthy sees that the "rock" Posthumus must think he stands on is that to which he anchors later (5.5.394), that is, Imogen herself. Hamilton reads these lines as an intervention in the debate on church and state under James I (147).

17. Works from 1606 to 1608 by Francis Bacon—including an early version of his essay "Of the True Greatness of the Kingdom of Britain" (1612), which is entitled "Of the Greatnesse of Kingdomes"—take up the prospect of a British empire created not by conquest but by trade and commerce (12: 376-78). It is typically the province of a tough and poor citizenry, uninterested in luxury and disciplined by a rural life. In "Of the Greatnesse of Kingdomes" Bacon returns to a topic he addressed as early as 1606 in a speech to Commons (13: 221-23)—the need for restraint in taxation: "The blessing of *Iudah* and *Issachar* will neuer meet, to be both the Lions whelpe and the Asse laid betweene burthens: Neither will a people ouercharged with tributes, bee euer fit for Empire. Nobilitie & Gentlemen multiplying in too great a proportion, maketh the common subiect grow to bee a pesant and base swaine driuen out of heart, and but the Gentlemans laborer. . . . take away the middle people, & you take away the infantery, whch is the nerue of an Armie. . . . For it is the Plough that yeeldeth the best soldier; but how? maintained in plentie and in the hand of owners, and not of meere laborers" ("Of the Greatnesse of Kingdomes," 12: 377-78). In its final form, published in 1625, Bacon's treatise on empire puts a special emphasis on Rome's peaceful conquests by naturalization: "you will say that it was not the Romans that spread upon the world, but it was the world that spread upon the Romans; and that was the sure way of greatness ("Of the True Greatness of Kingdoms and Estates," 12: 182).

Works Cited

Agnew, Jean-Christophe. *Worlds Apart: The Market and the Theater in Anglo-American Thought, 1550-1750.* Cambridge: Cambridge UP, 1986.

Bacon, Francis. *The Works of Francis Bacon.* Ed. James Spedding, Robert Leslie Ellis, and Douglas Denon Heath. 15 vols. London, 1860.

Barnes, Barnabe. *Foure Bookes of Offices.* London, 1606. STC 1468.

Bergeron, David M. "Sexuality in *Cymbeline.*" *Essays in Literature* 10 (1983): 159-68.

Coke, Sir Edward. "Slade's Case." *Reports.* 7 vols. London, 1776-77. 2: fols. 94-95.

Erasmus, Desiderius. *Institutio principis christiani. Opera omnia.* Ed. J. H. Waszink et al. 21 vols. Amsterdam: North Holland, 1969-94. Sect. 4, 1: 136-219.

Fleming, Chief Baron. "Bate's Case." *Constitutional Documents of the Reign of James I, 1603-1625.* Ed. J. R. Tanner. Cambridge: Cambridge UP, 1930. 243-45.

Fortescue, Sir John. *The Governance of England.* Ed. Charles Plummer. Oxford: Milford, 1926.

Fulbecke, William. *Pandectes of the Law of Nations.* London, 1602. STC 11414.

Geller, Lila. "*Cymbeline* and the Imagery of Covenant Theology." *Studies in English Literature* 20 (1980): 241-55.

Goldberg, Jonathan. *James I and the Politics of Literature: Jonson, Shakespeare, Donne, and Their Contemporaries.* Baltimore: Johns Hopkins UP, 1983.

Guy, John. "The 'Imperial Crown' and the Liberty of the Subject: The English Constitution from Magna Carta to the Bill of Rights." *Courts, Country and Culture: Essays on Early Modern British History in Honor of Perez Zagorin.* Ed. Bonnelyn Young Kunze and Dwight D. Brautigam. Rochester: U of Rochester P, 1992. 65-87.

Hamilton, Donna B. *Shakespeare and the Politics of Protestant England.* Lexington: U of Kentucky P, 1992.

Holinshed, Raphael. *Chronicles of England, Scotland, and Ireland.* 6 vols. London, 1802.

Holmes, Clive. "Parliament, Liberty, Taxation, and Property." *Parliament and Liberty from the Reign of Elizabeth to the English Civil War.* Ed. J. H. Hexter. Stanford: Stanford UP, 1992. 122-54.

Hutson, Lorna. *The Usurer's Daughter: Male Friendship and Fictions of Women in Sixteenth-Century England.* London: Routledge, 1994.

James I. *The Trew Law of Free Monarchies. Political Writings.* Ed. J. P. Sommerville. Cambridge: Cambridge UP, 1994. 62-84.

Judson, Margaret Atwood. *The Crisis of the Constitution: An Essay in Constitutional and Political Thought in England, 1603-1645.* New York: Octagon, 1971.

Lawrence, Judiana. "Natural Bonds and Artistic Coherence in the Ending of *Cymbeline*." *Shakespeare Quarterly* 35 (1984): 440-60.

Marcus, Leah S. *Puzzling Shakespeare: Local Reading and Its Discontents.* Berkeley: U of California P, 1988.

Moffet, Robin. "*Cymbeline* and the Nativity." *Shakespeare Quarterly* 13 (1962): 206-18.

Oakley, Francis. "Jacobean Political Theology: The Absolute and Ordinary Powers of the King." *Journal of the History of Ideas* 29 (1968): 323-46.

Parker, Patricia. "Rhetorics of Property: Exploration, Inventory, Blazon." *Literary Fat Ladies: Rhetoric, Gender, Property.* London: Methuen, 1987. 126-54.

Plucknett, Theodore F. T. *A Concise History of the Common Law.* 5th ed. Boston: Little, Brown, 1956.

Rossi, Jean Warehol. "*Cymbeline*'s Debt to Holinshed: The Richness of III.1." *Shakespeare's Romances Reconsidered.* Ed. Carol McGinnis Kay and Henry E. Jacobs. Lincoln: U of Nebraska P, 1978. 104-12.

Saltern, George. *Of the Antient Lawes of Great Britaine.* London, 1605. STC 21653.

Shakespeare, William. *Cymbeline.* Ed. J. M. Nosworthy. London: Routledge, 1991.

Simonds, Peggy Muñoz. *Myth, Emblem, and Music in Shakespeare's* Cymbeline: *An Iconographic Reconstruction.* Newark: U of Delaware P, 1992.

Simpson, A. W. B. *A History of the Common Law of Contract: The Rise of the Action of Assumpsit.* Oxford: Clarendon, 1975.

Spenser, Edmund. *The Faerie Queene.* Ed. Thomas P. Roche, Jr. New Haven: Yale UP, 1978.

Stone, Lawrence. *The Family, Sex, and Marriage in England, 1500-1800.* New York: Harper, 1977.

———. *Road to Divorce: England 1530-1987.* Oxford: Oxford UP, 1990.

Thomas Aquinas. "Commentary on the Sentences of Peter Lombard." *Selected Political Writings.* Ed. A. P. D'Entrèves. Trans. J. G. Dawson. Oxford: Blackwell, 1954. 180-87.

Thompson, Ann. "Person and Office: The Case of Imogen, Princess of Britain." *Literature and Nationalism.* Ed. Vincent Newey and Ann Thompson. Liverpool: Liverpool UP, 1991. 76-87.

Thornborough, John. *A Discovrse Plainely Prouing the euident vtilitie nd vrgent necessitie of the desired happie union of the two famovs Kingdomes of England and Scotland.* London, 1604. STC 24035.

———. *The Ioiefull and Blessed Reuniting of the two mightie & famous kingdomes, England and Scotland into their ancient name of great Brittaine.* London, 1605. STC 24036.

Tyndale, William. *The Obedience of a Christian Man. The Works of the English Reformers: William Tyndale and John Frith.* Ed. Thomas Russell. 3 vols. London, 1831. 1: 141-374.

Promissory Performances

LUKE WILSON

To BEGIN WITH, a list of some of the things *performed* in Shakespeare: a task, a word, a promise, pleasure, achievements, murthers, rites, work, a charge, a coronation, a part, assistance, bloody office, the "statue" of Hermione, sorrow, business, the king's will, observation, the figure of a Harpy, a charge, a tempest, a dreaded act, a kindness, a bidding, heaving spleens, an oath, an ability, friendship, an antic round, a behest. All these are things performed, yet only a few of them—the part, the antic round, the figure of the Harpy—have any clear reference to theatrical practice; in the majority of usages performance is responsive to a prior directive of some kind: task, word, promise, charge, office, business, will, bidding, behest.[1] Indeed, legal and quasi-legal use of the terms "perform" and "performance," often set in conceptual opposition to the "promise" of which they designate the fulfillment, begins no later than the thirteenth century, while some of the earliest instances of "perform" as a verb meaning, roughly, "to play a role in a dramatic production" only begin occurring with Shakespeare. In the Induction to *Taming of the Shrew* (1593-94), for example, the unnamed Lord recalls the earlier theatrical achievement of one of his players, whose performance he now commands for the entertainment of his guest Christopher Sly.

> This fellow I remember
> Since once he play'd a farmer's eldest son.

59

> 'Twas where you woo'd the gentlewoman so well.
> I have forgot your name; but sure that part
> Was aptly fitted and naturally perform'd.
>
> (Ind.1.83–87)

Even in Shakespeare, however, legal or quasi-legal uses predominate, and here, where the player's performance of a "part" clearly extends toward an emergent, specifically theatrical meaning, the older usage remains in play: the recollected performance of the player combined the satisfaction of an ambiguously social and legal obligation—similar to the "duty" acceptance which the Player craves of the Lord one line earlier—with the playing of a dramatic role.

Despite the occasional instance where the verbal form seems to import a specifically theatrical sense, moreover, I find nowhere in Shakespeare any nominative usage through which a specifically *theatrical* performance is visible as a conceptually stable idea.[2] Roughly during the span of Shakespeare's productive life, it would seem, the terms began to acquire specialized theatrical meaning; and I suggest that Shakespeare's own practice furthered decisively the process by which the theater absorbed and transformed them. That what we would describe as theatrical performances were occurring regularly before those involved described them that way, and that at a certain time they began to do so, does not *necessarily* tell us anything about how such performances themselves actually evolved. But it does indicate, at a minimum, something of how theatrical discourse conceptualized what it meant to play a part upon the stage. Arguably, the theater's appropriation of "performance" during Shakespeare's career, and its continuing relation to the legal and quasi-legal context from which the term had emerged, represents one part of a much more extensive process by which the Tudor and Stuart theater absorbed, transformed, and was itself transformed by legal language and legal conceptualizations of human action.

In *The Tempest*, for example, Shakespeare seems *thematically* interested in this interleaving of dramatic and obligational contexts. When Antonio first broaches his plot to Sebastian, his point of departure is Claribel, queen of Tunis, "she that from whom / We all were sea-swallow'd, though some cast again, / And by that destiny, to perform an act / Whereof what's past is prologue; what to come, / In yours and my discharge" (2.1.245–49). While the passage certainly contains a series of theatrical puns, as Frank

Kermode remarks in his New Arden edition, some of the links in the series seem to stand just at the threshold of ambiguity. That the *Oxford English Dictionary* does not record "cast" as a theatrical noun before 1631, or its corresponding verb form until the early eighteenth century, should not weigh too heavily here; Antonio's punning on the term is unmistakable given the terms "act" and "prologue," both having long since acquired specifically theatrical usages.[3] On the other hand, while Kermode includes the substantive "discharge" in the theatrical punning, the *OED* attaches no specifically theatrical meaning to the term, listing meanings ranging from the strictly legal (exoneration from blame; release from, or performance or execution of, obligation; payment of a pecuniary debt) to a bodily or material emission or disburdening.[4] If Antonio means the term in a theatrical sense, as he seems to, he is in the process of creating a new and specific meaning for it.

We can see this process in the relation between Antonio and his puns, which carry a semantic burden he seems only vaguely aware of even as he sets in motion a plan designed to cast it off, to discharge himself of it. If to be "cast" is to be offered the chance to play a new role, in its active form the same verb suggests the setting aside of an old one—and in this case it is the old Antonio who, along with the rest of his cast, is discarded and cast off. "Cast" refers both to the discharge of a precedent burden (*OED*, esp. III), and to a protentional shaping that looks to the future (*OED*, VII.43, "to machinate, contrive, devise, scheme"), as in the casting of a horoscope, or of an actor in a part, or as in the accountant's casting (reckoning or calculation) of a column of numbers, or the compositor's estimation of the space a manuscript is likely to occupy when set in type.[5] Antonio's use of the substantive "discharge," then, which as we have seen has yet to secure a specifically theatrical meaning, recapitulates this ambiguity, and (insofar as it foreshadows the theatrical) moves it more firmly into the future, while nevertheless retaining the anxiety with which "discharge" is freighted, about the satisfaction of or escape from an obligation incurred in the past. Antonio poses to Sebastian the prospect before them both as an opportunity to create for themselves new identities and destinies, and as a new-found ability to free themselves from the political hindrances represented by Claribel, Ferdinand, and Alonso. These come in fact to much the same thing; hence the Janus-faced bearing of "cast" and "discharge," and hence also the characteristically Shakespearean temporal imbrication of "what's past is prologue," as though Antonio's predicament has to do with his subjectivity being spread out across overlapping but finally incommensurable ontological estates.

Ariel's performances, as we will see, represent the discharge of duties Prospero has charged him to perform. Is there then a similar "charge" from which Antonio's (theatrical) plot may be said to derive? We can, again, regard it as the encumbrance of circumstance the shipwreck appears to enable the two conspirators to slough off and leave behind them, as if they were snakes "casting" their skins (*OED* II.20.a). But rather than accounting for the ambiguity of "cast" and "discharge" by positing a depth and coherence of character, in the manner so persuasively faulted by Margreta de Grazia, we may do so in a metatheatrical context, as the textual register of a perception Antonio cannot possibly be aware of as a *character*, that the role he is undertaking to perform is, after all, really of Prospero's design. In this reading, the awareness of a burden may be attributed not to Antonio but to the actor personating him, who discharges, for compensation and on the basis of a legally binding contractual agreement, a part in Shakespeare's play. Antonio's predicament is not only *like* the economic and professional predicament of the player; it *is* that predicament.[6]

Antonio's language here does more even than simply figure the economic and professional plight of the player, a version of whose economic and professional concerns are built into the words he is given to utter on the stage. The "depth" arranged by the words represents, then, neither a subjectivity effect originally "built into" Antonio nor the critical construction of such an effect, for whatever reason, after the fact, as de Grazia might argue. It discloses, rather, the depth and complexity of the *compositional* process itself, the way in which Shakespearean representation here anticipates the plight of the actor, and gives him the words he needs to register that plight even at the risk of generating a mimetic discontinuity. If such an anticipation may be understood as expressing some sort of empathetic identification with the plight of the player (which isn't incredible given Shakespeare's own identity as a player), it could equally well serve a preemptive, or otherwise aggressive, purpose, whether or not such a purpose were in the least degree conscious.

The terms of Antonio's plot, which is both insurrectionary and the performance of theatrical *labor*, may be compared to Prospero's employment contract with Ariel, where the element of mutual promise (as promise is opposed to performance) emerges more clearly. While Prospero repeatedly speaks of Ariel having "performed" various tricks that may seem to us specifically theatrical, he does so in contexts in which Ariel's obligation to him predominates. "Hast thou, spirit, / Perform'd to point the tempest that I bade thee?" (1.2.193-94), he asks; and Ariel's answer shows that he has performed both transitively and intransitively: "now on the beak, / Now in the waist, the deck, in every cabin, / I flam'd amazement . . ." (1.2.196-98). Later in the same scene Prospero tells Ariel that his "charge"—here the disposition of the ship's crew safely on land—"Exactly is perform'd: but there's more work" (1.2.237-38). Again the reference is more directly to the fulfillment of an obligation than to the acting of a dramatic part. And when Ariel complains at the prospect of further labor, he does so in terms that link promise and performance in the conventional manner: "Let me remember thee what thou hast promis'd, / Which is not yet perform'd me" (1.2.243-44). Ariel *owes* Prospero these performances, just as Prospero in turn owes it to Ariel to perform his promise of freedom; it is primarily in this sense that they are performances. Later on, however, when Prospero commends Ariel's performance—"Bravely the figure of this Harpy hast thou / Perform'd" (3.3.83-84)—the two aspects of Ariel's performance are abruptly juxtaposed and the pun hitherto latent suddenly emerges; that performance is simultaneously the theatrical personation of the Harpy and the execution of Prospero's command, a command that is not unilaterally imposed but rather one component in an agreement *figured* as contractual (whatever form of coercion it may in fact be founded on).[7] An emergent concept of theatrical performance is predicated here on the quasi-contractual understanding by which Ariel has agreed to perform some last acts of magic for Prospero in exchange for his freedom; this is the *consideration* (in the technical legal sense of the term) for which he performs.

The obligational context out of which specifically theatrical "performance" seems to emerge anchors such performance in an antecedent *promise*; but in the shift toward a theatrical meaning this element of promise loosens its hold and falls away. Performance in this sense is hereafter no longer to be the performance of a promise or obligation but rather of a script, a part, a character, the figure of a Harpy; and eventually it aspires to grow into a purely intransitive use that is also purely theatrical. In this shift the relation between performance and what is performed is of course radically altered: to do a deed is not the same as to "do," say, Hamlet; to perform a promise is not the same as to "perform," intransitively, in a play. As we will see, however, the promissory sense of performance, and with it the oblique reference to the obligated performance of dramatic labor, remains in play, particularly in the acting out on stage of promises, obligations, and their performance or non-performance.

Even if a specifically theatrical sense of performance does not escape its origins in obligated (i.e., promissory) performance, however, its obligational component is modified in two ways. First, it surrenders a certain amount of its obligational force to a performance understood in mimetic terms, having to do with the player's responsibility to the script, or to his character, or to the theater as a set of conventional institutional rules, norms, and dicta. Second, in theatrical performance, obligation of the promissory kind, rather than being eliminated, becomes more firmly contractual: it is revealed as reducible to a monetary equivalence, and what had remained occulted in an ideology of status relationships is thus demystified, or rather remystified according to a more openly contractualist ideology. Where the player's performance for the Lord in *Shrew* is represented as only implicitly contractual, the terms mandating a player's performance for a London acting company in the 1590s and 1600s would have been a good deal more explicit. Of such contracts little is known, though it is not disputed that they were, under the name of "compositions," the normal means of creating a legal relation between a sharer and a company. The one such composition of which we have record stipulates the terms under which Robert Dawes signed on with the Lady Elizabeth's men in 1614; it "not only made him a partaker in the contractual and financial liabilities of the company, but also exposed him to penalities if he missed plays or rehearsals, or came late or in a state of intoxication, or took apparel or other common property away from the theater" (Chambers 1: 352).[8]

The contractual relationships under which performance occurs are no longer those between the player and the patron who commands a performance (or at least, no longer exclusively: players still belong to companies sponsored by the aristocracy, and the performances at court remain command performances), but between the player and the company with which he has contracted to perform, and between the company and the audience members who have bargained to be entertained or instructed.[9] In these new economic relationships, of course, the player acquires new capabilities, as well as new obligations and liabilities, as an economic agent. As a subject *socially* subordinate to the patron for whom he performed, the player's promissory capacity had been reified, more thoroughly inscribed in relationships of status than had become possible by the end of the sixteenth century.

If the ambiguity apparently arising around this time in what it means to "perform" in the theater is properly understood as opening up or opened up by a relatively new sense of economic agency on the part of the theatrical practitioner (and primarily of the player)—and this hypothesis is supported by the simultaneous emergence of the term "agency" in both the legal sense (*OED* B.4.a) of one who acts for or on behalf of another and in the more general sense (*OED* B.1.a) of one who (or that which) exerts power (as opposed to being either a patient or an instrument)—it would seem also to participate in what Robert Weimann calls the "bi-fold authority" of the Renaissance stage. In Weimann's terms the ambiguity could be said to rehearse the shift from the *performing of* authority to the *performing* authority, or, to put it another way, from the command performance to the commanding performance. If this is an accurate description, then the development of a specifically theatrical sense of what it means to "perform" corresponds to and articulates an interesting moment in the history of the phenomenology of performance, where an actor and his audience (gradually? suddenly?) cease to fix on him as an employee of the authority for whom he performs, and instead begin to identify him in a new way with the character he personates; by the 1610s the actor has come a long way from the conventional self- and audience-consciousness we see in academic plays of the early to mid-1500s (Bevington 37), despite the persistence of the *platea*-based actor-audience relationships described by Weimann (*Popular* 73–85). The actor thus seems to have been perceived as obligated to the figure he performed at the same time that his obligation *to* perform now made him appear an autonomous economic agent, exchanging his performance for monetary compensation. As Weimann puts it, theatrical authority resides both in the representations of the player and in his acts of representation themselves: authority is thus "both an object and an agent of representation" ("Towards a Literary Theory" 271).

It's not quite right therefore to say that the move from the legal to the theatrical is a move away from promise. Even so, if the word was to secure for itself a specifically theatrical meaning, that meaning would have to exclude or repress its obligational origins: the performance of a dramatic part must be accorded a value above the mere mercenary performance of a promise. Thus a remystification of performance is built into the theatrical version of the term to the extent that this version insists on its claim to function intransitively, as if to say, "Oh, we don't perform anything in particular, we can't be bothered to behave transitively; we just *perform*."[10]

These shifts in the basis of the structures of agreement on which theatrical performance is founded both signal an evolution in conceptions of theatrical performance itself (a matter too large to be properly handled here) and overdetermine the representation of contractual relationships on the stage. I wish to focus in this essay on the latter, and more manageable, of these consequences. When contractual language appears in such contexts, it is implicitly metatheatrical, commenting on the very contractual presuppositions and cognitive structures that have gone into the production of theatrical practice in the first place, and produces in turn a materialization of cognitions, mental acts, intentions, promises, and speech acts generally. Such acts come to shoulder an institutional, a *material* weight: any promise represented theatrically potentially has a bearing on the promissory, contractual, obligational structures that subtend and enable the theatrical performances themselves.

Oddly enough, this process of the materialization of performance within theatrical language appears to have been enabled at least in part by contemporary developments in contract law, which might be described as moving in a contrary direction, from *things* to states of mind. This is true, certainly, of what is perhaps the most significant transformation in the private law of the period, namely the rise of the action of *assumpsit*, which put the notion of promising at the center of common-law analysis of contract; under *assumpsit*, "performance" was conceptualized as a matter of (the fulfillment of) a promise. Legal historians have had a great deal to say, of course, about the rise of *assumpsit* during the sixteenth century as the dominant form of action under which contract disputes were adjudicated, and especially about the key role played in the consolidation of the dominance of the action over the rival action of debt by the ruling in Slade's case (1597–1602).[11] Only a few facets of this complex issue require recapitulation here.

Assumpsit (literally, "he or she promised") made the remedy for breach of contract depend on prior *promises* to perform rather than on other factors, at the same time that it tended to turn such promises into highly manipulable legal fictions. The action made accounts of intentional states the currency of contract litigation, the means by which one could advance one's interests, and consequently it focused attention on the development and manipulation of such accounts.

The issue in Slade's case was whether a simple bargain and sale involved an *assumpsit*—whether, in other words, when you made a bargain you also implicitly *promised* to uphold your part of it—and whether therefore the case was actionable as an *assumpsit*. The particular transaction in question could also have founded an action of debt, and the question arose whether *assumpsit* should be allowed, in view of the double remedy doctrine, which forbade an action on the case where one of the traditional actions listed in the Register of Writs was available.[12] In the event, the case was decided in favor of the plaintiff, and firm precedent was established for the use of *assumpsit* in lieu of debt. In his report of the case, Edward Coke gives what he, at any rate, took to be the reasoning on which the decision was based, asserting that "every contract executory imports in itself an *assumpsit*, for when one agrees to pay money, or to deliver any thing, thereby he assumes or promises to pay, or deliver it" (4 Coke 94a-94b in *English Reports*, vol. 76). Or, as A. W. B. Simpson glosses Coke's conclusion, "wherever a situation has arisen where the writ of debt *sur contract* would lie against a person, and that person has not paid the debt ('executory') an *assumpsit* to pay the money will be implied" ("Slade's Case" 391).

As I have argued in more detail elsewhere, the shift from debt to *assumpsit* tended to complicate the temporal structure of contractual obligations, even apart from their litigation, at least insofar as experience of legal expectations fed back into habitual ways of imagining what it meant to make a bargain, agree to perform, and so on. This was because debt is fundamentally *atemporal*, a description of the spatial relations between objects rather than of the persons between whom those objects pass (Spinosa): you have the corn you agreed to sell me; I *should* have it, since I gave you money, it having passed legally from you to me at that time, whether you gave it to me or not. As Bacon put it in arguing for the defendant in Slade's case:

For a bargain is in any manner a thing executed and not executory as an *assumpsit* is. For a bargain changes the property of each part, and therefore in action of debt it is alleged that the defendant detains the money or thing demanded as if it were his before; to wit, that the plaintiff had the property of it by the contract. Wherefor Bracton says that *contractus est permutatio rerum*. And therefore when the plaintiff demands only that which was his before, it cannot be said that he is deceived by the defendant; but that the defendant detains that of which the property was in the plaintiff.[13] (Baker, "New Light" 60)

Conceptualized in terms of the action of debt, then, "*contractus est permutatio rerum*" [contract is the exchange of things], and it has therefore no temporal dimension; the purpose of litigation is simply to catch the *de facto* up with the *de jure*, the latter being identified, in a thoroughly nominalistic way, with what's understood to be the *truth* of the case. Since the transaction occurs in an instant, no interval can insert itself between promise and performance or open a space for agency there; and there can be no articulation of intentions, states of mind, and so on, only a condition which signifies by its structure that money or goods bargained for are not in the possession of the person who has a right to them.

Conceptualized as the work of social actors, on the other hand—that is, as *assumpsit*—contracts are *necessarily*, if only in a minimal sense, executory, incomplete at the time of the bargain and complete only upon bilateral performance. At the same time that Coke's argument closes the gap between the objective act of entering into a debt relation and the subjective act of making a promise, it also delineates the implicit temporal structure of the *assumpsit*, in which the promise and the interval that divides it from performance, logically implied in the qualification "executory," are mutually affirming. If you have a promise you have an interval; if you have an interval it becomes relevant to ask if there has been a promise. The action of *assumpsit* distracts or distends the structure of the contract into a futurity that precipitates in discursive form the promises, intentions, deceits, motives, and considerations according to which the action organizes itself.

To insist that these effects had no precedents or equivalents in earlier English law would be to oversimplify legal history. And, in practice, contractual agreements tend to create temporal tensions associated with performance quite apart from any litigation and regardless of how the action of debt was itself conceptualized by Henry de Bracton or Francis Bacon. But this is clearly a period during which ways of thinking about time, intention, and person in the law were undergoing relatively rapid transformation; a similar shift of attention is evident in criminal law, from the offense, understood as a material damage, to the persons involved and their responsibilities (Watkin). What is new about the rise of *assumpsit* is that the action in all its complex varieties objectifies in legal procedure strategic uses of time that may or may not have been similar to those which immemorially had figured in exchange relationships, but which were at any rate probably endowed with a greater formal consistency owing to their new discursive articulation.

An intentional temporality thus came to be institutionalized in the common law of contract around the same time that the theater began to acquire (or at least to formulate linguistically) its own sense of what it meant to "perform," a sense that both adapted the legal origin of the term to the specific contractual conditions governing theatrical labor, and began to mark out the linguistic space in which "performance" was to become purely a term of art, cut off from its contractual origins altogether. If fairly technical changes in contract law made temporal intervals and the subjective agencies enabled by and operating within them more important than they had been, something of the same thing may be said for the dramatic representation of human cognition and purposive action. And because theatrical representation both represents human agency in time and requires human agency in time to represent it, the theater was in a unique position to read the economic and legal conditions of its own production, especially as those conditions involved the performance of contractually incurred obligations, into its complex phenomenologies of fictional subjects distended in time.

This is an enormous subject, of course, and I'd like to single out a particular dimension of it, namely the complicated relation between temporal distention and the forms of legal liability. That such distension will be irreversible, that time will run out without a resolution, that you will not be able to perform what you've promised, your part, in a play or of a bargain, may be understood as yet another of the many forms of liminality, the detection of which in Renaissance English theater has so often framed critical inquiry.[14] This early modern theatrical ending-up-where-you-shouldn't-be can be conceptualized both in terms of a criminal subjectivity founded, as I've argued elsewhere, on the criminal-law principle of *mens rea* or guilty mind, and as the effect of a strictly *civil* liability (Wilson, "*Hamlet*, Hales").[15] While the history of the procedural and jurisdictional differences between civil and criminal actions in the common law is too large a topic to be considered here, the relation between criminal and civil liability can be described roughly as follows. Criminal culpability was understood in relation to the person of the king: the subject's guilt (and the subject himself) arose as an infraction, or the potential for an infraction, against the property of the king; and this was as true for felony as for treason. Civil liability, on the other hand, arose as a result of contractual and tortious disputes disturbing the subject's relationships with other subjects. The principle of criminal intent (*mens rea*) developed in the English common law during the twelfth century via the influence of Roman and canon law ideas (Sayre; Pollock and Maitland 2: 476–78; Baker, *Introduction* 596–99).[16] The standards governing blameworthiness were different, however, in civil matters. In fifteenth- and early sixteenth-century actions of trespass *vi et armis*, for example, which asked for monetary damages in recompense for some bodily harm done by the defendant, judges did not allow lack of intent to commit the wrong complained of as an extenuation, as it would have in certain cases of felony; that a fatal archery accident was unintended might excuse the perpetrator of felony homicide, but it would have been irrelevant to the question of whether the perpetrator was to be required to pay damages (Baker, *Introduction* 457). Strict civil liability, while it exposed the legal subject to monetary responsibilities stemming from incidents he had not intended, nevertheless typically required a causal chain to link the defendant to the harm done; when the causal chain had been interrupted, as by some event that would have happened anyway, or that was beyond the defendant's control, the defendant had a good chance of escaping responsibility (Baker, *Introduction* 456–57).

Criminal and civil liability, then, developed according to different conceptual, institutional, and political pressures, which by the sixteenth century had produced differentiating features in each. Even so, the two forms of liability grew up together even as they were growing apart, and it seems probable that ad hoc differences in practice pre-dating the relatively late emergence of the doctrinal division of the criminal from the civil separated themselves out onto either side of this division as it emerged, and grew more marked as a result of doctrinal imperative. Legal liability in all its different forms, in other words, is likely to have developed out of an undifferentiated, if inconsistent, whole. Such a hypothesis is supported at the widest level of historical generality by Marcel Mauss's argument that the Latin term *reus*—"accused" or "under obligation" in Roman law—seems originally to have derived from a genitive in *-os* of *res*, thing: a man accused is a man *reus*, "of the thing"; he has failed to fulfill his part in a contractual agreement, yet retains the thing as a benefit he is not entitled to. Mauss, whose argument emphasizes the animation of things in primitive systems of exchange, reads the genitive the other way around, suggesting that "[i]t is the man possessed by the thing"—as though the spirit of the thing itself has a claim on him and demands that the thing be returned to its proper owner (52).[17] Even more derivative is the Anglo-American common-law usage of *reus* to mean "guilty" in the terms *mens rea* (guilty mind) and *actus reus* (guilty act):

> First, the contracting party is *reus*, he is above all the person who has received the *res* of another, and thereby becomes his *reus*, i.e. the individual who is linked to him by the thing itself, namely by his spirit. . . . We would trace the genealogy of the meaning in a way that is directly the opposite to that ordinarily followed. We would say: (1) the individual possessed by the thing; (2) the individual involved in the matter caused by the *traditio* of the thing; (3) finally, the guilty one and the one responsible. From this viewpoint all the theories of "quasi-offense" as the origin of a contract, of *nexum* and *actio*, become a little clearer. (Mauss 51–52; note numbers omitted)

It was the state of having the thing, then—or, perhaps, as Mauss suggests, of being had by the thing—that once gave rise to the notion of being guilty, whether that thing were a gift that has not been reciprocated, or something acquired by a contract whose terms you've failed to honor, or, in the case of early English homicide law, the *wergild* you are obligated to pay as a result of having killed someone. To the giver, or the person with whom you have contracted, or the dead man's kin, you are identified with the thing given or otherwise (presumptively) conveyed, the *res*, since that *res* is the link between you; and so by extension *you* are *reus*, guilty.

It would probably not be too much of a simplification to say that during the early modern period the extent to which one was *reus* became more and more measured in terms of *mens*. This is generally true, as we have seen, of contract law, in the supercession of debt by *assumpsit*, from an objective account of *res* and where they are to a subjective account of persons, their mental states and legal obligations. And while, as Plucknett remarks, the adherence of early English criminal law to the principle of absolute liability should not be overstated (*Concise History* 463–65), it is clearly true of the criminal law as well.

The primitive shift from *res* to *reus* identified by Mauss marks as well a relocation of agency and animation. If the action of debt tends to objectify exchange relationships, we can see that it also fetishizes the *res* and attaches a peculiar importance to the notion that it belongs, as though inherently, by virtue of its internal properties, in one place rather than another. Similarly, in the Maori gift economies and Roman contracts Mauss discusses, agency is distributed between person and *res* rather than invested entirely in a subject possessing absolute sovereignty over inanimate objects. If mental states are thus reified, in effect standing in for the *res* they have displaced, these reifications—which, as such, are often openly fictional—tended to play a complicated part in the juggling of liabilities that the historical evolution of legal thought often necessitated. Early modern English criminal law, for example, retains, strategically as it were, some components of a fusion or confusion between person and thing that had otherwise for the most part been left behind. We know from Elizabethan and Jacobean assize court records, for example, that when juries chose to free a defendant manifestly guilty of manslaughter or even of murder, they sometimes chose to attribute the crime to a fictional person—a John a Nokes, William Nemo, or John in the Wind.[18] In some cases, however, the jury suited the name to the manner of death, as when at the East Grinstead Assizes in Sussex in February 1593 a jury found that Catherine Lucas of Arlington was not guilty of assaulting Alice Tuppen, also of Arlington, "with a 'wool card', inflicting injuries from which she died": appropriately, the jury found that "John Card killed her" (Cockburn, *Calendar, Sussex Indictments Elizabeth I* 265–66). And, also at East Grinstead, in June 1589, a jury found that "Thomas Staff," not Elizabeth Reader, had beaten ten-year-old Edward Cooper with "a staff (1*d*.)," as a result of which he died two days later (Cockburn, *Calendar, Sussex Indictments Elizabeth I* 225).

This fairly unusual practice of naming the fictional killer after the accidental instrument causing the death appears to be akin to the ancient law of deodand, which required that in cases of accidental death the instrument (cart, axe, knife, rope) involved be forfeited as an appeasement to God, the *precium sanguinis*, in effect holding it responsible for the death.[19] But it goes significantly further, for in the assize records, while the indictment typically fixes the money value of the *res* used to kill (e.g., "with a staff [1*d*.]"), indicating the persistence of deodand as simultaneously an economic and a symbolic state strategy, the jury itself, almost certainly with the complicity of certain officers of the court, if not the court itself, institutes its own *ad hoc* conflation of person and thing, not in order to render to God (or the king) compensation for the loss of a soul (or subject), but on the contrary, precisely to protect a person from the same authority.

But the law requires that if the jury find that the person indicted did not commit the crime, it must make a statement as to who did. If you don't want to blame one person you have to blame someone else, preferably someone who does not exist (a William Nemo or John in the Wind); and this object of blame seems to get mixed up with the deodand, a *thing* that *does* exist and which may figure in the causal chain out of which a death occurred for which no person seems responsible. The difference between the deodand, which invests *things* with agency, and the device of the fictional killer, by which agency (and liability) are displaced onto a person who does not exist, is smaller than it may appear, since both devices are fictions (in the strictly legal sense of the term) of agency: a thing has no more (and no less) agency than a person who does not exist—or, at any rate, that is what the devices' status as fictions meant to contemporary practitioners who (we may be sure) recognized them as such. The fictionality is compounded where, as in the case of John Card or Thomas Staff, the two devices combine, investing a fictional entity both with the subjectivity to which blame or liability may be attached and with the agency attaching to a manifestly proximate cause. Such a combination, of relatively rare occurence in the assize records, is more a legal curiosity than a component in a socially or politically significant strategy. Yet that it occurs at all seems to me significant, even if the precise mechanism enabling it remains obscure. It is as though the ancient suspicion on which the deodand seems originally to have been based—that whatever moves must be animated—having been repressed even as the deodand was insti-tutionalized as a profitable source of royal revenue, seizes on the pretext of the fictional killer to reassert itself in the peculiarly instrumental surnames these killers are sometimes assigned. Thus the distinction between persons and things normally obtaining in the early modern legal economy gives way here momentarily, and animate things are readmitted either—it's hard to tell—as the return of repressed vestigial elements or as devices deployed in particular political and legal strategies.

Similarly, if in the "primitive" gift economies Mauss discusses, a person's legal status is described in terms of his having or not having the *res*, *res* themselves tend, conversely, to be imagined as animated. The identity of the person under these conditions may be described in terms of his rela-tionship to the objects circulated in systems of exchange, and specifically in terms of the distribution of animation between persons and things. Because a person's relationship to things varies as a function of time, identity under the aspect of exchange must be a understood in temporal terms. Where the contractual temporality associated with *assumpsit* comes into being as a cause or effect of the development of increasingly sophisticated discursive renderings of purposive mental states, the exchanges which constitute systems of gift-giving seem to presuppose from the start a temporal dimension. As Pierre Bourdieu points out, the possibility of the repression of the coercive nature of the whole system of giving and return-giving depends on difference and deferral: the return-gift must both differ from the original gift and not come too soon; immediate return of an identical gift, for example, constitutes a refusal of the gift itself (*Outline* 4-6).[20] The person, or the person *as* guilty, as a *mens rea* or guilty mind, arises then at the point at which the delay in the return exceeds a temporal limit established tacitly and ad hoc, beyond which non-reciprocation becomes irreversible and irremediable. The self, constituted as a potentially guilty subject, is distended in a temporal space, opened within exchange relationships, that is also—whether that space is exceeded or not (whether the self is guilty or not)—a *tactical* space whose properties can be manipulated in the service of particular social objectives. Thus the emergence in both gift and contract economies of the "guilty person" out of *res*, the thing given and not reciprocated, corresponds, in the opportunities it offers for tactical engagement, to the procedural institutionalization of temporality and tactic in the law of *assumpsit*.

We saw how Antonio's desire to perform expressed a characterologically impossible need to escape from a burden not "he" but the player performing him suffered under, and how this predicament speaks a concern with the acting of another's agenda and with the conditions of theatrical labor specifically. Where mimesis gives way to representation—where the actor speaks out from inside his character—character thins out and agency becomes palimpsestic, revealing agency-for-another lurking behind agency-for-oneself, the player and playwright speaking out of the mouth of the character.[21] This can happen, for example, where representation dispenses temporarily with the mimetic decorum it has adhered to provisionally, as when Iachimo spends three hours in Imogen's chamber in the course of a few minutes of theater time, or when Time, personified, addresses the audience at the opening of act 4 of *The Winter's Tale*, becoming the direct sign of Shakespeare's dramatic agency, even in some sense agency itself ("*I mentioned* a son o' th' King's, which Florizel / I now name to you" [4.1.22–23; emphasis added]).[22] In such cases, it seems, theatrical performance works as the violation of a sort of mimetic contract and the collapse of the illusion, such as it is, of character.

We tend to associate such failures of character with "bad" Shakespeare, as in the case of *Timon of Athens*, whose title character critics have traditionally reproached with a lack of characterological density that goes hand in hand with the incoherence of the play as a whole. The state of the text in which *Timon* has come down to us, however, fixes in discourse a stage at which the process of composition is incomplete, and at which it is called on to perform what it has not yet finished promising. I'd like by way of conclusion to suggest some connections between Timon's characterological failure, his disastrous failure to master the temporal aspect of exchange, and Shakespeare's own compositional predicaments. Not accidentally, it is also in *Timon* that we encounter Shakespeare's most extensive exploration of the promise-performance pair.

At the opening of act 5, for example, the Poet and the Painter seek out Timon in his cave, having heard he is once again a rich man. They have nothing to present to him, but hoping nevertheless to resuscitate his failed gift economy, the Painter resolves simply to promise him "an excellent piece" (5.1.19) and continues:

Promising is the very air o' th' time; it opens the eyes of expectation. Performance is ever the duller for his act; and, but in the plainer and simpler kind of people, the deed of saying is quite out of use. To promise is most courtly and fashionable; performance is a kind of will or testament which argues a great sickness in his judgment that makes it. (5.1.22–29)

While I don't wish to complicate this passage unnecessarily, I do think it is less clear, more confused and confusing, than it may initially appear. Certainly, we can't miss the play's characteristic cynicism and class consciousness (Cohen) in the Painter's distinction between the lower orders, who actually imagine that performance ought to follow promise, that one ought to do what one promises to do, and those "courtly and fashionable" persons for whom performance is a tiresome and nonessential addition to the pleasure of promising. The notion that promises are things of air is one Shakespeare evidently liked; we may compare Hamlet's remark to Claudius: "I eat the air, promise-cramm'd" (3.2.94–95). But the passage begins to lose its coherence when it shifts conceptually from promise to performance. "Performance is ever the duller for his act," says the Painter; the neuter possessive pronoun "his" must take either "performance" or the "promising" of the previous sentence as its antecedent. In his New Arden edition, H. J. Oliver assumes that it is the "act" of *"performance"* that makes the latter "ever the duller." But what sense does it make to say that a performance is acted? Performance can't *have* an act: it *is* an act; there is no room for assigning attributes here, nothing extra to add or take away.

On the other hand, if the antecedent is the "promise" of the preceding sentence, then the second sentence says something like: "Performance is ever the duller for the acting out of the promise"—which means no more than that because a performance is what it is—the acting out of a promise—it is, and simply for that reason, ever duller; but, then, duller than what? Does the Painter mean that promising is to be preferred to performance because the latter, the realization of a promise in practice, will be a disappointment, a weak approximation of a promise which, unperformed, can take refuge in the abstract and ideal? Maybe. But that would be to say that the *promise* is made duller—reduced into the confines of an imperfect practice—when it is performed, and nothing of the kind is being said here. It is the *performance* that is made duller, but, according to this reasoning, performance is already dull since its dullness is what defines it in relation to the promise.

Now, these complications are typical of Shakespeare's writing even where he must have had the chance to make thorough revisions; and, as we know, he probably abandoned *Timon* at a rather preliminary stage in the process of composition.[23] But this is precisely why they are interesting, since, I suggest, they not only take up their place as linguistic or even characterological incoherencies, but also as indicators of Shakespeare's own compositional practice, and of a difficulty that seems to have elicited a connection between the narrative concerns of *Timon* and the nominally distinct activity of composing the play.

All this complication suggests that Shakespeare was preoccupied in this play with the tendency of the relation between promise and performance to collapse or to produce a conceptual impasse. Acting a performance seems to get mixed up with the act of promising to perform; there is in this a tendency toward reifying performance in such a way as to make it some-thing verbs can operate on, as, for example, something which can be acted upon *by being acted*. I think this tendency shows Shakespeare thinking about the relation between theatrical and promissory performance, acting and action. Moreover, in the context of the argument with which this essay began, concerning the possible historical evolution of the theatrical from the promissory, the confusion of the passage as a whole reflects the erratic behavior of the notion of performance at the threshold of its formulation as a substantive with specifically theatrical meaning.

This oblique approach to theatrical practice via promissory practice is also suggested in the Painter's remark that, except among the plainer sort of people, "the deed of saying is quite out of use." This strikingly compressed phrase, "the deed of saying," expresses at least two distinct actions: the doing or performance of what's been said or promised; and the doing *of* the *promising*, that is, the promising *as* a doing, as a performative speech-act. The primary meaning is no doubt the first of these (though in what sense I mean "first" here, whether in terms of Shakespeare's "final authorial intentions" or on the contrary in compositional or genetic terms, is perhaps open to question). Yet the expression plays with the idea of collapsing both, the saying and the subsequent doing, around a genitive construction that fuses promise and performance in a kind of simultaneity that elides without extinguishing precisely the temporal gap which, as we have seen, defines the two terms in their relation to one another.

The *form* of this simultaneity corresponds to what J. L. Austin, referring of course to *Hamlet*, calls "suiting the action to the word," as when the lawyer says, "I rest my case" (65). This is a peripheral category for Austin, of course, since it lacks the structure of the true performative, in which saying and doing are two ways of describing the same event, and in which for that reason any temporal relation, including simultaneity, is logically foreclosed. Rather, the structure of the "deed of saying" duplicates the structure of theatrical performance itself, the art in which Hamlet instructs the player, that of "suiting the action to the word."

Theatrical performance brings promise and performance, saying and doing, into *temporal* juxtaposition, both in the sense that it is the continual, incremental performance of an antecedent yet constantly renewed promise ("promise *of* performance" operating here as a *subjective* genitive), and in the sense that it occurs in the interval *between* an initial promise and a subsequent performance ("promise of performance" as *objective* genitive), an interval which has been absorbed into theatrical performance and reestablished as a specifically theatrical duration. Similarly, while theatrical performance is a potential implicit in the script as promissory performance is implicit in a promise, that script itself represents a *compositional* performance as well.

The legal basis of the promise-performance pair seems close to the surface here, and indeed in the next sentence the buried corpse of the law sticks out a toe, when the Painter tells his fellow that while promising is a courtly and fashionable thing to do, "performance is a kind of will or testament which argues a great sickness in his judgment that makes it." The judgment of the person who elects performance is as moribund as the body of the man who makes his will. In this new turn, performance lines up with death in the sense that each is a termination, a resolution of outstanding debts and imbalances—or, to adapt the legal term in the way we see Shakespeare doing in *Hamlet*, a *quietus est*. But this odd twist also shows performance reversed into a secondary, delegated form of promise, a promise to heirs and a command to executors involving intentions to be followed out after the intender is dead. Doing reverts to an intention that a particular series of acts be done. Performance remains a deed, but only in the sense of a testament, a *written* "deed" the performance of which is again deferred.

That Shakespeare's imagination sends us back to promise, back to text, means both that in some sense performance fails and reverts to promise, and that Shakespeare is manipulating the pair of terms so as to cause them to be reversible: performance is approached only to be turned back into promise in a new guise. And it's precisely this reversal of direction that is possible in the rehearsal and composition of a dramatic script; indeed, in this passage in *Timon* the things to be promised are precisely works of art—poems and paintings.[24] Plays go unmentioned, but the theater, where production and performance maintain so tense a temporal relationship, is clearly the most suited generic paradigm. *Perhaps* it is only an accident that Shakespeare does not seem to have finished *Timon*, or that it was not performed (as far as anyone has been able to determine) during his lifetime; yet surely it is remarkable that the play was thus an unperformed promise of performance.

Shakespeare's preoccupation in this play with the non-performance of promises reaches a kind of limit-case of complexity in act 4, in Timon's tangled challenge to Alcibiades: "Promise me friendship, but perform none. If thou wilt not promise, the gods plague thee, for thou art a man! If thou dost perform, confound thee, for thou art a man!" (4.3.74–77). Timon's demand calls for a double or nested promise—"Promise (to promise me friendship and not to perform it) and perform what you promise"; and this is a demand that raises questions of what such a promise can mean in ways more interesting, I think, than what this is not, namely, the simple paradox "Promise not to perform this promise," in which the solicited promise excludes time altogether, since logical contradiction makes it impossible to proceed to performance, and therefore prevents the production of a performative interval.[25] Here, on the contrary, the implicit promise can only be performed by the non-performance of the explicit promise. And this will take time.

In gift economies obligation is socially imposed via acts of giving initiated by others, and the category of the voluntary, though of course essential to the ideology of giving, has in fact no place whatsoever, since for the receiver the gift arrives from without, as an (often unwelcome) surprise, and since for the giver the impulse to give is simply a coerced response to the prior receipt of a gift. Gift economies, therefore, have no use at all for the notion that promises are made or ought to be kept; the interval between gift and return-gift is not in this sense an *intentional* interval. It is so, however, in a different sense, to the extent that it's meaningful to talk about the intentions of the actor in social strategizing. As Bourdieu insists, the collective misrecognition that enables the gift economy to endure is sustained by *time*, specifically the interval between gift and return-gift; for this reason both gift and contract economies provide an environment in which social actors can make tactical use of time. Because in gift economies the determination of such intervals is necessarily tacit, the maintenance of a temporal equilibrium is both more tricky and more critical; and a distortion of the system's temporal structure can prove fatal to it, as Timon learns to his confusion.

Timon's behavior destroys collective misrecognition not because he returns identical gifts immediately (though he is certainly uncomfortable with having the gift, being *reus*: "there's none / Can truly say he gives, if he receives" [1.2.10–11]) but because he gives what is not his to give, indeed, what should be given *him*; there is thus a perverse logic to his friends' refusal to help him out: it is as if the return-gifts they might have given him have already been given, but, as if in some confusion of sequence and agency, *to* them rather than *by* them. The resulting collapse in exchange relationships disturbs the temporal medium of the gift economy. Timon's literally preposterous behavior—his giving away to those from whom he has borrowed what he has borrowed from them—has, in some obscure temporal economy, swallowed up the time formerly available for use in strategies of delay and precipitancy.

If the economic crisis in *Timon* is properly described as precipitated by a conflict between Timon's gift economy and the usurious money economy of his "friends" (Chorost), it is only after Timon has reoriented himself toward the latter that the language of promise and performance creeps into his utterances.[26] The gift economy does not depend on promise; promise enters the picture when the coercive state of things becomes explicit; where coercion remains covert, inscribed only in the deep structure of disembodied practices themselves, there will be no promises, since to say one is bound will be to violate—*if* one meant it and was understood to mean it—the tacit agreement on collective denial. *Timon*'s move from gift to contract, from tacit coercion to explicit promise, from implicit practice to explicit law, corresponds, I would like to think, to the shift from status-oriented theatrical practice to the contractualism that had come to dominate the business of the theater during the years Shakespeare wrote. Thus Timon's bitter subscription to a contract economy, with its system of promises and consideration, and the simultaneous collapse of the temporal dimension of the gift economy narrate cryptically, I suppose, the production of a specific theatrical temporality, or, more exactly, the *failed* production of such a temporality and, along with it, the failure of the play and of Timon as a character. In some surely more-than-figurative sense, the time lost from the gift economy reappears in the nearly self-canceling tangle of promises and performances I have been discussing, and has also been invested in the deferred performance of Timon's own corporeality, where it waits to be uncorked in a theatrical performance that was not to be (as far as we know) until Shakespeare and the rest of the King's Men were long since dead. The unperformed *Timon*, in other words, rehearses the construction of the temporal space of theatrical performance; and in this sense the rough, incomplete textual draft in which the play has come down to us is itself something like what Timon demands of Alcibiades: I mean, of course, the performance of a non-performance.

Notes

This essay has its origin in some opening remarks in Wilson, "*Hamlet*: Equity, Intention, Performance," and incorporates some of the language in the first paragraph and the first three notes. Parts of the discussion of *assumpsit* and debt appear in Wilson, "Ben Jonson and the Law of Contract." I presented earlier versions of the essay at the Modern Language Association Convention in 1992, and at the third triennial History and Literature Conference at the University of Reading, England, in 1995.

1. In compiling this list I've relied on Spevack. Quotations from *The Tempest* (ed. Kermode) and *Timon of Athens* (ed. Oliver) are based on the New Arden editions. Quotations from other Shakespeare plays are based on the *Riverside Shakespeare*.

2. This is true, I think, even of the "performance," participation in which the Chorus requires of the audience of *Henry V*: "Still be kind, / And eche out our performance with your mind" (3.Cho.34-35). In this instance the usage of the word bears semantic traces both of an implicit representational *contract* between actors and audience—the terms of which engage all the Choruses of that play—and of a more general and even less theatrically specific meaning. The *OED* cites this passage as instancing the general sense of "notable deed or achievement" (2.b), without any direct implication of theatrical context at all; and though we may find such an exclusion peculiar now, it probably was not then, the word having at the time practically no prior *specific* connection to what went on in the theater. This is probably the case, too, in *A Midsummer Night's Dream* (1595-96), when Bottom, upon being informed that he is to play Pyramus the suicidal lover, remarks, "That will ask some tears in the true performing of it" (1.2.25-26); here it seems almost accidental that the "performing" spoken of involves a theatrical impersonation; the word seems just on the verge of responding to the specifically theatrical dimension of its context. The decisions made by the *OED* editors do not help us much, since while they classify the usage of "performance" in *Henry V* as without specifically theatrical meaning, they identify the passage cited from *The Tempest*, where Ariel performs the figure of a Harpy, as one of the earliest uses of the verb *with* such meaning. Clearly these are some of the textual moments at which the more specific meaning comes into being, miraculously precipitated out of a contractual and obligational context. The obligatory aspect of theatrical "performance" also surfaces in *Coriolanus*, when Coriolanus, pressured to appear before the common people to answer their accusations, submits in theatrical terms: "You have put me now to such a part which never / I shall discharge to th' life" (3.2.105-06). Volumnia, urging her son to participate in what is in effect a command performance, develops the metaphor: "To have my praise for this, perform a part / Thou hast not done before" (3.2.109-10). The verb here has a specifically theatrical component, as nearby theatrical terms ("prompt," "part") make clear. Yet while the theater metaphor is clearly in play, the passage's emphasis falls as much on an obligation amounting to coercion as on insincere display. Coriolanus is not merely a reluctant actor or player; what such acting *is*, in relation to social and legal obligation, remains at this time confused. On the older and closely related, ritually oriented sense of "perform" in Shakespeare, see Wilson, "*Hamlet*: Equity, Intention, Performance," 105n2, and on the frequency of "perform" and its cognates in Shakespeare's plays overall, 105n3.

3. "Cast" in this case suggests that certain actors in the drama about to unfold have been disgorged from the sea and onto the stage in order to play their parts. It may be compared to *Hamlet*, 1.4.48-51, where Hamlet suggests that his father's ghost has been vomited ("cast") out of the "ponderous and marble jaws" of his sepulchre. There is in both the sense that to be cast theatrically is to be thrown forth onto the stage to take on a new life, though clearly the theatrical meaning owes a good deal to the process of molding or casting metals into various shapes. To be cast in a part is both to be vomited forth as a revenant or as otherwise assuming a new identity, and to be molded into a new form.

4. Even Antonio's use of the term falls under the general, quasi-legal heading "Fulfilment,

performance, execution (*of* an obligation, duty, function, etc.)" (*OED, s.v.* discharge, *sb.* 6).
Similarly, when Snout the tinker ends his performance in *Pyramus and Thisbe* with the
pronouncement "Thus have I, Wall, my part discharged so; / And being done, thus Wall away
doth go" (*Midsummer Night's Dream* 5.1.204-05), it seems to be the *obligational* dimension
of this performance, like the player's in *Shrew*, that is in question; Snout's performance of
Wall is above all an obligation he is anxious to discharge. See also *Coriolanus* 3.2.106.

5. Cf. *OED* VII.44.a, "to design, purpose, intend, determine (*to do* a thing)." The printing-
house phrase "casting off" perhaps combines these senses in one expression.

6. In thinking about theatrical labor in *The Tempest* I am indebted to Bruster, "Local
Tempest." Although Bruster discusses in detail some of the ways in which the play reflects on
the conditions under which playwrights and players worked in Shakespeare's theater, he does
not consider directly the dramatic implications of the contractual conditions under which
theatrical practice was carried out.

7. This passage is the *OED*'s earliest example of the use of "perform" to mean "to act, play
(a part or character)"; but in the context of the other, closely parallel uses of the word in this
play, the new meaning is not so clearly indicated as the *OED*'s classifications would seem to
suggest.

8. On the Dawes contract, see Bentley 47-51. Chambers (1: 354) notes that legal relations
depended entirely on such compositions rather than on the warrant of appointment by which
the company attached itself to the sponsorship of an aristocratic patron. Contracts entered
into between the companies and "hirelings" or journeymen were probably less formal but
are likely to have included similar provisions. In the case of the Admiral's Men, both hirelings
and sharers were legally bound not to the company by means of a composition, but to Philip
Henslowe by means of a contract for service (3: 363).

9. Contracts, and therefore contractual disputes, between playgoers and members of the
theatrical professions are unlikely to exist, though there seems to be no reason why, in theory,
such disputes might not have been litigated as actions on the case for *assumpsit*—except, of
course, that the sums involved were so small. Contracts between playwrights and companies,
on the other hand, seem not to have been unusual; the few that are extant are those that were
the subject of legal disputes. The contract of this kind about which most details are known
was one between Richard Brome and the Salisbury Court Theater in the 1630s, litigated in the
Court of Requests (Haaker); on this contract as well as on dramatists' contractual obligations
generally, see Bentley 111-44. Maguire discusses a contractual dispute involving Dryden in
1668. On a disputed contract for plays in the 1570s, see Benbow.

10. Of course, theatrical performance remains *economic*; the actor is likely to be contractually obliged to perform, and if so must do so to get whatever compensation is due him.
The correspondence between the two forms of performance eventually becomes effectually
accidental, even though the usage in theatrical contexts had originally been overdetermined.

11. The primary sources of information about Slade v. Morley are Coke's report of the
case, 4 *Reports* 91a-95b in *English Reports,* vol. 76; and the additional reports excerpted and
discussed by Baker, "New Light." See also Simpson, *History* 292-302; Simpson, "Place"; Lücke;
Baker, *Introduction* 360-426; Plucknett 627-70; Fifoot 217-443. More recently, literary critics
have interested themselves in Slade's case also. See Wayne; Spinosa; Wilson, "Ben Jonson."
What follows is an abbreviated version of the argument set forth at greater length in this latter
essay.

12. Also, since debt allowed the defendant the right of compurgation (wager of law), and *assumpsit*, owing to its origin in the tortious writ of trespass, did not, the question arose whether, if *assumpsit* were allowed, the defendant was being wrongfully denied this ancient right of all Englishmen.

13. Bracton (and Bacon) probably had in mind *permutatio*, one of the so-called "innominate contracts" in Roman law, and equivalent to barter or exchange. See Nicholas 174, 189-91; Buckland 520-21.

14. On the senses of "part" in Shakespeare, specifically in *The Winter's Tale*, see Cavell 200.

15. For similar claims regarding the relation between theatrical representations of subjectivity and legal conceptualizations of the person, see also Dolan; Maus.

16. On the appearance in the *Leges Henrici Primi* of the doctrine that *actus non facit reum nisi mens sit rea*, in close proximity to the precisely contrary proverb that *qui inscienter peccat, scienter emendet*, see Pollock and Maitland 2: 476. The author of the *Leges* seems in fact to have borrowed the phrase, whose meaning is in any case somewhat out of place in this context, from St. Augustine, *Sermones*, no. 180, cap. 2, where it concerns perjury specifically: "Ream linguam non facit nisi mens rea" (Migne 38: 974).

17. Mauss's assertion of the animation of things exchanged, based on his research into the Maori concept of the *hau* of the gift, has been challenged by later anthropologists. See, for example, Sahlins 149-83.

18. The extant assize records for the home counties are collected and translated in Cockburn, *Calendar*. On fictional killers see Cockburn, *Calendar*, vol. 1; Cockburn, "Early-Modern Assize Records"; Cockburn, *English Assizes*; Knafla.

19. Pollock and Maitland 2: 473-74; Baker, *Introduction* 437. John Cowell provides a good early seventeenth-century account of the law of deodand:

Deodand . . . is a thing given or forfeited (as it were) to God for the pacification of his wrath in a case of misadventure, whereby any Christian soule commeth to a violent ende, without the fault of any reasonable creature. For example, if a horse should strike his keeper and so kille him; if a man in dryving a cart . . . should so fall, as the cart wheele running over him, should presse him to death. . . . In the first of these cases the horse, in the second the cart wheele, carte and horses . . . is to be given to God: that is, to be sold and distributed to the poore, for an expiation of this dreadfull event, though effected by unreasonable, yea sensles and dead creatures. (Y3)

Cowell adds that this really means the value of the items are "forfeited to the king by lawe, as susteining Gods person . . ." (Y3v). That the indictments collected by Cockburn give the value of the instrument of death reflects the persistence of the deodand in the Renaissance. In fact, homicide indictments continued into the nineteenth century to indicate such values. The law of deodand was not taken off the books until 1846, after it began to be applied to locomotives involved in accidental deaths (Baker, *Introduction* 437; Gray 47-48). See also Dalton 218; and Coke, *Third Institutes* 57-58: "Deodands when any moveable thing inanimate, or beast animate, doe move to, or cause the intimely death of any reasonable creature by mischance in any country of the realm (and not upon the sea, or upon any salt water) without the will, offence, or fault of himself, or of any person." Fernando Pulton repeats "the old rule, Omnia que mouent ad mortem sunt Deodanda" (128). John Chipman Gray remarks that the law of deodands arises in relation to the "imagination that there must be life in a moving object" (48); on the importance of *motion*, see also Holmes 23-24. We learn in *The Doctor and Student* that liability does not travel across the proprietary link connecting a thing and its owner, the obdurate inanimacy of the thing in effect absorbing blame by becoming the deodand: "And so it is where a man killeth another with the sword of John at Stile, the sword shall be forfeit as a *deodand*, and yet no fault is in the owner" (St. German 266). In the assize indictments the deodand as such both supplies a supplementary diversion of liability and translates that liability into explicitly monetary terms.

20. Elsewhere Bourdieu positions gift-giving in relation to other forms of exchange, and shows the particular dependence of the misrecognition of the gift economy on temporal intervals:

[T]he counter-gift must be deferred and different, because the immediate return of an exactly identical object clearly amounts to a refusal. Thus gift exchange is opposed to swapping, which, like the theoretical model of the cycle of reciprocity, telescopes gift and counter-gift into the same instant. It is also opposed to lending, in which the return of the loan, explicitly guaranteed by a legal act, is in a sense already performed at the very moment when a contract is drawn up ensuring the predictability and calculability of the act it prescribes. . . . the functioning of gift exchange presupposes individual and collective misrecognition of the truth of the objective 'mechanism' of the exchange, a truth which an immediate response brutally exposes. The interval between gift and counter-gift is what allows a relation of exchange that is always liable to appear as irreversible, that is, both forced and self-interested, to be seen as reversible. (*Logic* 105).

Along mostly independent lines, Jacques Derrida's work on gifts in *Given Time* runs in the same direction but ends in a characteristic reversal, by which it is precisely the "temporalization of time (memory, present, anticipation; retention, protention, imminence of the future; 'ecstasies' and so forth)" (14) that finally undermines (the misrecognition enabling) the gift, inasmuch as "[t]he simple intention to give, insofar as it carries the intentional meaning of the gift, suffices to make a return payment to oneself" (23).

21. My use here of the terms mimesis and representation derive from Weimann ("Towards a Literary Theory"), as does the implied association of the two forms of agency with *locus* and *platea*, from his discussion of *Figurenposition* in *Shakespeare and the Popular Tradition*.

22. For a still-persuasive account of dramatic conventions concerning time and character, see Bradbrook.

23. The question of the possible divided authorship of *Timon* is still unresolved. In keeping with recent statistical analysis suggesting that the case for partial authorship by Middleton remains inconclusive (Smith), I assume Shakespearean authorship throughout, though nothing I say is necessarily incompatible with divided authorship.

24. Note that "perform" could be used, as it is of Hermione's supposed statue in *The Winter's Tale* (5.2.96-97: " . . . now newly perform'd by that rare Italian master, Julio Romano"), to denote specifically the execution of a work of art.

25. On the functions of paradox in *Timon*, see Scott.

26. Renaissance gift-giving practices concern me only peripherally here. But for discussions of the gift economy in *Timon*, see Chorost, Kahn, and especially Wallace, who reads Arthur

Golding's 1578 translation of Seneca's *De Beneficiis* as a gloss on the play. On gift-giving in the Renaissance generally, see Montrose, Fumerton, and Davis.

Works Cited

Austin, J. L. *How to Do Things with Words.* 2nd ed. Ed. J. O. Urmson and Marina Sbisà. Cambridge: Harvard UP, 1975.

Baker, J. H. *An Introduction to English Legal History.* 3rd ed. London: Butterworths, 1990.

———. "New Light on *Slade's Case.*" *Cambridge Law Journal* 29.1 (1971): 51-67 (pt. 1); 29.2 (1971): 213-36 (pt. 2).

Benbow, R. Mark. "Dutton and Goffe versus Broughton: A Disputed Contract for Plays in the 1570s." *Records of Early English Drama* (1981.2): 3-9.

Bentley, G. E. *The Profession of Dramatist in Shakespeare's Time, 1590-1642.* Princeton: Princeton UP, 1971.

Bevington, David M. *From* Mankind *to* Marlowe: Growth of Structure in the Popular Drama of Tudor England. Cambridge: Harvard UP, 1962.

Bourdieu, Pierre. *The Logic of Practice.* Trans. Richard Nice. Stanford: Stanford UP, 1990.

———. *Outline of a Theory of Practice.* Trans. Richard Nice. Cambridge: Cambridge UP, 1972.

Bradbook, M. C. *Themes and Conventions of Elizabethan Tragedy.* Cambridge: Cambridge UP, 1935.

Bruster, Douglas. "Local *Tempest:* Shakespeare and the Work of the Early Modern Playhouse." *Journal of Medieval and Renaissance Studies* 25 (1995): 33-53.

Buckland, W. W. *A Text-Book of Roman Law from Augustus to Justinian.* Cambridge: Cambridge UP, 1921.

Cavell, Stanley. *Disowning Knowledge: In Six Plays of Shakespeare.* Cambridge: Cambridge UP, 1987.

Chambers, E. K. *The Elizabethan Stage.* 4 vols. Oxford: Clarendon, 1923.

Chorost, Michael. "Biological Finance in Shakespeare's *Timon of Athens.*" *English Literary Renaissance* 21 (1991): 349-70.

Cockburn, J. S., ed. *Calendar of Assize Records.* 10 vols. London: HMSO, 1975-85.

———. "Early-Modern Assize Records as Historical Evidence." *Journal of the Society of Archivists* 5.4 (1975): 229-30.

———. *A History of English Assizes, 1558-1774.* Cambridge: Cambridge UP, 1972.

Cohen, Derek. "The Politics of Wealth: *Timon of Athens.*" *Neophilologus* 77 (1993): 149-60.

Coke, Edward. *The Third Part of the Institutes of the Laws of England Concerning High Treason and Other Pleas of the Crown and Criminal Causes.* 1628. London: W. Clarke & Sons, 1809.

Cowell, John. *The Interpreter.* 1607. Menston: Scolar, 1972.

Dalton, Michael. *The Countrey Iustice, Conteyning the practice of the Iustices of the Peace out of their Sessions.* London, 1618.

Davis, Natalie Zemon. "Art and Society in the Gifts of Montaigne." *Representations* 12 (1985): 24-32.

de Grazia, Margreta. "The Motive for Interiority: Shakespeare's *Sonnets* and *Hamlet*." *Style* 23 (1989): 430-44.

Derrida, Jacques. *Given Time. I: Counterfeit Money*. Trans. Peggy Kamuf. Chicago: U of Chicago P, 1992.

Dolan, Frances E. *Dangerous Familiars: Representations of Domestic Crime in England, 1550-1700*. Ithaca: Cornell UP, 1994.

English Reports. 176 vols. Edinburgh: William Green & Sons, 1907.

Fifoot, C. H. S. *History and Sources of the Common Law: Tort and Contract*. London: Stevens, 1949.

Fumerton, Patricia. "Exchanging Gifts: The Elizabethan Currency of Children and Poetry." *ELH* 53 (1986): 241-78.

Gray, John Chipman. *The Nature and Sources of the Law*. 2nd ed. New York: Macmillan, 1948.

Haaker, Ann. "The Plague, the Theater, and the Poet." *Renaissance Drama* ns 1 (1968): 283-306.

Holdsworth, W. S. *A History of English Law*. 9 vols. Boston: Little, 1926.

Holmes, Oliver Wendell. *The Common Law*. Ed. Mark DeWolfe Howe. 1881. Boston: Little, Brown, 1963.

Kahn, Coppélia. " 'Magic of bounty': *Timon of Athens*, Jacobean Patronage, and Maternal Power." *Shakespeare Quarterly* 38 (1987): 34-57.

Knafla, Louis A. " 'John at Love Killed Her': The Assizes and Criminal Law in Early Modern England." *University of Toronto Law Journal* 35 (1985): 305-20.

Lücke, H. K. "Slade's Case and the Origin of the Common Counts." *Law Quarterly Review* 81 (1965): 422-45 (pt. 1); 81 (1965): 539-61 (pt. 2); 82 (1966): 81-93 (pt. 3).

Maguire, Laurie E. "A King's Men's Contract and Dramatic Output." *Notes and Queries* ns 32 (1985): 73-74.

Maus, Katharine Eisaman. *Inwardness and Theater in the English Renaissance*. Chicago: U of Chicago P, 1995.

Mauss, Marcel. *The Gift: The Form and Reason for Exchange in Archaic Societies*. Trans. W. D. Halls. New York: Norton, 1990.

Migne, Jacques-Paul, ed. *Patrologiae Cursus Completus*. Paris: Garnier Fratres, 1865.

Montrose, Louis Adrian. "Gifts and Reasons: The Context of Peele's *Araygnement of Paris*." *ELH* 47 (1980): 433-61.

Nicholas, Barry. *An Introduction to Roman Law*. Oxford: Oxford UP, 1962.

Plucknett, T. F. T. *A Concise History of the Common Law*. 5th ed. Boston: Little, Brown, 1956.

Pollock, Frederick, and Frederic William Maitland. *The History of English Law before the Time of Edward I*. 2nd ed. Intro. and bibl. S. F. C. Milsom. 2 vols. Cambridge: Cambridge UP, 1968.

Pulton, Fernando. *De pace regis et regni. viz. A Treatise declaring which be the great and generall Offenses of the Realme*. London, 1609.

Sahlins, Marshall. "The Spirit of the Gift." *Stone Age Economies*. Chicago: Atherton, 1972. 149-83.

St. German, Christopher. *The Doctor and Student*. Rev. William Muchall. Cincinnati: Robert Clarke, 1874.

Sayre, Francis Bowes. "*Mens Rea.*" *Harvard Law Review* 45 (1932): 974-1026.

Scott, William O. "The Paradox of Timon's Self-Cursing." *Shakespeare Quarterly* 35 (1984): 290-304.

Seneca. *The woorke of the excellent Philosopher Lucius Annæus Seneca concerning Benefyting, that is too say the dooing, receyving, and requyting of good Turnes.* Trans. Arthur Golding. London, 1578.

Shakespeare, William. *The Riverside Shakespeare.* Ed. G. Blakemore Evans. New York: Houghton, 1974.

———. *The Tempest.* Ed. Frank Kermode. London: Methuen, 1954.

———. *Timon of Athens.* Ed. H. J. Oliver. London: Methuen, 1959.

Simpson, A. W. B. *A History of the Common Law of Contract: The Rise of the Action of Assumpsit.* Oxford: Oxford UP, 1975.

———. "The Place of Slade's Case in the History of Contract." *Law Quarterly Review* 74 (1958): 381-96.

Smith, M. W. A. "The Authorship of *Timon of Athens.*" *Text* 5 (1991): 195-240.

Spevack, Marvin. *The Harvard Concordance to Shakespeare.* Cambridge: Harvard UP, 1973.

Spinosa, Charles. "The Transformation of Intentionality: Debt and Contract in *The Merchant of Venice.*" *English Literary Renaissance* 24 (1994): 370-409.

Wallace, John M. "*Timon of Athens* and the Three Graces: Shakespeare's Senecan Study." *Modern Philology* 83 (1986): 349-63.

Watkin, Thomas Glyn. "Hamlet and the Law of Homicide." *Law Quarterly Review* 100 (1984): 282-310.

Wayne, Don E. "*Drama and Society in the Age of Jonson*: An Alternative View." *Renaissance Drama* ns13 (1982): 103-29.

Weimann, Robert. *Shakespeare and the Popular Tradition in the Theater: Studies in the Social Dimension of Dramatic Form and Function.* Ed. Robert Schwartz. Baltimore: Johns Hopkins UP, 1978.

———. "Towards a Literary Theory of Ideology: Mimesis, Representation, Authority." *Shakespeare Reproduced: The Text in History and Ideology.* Ed. Jean E. Howard and Marion F. O'Connor. New York: Methuen, 1987. 265-72.

Wilson, Luke. "Ben Jonson and the Law of Contract." *Cardozo Studies in Law and Literature* 5 (1993): 281-306.

———. "*Hamlet*: Equity, Intention, Performance." *Studies in the Literary Imagination* 24.2 (1991): 91-113.

———. "*Hamlet,* Hales v. Petit, and the Hysteresis of Action." *ELH* 60 (1993): 17-55.

"Good queen, my lord, good queen": Sexual Slander and the Trials of Female Authority in The Winter's Tale

M. LINDSAY KAPLAN AND KATHERINE EGGERT

T HE LEGAL HISTORY of early modern Englishwomen has not yet been written, though recent contributions suggest that scholars are beginning to rectify this oversight.[1] One productive point of entry into this important field is presented by defamation, generally defined in early modern England as an injury inflicted by the false and malicious imputation of a crime. The popularity of this charge and its redresses is registered in the records for both common law and ecclesiastical courts in this period, both of which evidence dramatic increases in slander cases. The value of slander for the exploration of early modern women's legal concerns is multiple. First, defamation gives us an indication—albeit more reflective, perhaps, of public opinion than actual indictment rates—of the types of crimes women were thought to commit. After all, slanderous accusations have to have some plausibility in order to be damaging. Second, defamation is an injury that women both commit and complain about in significant numbers. Finally, the form of and redress for defamation are, for the most part, gendered. Imputations of bankruptcy, for example, which could have damaged a merchant and thus were actionable for a man, would probably have had little effect if directed toward a woman. In contrast, allegations of whoredom—which, while occasionally leveled at men, were not usually thought to injure male reputations—were overwhelmingly cited by women in the slander suits they brought.[2]

89

In this essay, we would like to make a foray into a gendered legal history of early modern England through the problem of slander as experienced by contemporary women and as represented and commented upon in Shakespeare's play *The Winter's Tale*. Not only does the play concern itself with slanders to women's reputations, it also engages a series of other transgressions particularly associated with women: adultery, petty treason, bastardy, infanticide, scolding, and witchcraft.[3] All the female offenses aired in the play thus reveal a pairing of common concerns about women in the period, their sexuality and their authority (a circumstance discussed by early modern commentators never as autonomy *from* men, but always as power *over* men). Female criminality was on the whole popularly defined in terms of either inverting gender hierarchy, as in petty treason or scolding, or transgressing sexual mores, as in bastardy or prostitution, or both, as in adultery or witchcraft. In fact, anxiety about female sexuality might be considered a displaced version of anxiety about female authority, insofar as a causative relation between these two can ever be established. Accusations of sexual impropriety often were unsubtly coded attacks on women's perceived dominance over men in a nonsexual sphere. In a period when a woman's reputation rested largely on her sexual behavior, there was insufficient language, besides that of promiscuity, to classify and to discourage the exercise of female authority. The next best category of opprobrium would be to characterize her behavior as male (Amussen 119–20).

England's ongoing concern with female dominance and female sexuality was only highlighted and exacerbated, in the second half of the sixteenth century, by the peculiar status of its monarch. Although Elizabeth Tudor preferred to promote herself as a singular woman, one whose sexual and legal autonomy was available to no one else, in fact her position as sole monarch and *femme sole* posed a significant challenge, as many critics have pointed out, to contemporary assumptions about the subordination of women. In her recent book on Elizabeth's multivalent presentations and representations, Carole Levin outlines Elizabeth's complex restructuring of gender hierarchies and the anxiety over an unfettered feminine sexuality she thus elicited. Far from simply categorizing the queen's monarchical persona as masculine, as some critics have tended to argue,[4] Elizabeth and her subjects also considered her rule to be precisely that of a woman over a kingdom of men; as a result, as Levin puts it, although "[h]er people might regard her body politic as both pure and virginal, and the incarnation of the sacred principle of male monarchy, . . . the rumors and seditious words so carefully gathered [by Elizabeth's detractors] suggest a perception of her body natural as potentially corrupt in a manifestly female way" (147). As critics such as Levin, Susan Frye, and Leah Marcus (*Puzzling* 59–73) have contended and as we discuss below, Elizabeth's queenship elicited her subjects' fantasies and fears that she was, as Shakespeare's Cleopatra puts it, "no more but e'en a woman," and that a woman ruling over men would necessarily subject her entire realm to unbridled feminine sexual desire. Those fantasies and fears were expressed and repeated in a number of different venues, including the courts of law, which during Elizabeth's reign heard cases that, had the female reputation at issue been not the queen's but a mere woman's, would have been considered under the rubric not of treason but of sexual slander.

Our discussion of a Jacobean play depends, however, on considering not what Elizabeth's sexual reputation underscored while she lived, but how her sexuality might have been remembered. Although Elizabeth's cherished virginity remained the topic of both idle curiosity and scurrilous attack well into the Stuart era (if not, indeed, into our own), the death of the queen tended to polarize the discussion of her sexual nature into clearer terms than the ones in circulation while she was alive. Elizabeth's disturbing presentation of herself as both virginal and sexual bifurcated after her death into opinion about whether she was virginal *or* sexual, so that on the one hand Elizabeth was apotheosized as the saint who through her refusal to marry had kept England Protestant and free,[5] while on the other hand she was still the object of detraction by persons such as "one Sheapheard, a barrister of Lincolns Inn, [and] a base Jesuited papist," who during James I's reign uttered "base and scandalous" words regarding the late queen's honor.[6] It is perhaps the case, then, that Elizabeth's passing offered a respite in which the late queen's sexuality could be named, codified, and contained. At the same time, however, Elizabeth's new status as a remembered personage gave England a neutral arena in which the debate over female sexuality and female authority, issues of increasing public anxiety as the seventeenth century wore on, could be creatively explored. That is, the threat posed by the desire and authority of real women is discussed in terms of the late queen so that it may be discussed at all. For these reasons, we contend, Shakespeare's *Winter's Tale* constructs its considerations of female sexuality around representations that remember and reevaluate Elizabeth. That reevaluation, we shall presently argue, in fact requires reaching back even farther in history, to Elizabeth's mother, Anne Boleyn, whose career provides a kind of prototype and a warning for all subsequent slandered women in positions of authority. Shakespeare's seventeenth-century recasting of sixteenth-century queens therefore serves as a larger commentary on the misrepresentations, if not defamations, that the law perpetrated against women in the early modern period in attempting to name and contain their behavior.

An account of how the law of defamation functioned for English women in the sixteenth and seventeenth centuries provides a necessary foundation for our argument. As we have already suggested, gender affected both the content of and the redress for defamation, due to a large extent to differences in the way male and female reputation was constructed. Susan Amussen observes:

The defamation cases [suggest] that "honesty" had one meaning for women and another for men. Women's honesty was determined and judged by their sexual behavior; men's honesty was judged in a wide variety of contexts with their neighbours, and bore a closer relation to our notion of honesty as "truthful." Reputation was a gendered concept in early modern England. (104)

The development of defamation law in sixteenth-century England indicates how the courts reflected and reinforced gender distinctions in rectifying damage to reputation. At the beginning of the century, the only redress for defamation was to be found at the ecclesiastical courts. The offense was defined as the malicious imputation of a crime; the punishment was excommunication, which could be revoked upon the guilty party's doing public penance (Helmholz xiv). However, as the century progressed, the common law began offering a remedy for defamation, based on the same definition of the offense, which understood its effects as financial and offered as punishment and redress damages paid by the offender to the victim. The two jurisdictions were distinguished by the content of the defamations spoken: the church courts handled imputations of "spiritual" crimes (i.e., offenses against ecclesiastical law) while the common-law courts offered redress for imputations of "temporal" crimes (offenses actionable in secular law). Hence, a defamation alleging sexual impropriety by either sex would go to ecclesiastical court while a slander imputing theft, for example, would be heard in a court of common law (Helmholz xli–xlvii).[7]

J. A. Sharpe speculates that the gendered nature of defamation reflects the differences in social roles for men and women:

> . . . it is difficult not to see the wider types of defamation against which men litigated as a consequence of their more varied involvement in the affairs of the world. Women . . . were allowed free access to everyday activities, but their role within them was limited. The rarity with which they were slandered as perjurers, cheats and usurers, for example, suggests that they were not allowed to participate very fully in business or legal matters. (*Defamation* 28–29)

The conception of women in terms of their sexuality reflects the limitations of their economic autonomy: the early modern English husband not only took control over his wife's property upon marriage, he also acquired property in her body. The children she produced belonged to him, and for middling and upper classes, the family's very continuity depended on her bearing a legitimate male heir to carry on the family name and control its financial holdings. Anxiety about female promiscuity thus fixates on the possibility that the wife's children might not be her husband's, and that his property might be transmitted to another man's son. A woman's assertion of independent sexuality in this way belies the important fiction that her husband owns her body, and the children she bears, by demonstrating that her sexual choices are beyond her husband's control. Thus sexual slander, while perceived as a problem by its victims, nevertheless performed a valuable patriarchal function: the threat of public humiliation and rejection, or even of disciplinary prosecution for the imputed behavior, served as a deterrent against sexual misbehavior both for victims of slander themselves and for either chaste or promiscuous bystanders (Ingram 305–07, 311–13). In fact, as Laura Gowing suggests, slanders against women's sexual reputations drew on directives for female chastity expressed in canonical and noncanonical sources: conduct and household manuals, sermons and ballads (9–10). Hence, defamation could function as a valuable force for policing female sexuality, not just as an action disruptive of the social order.[8]

It is, then, not surprising that Elizabeth, the self-styled Virgin Queen, repeatedly found herself the victim of sexual slander in the context of attempts either to rein her into an acceptable marriage or to unseat her. Rumors alleging Elizabeth's sexual misconduct circulated repeatedly throughout her reign, revealing that even the queen was not protected from her gender. Early in her reign, such rumors tended to emerge around discussions of the queen's marriage plans and England's concomitant fears over either foreign entanglements or subjection to a powerful domestic peer. Her affection for Robert Dudley (later earl of Leicester), for example, caused such a flurry of scandal in England and on the Continent that the representative for one of her wooers felt it necessary to inquire if Elizabeth were still a virgin (Neale 79-83). Outside of court, stories circulated to the effect that she had borne Dudley at least one illegitimate child. Such slanders regarding the queen and Dudley returned in the 1570s, 1580s, and 1590s, long after the end of her childbearing years and the earl's death (Samaha 69); as Levin explains, when Elizabeth's ability to marry and bear children was no longer an issue, "the rumors [of Elizabeth's sexual misconduct] served as a focus for discontent and fear for the succession" (67), and particularly as a focus for England's increasing desire to end female rule and institute normative male rule instead (Levin 100-20; Eggert, "Nostalgia" 524-26). In this way slanders against Elizabeth from late in her reign revived debates from early in her reign over the very possibility of a woman's public status. As a female ruler in her own right, she—like Mary Tudor and Mary Queen of Scots—contradicted the conventional wisdom that women could not rule over, and hence be superior to, men (Jordan 116-33). The general weakness and inferiority of women were cited by authors of treatises against queenship; one serious concern voiced was that once freed from male control, female lust would know no bounds.

In turn, the sexual scandals surrounding Elizabeth's own lineage also generated slander during her reign, slander that vented discontent against Elizabeth in the context of England's bitter religious controversies. In its belief that Henry VIII's divorce from Catherine of Aragon was invalid, the Roman Catholic church viewed his subsequent marriage with Anne Boleyn as adulterous and considered Henry and Anne's daughter Elizabeth a bastard. Charges against Elizabeth and Anne continued to surface well into her reign, as Catholic propaganda alluding to Elizabeth's adulterous origins and linking them with her own alleged promiscuity circulated with increasing frequency and virulence as the sixteenth century wore on. In 1588 William Allen, expatriate Catholic Cardinal of England, published in Antwerp his *Admonition . . . Concerning the Present Warres*, which not only charges Elizabeth with being the product of an incestuous union, asserting that Anne Boleyn was Henry VIII's daughter as well as his wife (Levin 80-81), but conflates that attack with vicious allegations against Elizabeth's own sexual conduct:

With [Leicester] . . . and diuers others she hathe abused her bodie, against Gods lawes, to the disgrace of princely maiestie & the whole nations reproche, by vnspeakable and incredible variety of luste, which modesty suffereth not to be remembred, neyther were it to chaste eares to be vttered how shamefully she hath defiled and infamed her person and cuntry, and made her Courte as a trappe, by this damnable and detestable arte, to intangle in sinne and ouerthrowe the yonger sorte of the nobilitye and gentlemen of the lande, whereby she is become notorious to the worlde, & in other cuntryes a comon fable for this her turpitude, which in so highe degre, namely in a woman and a Queene, deseruethe not onelie deposition, but all vengeaunce bothe of God and man, and cannot be tollerated without the eternal infamie of our whole cuntrie. . . . (xix, B2r)[9]

The illegitimacy of her birth and of her capacity to rule merge in this diatribe, which imagines Elizabeth's nymphomania transforming her realm into an effeminate "cuntry," emasculating and debauching its youth, and bringing infamy to England. Elizabeth's attackers hence transform the victim of slander into a source of defamation.

The treatment of Elizabeth's parentage in fact provides a paradigm for the ways in which sexual slander was used to control a woman's assertion of authority. It is now assumed by most historians of the period that Anne Boleyn was innocent of the charges that brought about her 1536 execution, a view apparently available in the Elizabethan period as well, since John Foxe styles her in his *Actes and Monuments* (1563) as a martyr whom he suspects was brought down by "some secret practising of the papists" (5: 136). However, popular stories of Anne as a treasonous witch and incestuous adulteress circulated from the time of her death well into the eighteenth century and are still current today (Warnicke 247). Henry VIII himself provided the basis for these slanders when, three years after his marriage to Anne, he charged her with adultery, incest, and treason, and had her executed and Elizabeth declared illegitimate. Foxe cites Anne's commitment to true religion as having provoked slander against her: "By reason whereof it may be easily considered, that this christian and devout Deborah could lack no enemies amongst such a number of Philistines, both within the realm, and without" (5: 136). Yet as the Second Act of Succession (1536) makes clear, it was Henry himself who removed the injunction against slanders of Anne and Elizabeth he had legislated earlier in the wake of criticisms over his divorce from Catherine of Aragon, in effect confirming and legalizing Catholic opinion in pardoning slanders against his second wife and her daughter:

. . . the kings most roiall maiestie, most gratiouslie considering, that diuers and manie of thi most louing and obedient subiects now latelie afore the begining of the present parlement, haue spoken [etc.] . . . against the said vnlawfull mariage, solemnized betweene his highnesse and the said ladie Anne, and to the preiudice, slander disturbance and derogation thereof, but also to the perill, slander and disherison of the ladie Elizabeth the kings daughter illegitimat borne vnder the same mariage, and to the let, disturbance and interruption of the said ladie Elizabeth to the title of the crowne. . . . Which words, dooings, [etc.] albeit they proceeded of no malice, but vpon true and iust grounds, . . . yet neuerthelesse the kings said subiects might heereafter happen to be impeached, troubled and vexed for such their words, dooings, acts, [etc.] . . . The kings highnesse therefore of his most bountifull mercie and benignitie is pleased and contented that it be enacted . . . that all and singular his louing subiects, which haue spoken, . . . [etc.] against [the marriage, Anne, or Elizabeth], or to anie of their slanders, perils, or disherison: . . . shall be freelie and cleerelie pardoned, discharged, and released by authoritie of this act, of all those and such treasons and misprisions of treasons aboue mentioned. (28 Hen. VIII c. 7)

While Henry apparently believed the charges to be true, a sense still lingered that imputations against Anne and Elizabeth had been considered defamatory in the past and might continue to be. Foxe tries to right this score by noting Henry's later change of mind as manifested in his last will, "wherein, expressly and by name, he did accept, and by plain ratification did allow, the succession of his marriage to stand good and lawful" (5: 136). Nevertheless, the Second Act of Succession remained on the statute books throughout Elizabeth's reign, licensing critics of her rule to deploy imputations of sexual impropriety against both Elizabeth and her mother.

The case of a king who falsely charges his wife with adultery, seeks to execute her, and bastardizes his daughter resonates strongly with the plot of *The Winter's Tale*, and in fact suggests a reading of the play as an allegory of Anne's downfall and Elizabeth's bastardization, seventy-five years after the fact. Horace Walpole expressed this opinion in 1769 in a digression from the main topic of his essay "Historic Doubts on the Life and Reign of King Richard the Third":

. . . there is another of Shakespeare's plays, that may be ranked among the historic, though not one of his numerous critics and commentators have discovered the drift of it; I mean *The Winter Evening's Tale*, which was certainly intended (in compliment to queen Elizabeth) as an indirect apology for her mother Anne Boleyn. . . . The subject was too delicate to be exhibited on the stage without a veil; and it was too recent, and touched the queen too nearly, for the bard to have ventured so home an allusion on any other ground than compliment. The unreasonable jealousy of Leontes, and his violent conduct in consequence, form a true portrait of Henry the Eighth, who generally made the law the engine of his boisterous passions. . . . The Winter's Evening Tale was therefore in reality a second part of Henry the Eighth. (108–09)

Walpole's comments obviously contain inaccuracies, from the title of the play, to the date of its composition (he imagines it written during Elizabeth's lifetime), to its place in the Shakespearean chronology. Nonetheless, we find Walpole's reading of the play intriguing, and we propose to consider it at some length in the following pages. In the end, though, we mean not to suggest that Hermione's family and fatal career precisely correspond at every point to Anne Boleyn's, but to argue that *The Winter's Tale* entertains reminiscences both of the long-dead Anne and of her lately deceased daughter Elizabeth in order to expand consideration of the plight of the sexually slandered woman outside these defunct episodes. We are, then, precisely not making a "topical" argument regarding Anne Boleyn and *The Winter's Tale*; rather, we are arguing that while the historical issues the play engages are still current enough in the early seventeenth century to be familiar and thus useful, their use lies in their presenting a concluded and thus less controversial episode through which difficult contemporary problems surrounding gender might be explored.[10] Charges in the play that initially seem utterly specific to Hermione, and that seem uniquely to resonate with Anne Boleyn's case, begin to attach themselves to different female characters, including women of different generations and stations than Hermione's. In this regard we find it significant that *The Winter's Tale* glosses its own ostentatious historical gap of sixteen years as a matter of comparison and substitution. Just as Time promises both to measure and to obliterate the distinctions between past and present—"so shall I do / To th' freshest things now reigning, and make stale / The glistering of this present, as my tale / Now seems to it" (4.1.12–15)—so, too, do the play's female characters interchangeably occupy the slandered or slanderable positions occupied in turn by Anne Boleyn, Elizabeth Tudor, and their successors in both royal and non-royal positions: adulteress, witch, scold, virgin, bastard, bride.

One might argue, to concur for the moment with Walpole, that Leontes's apparently unmotivated jealousy begins to cohere only as a recollection of Henry VIII's rejection of Anne Boleyn. Not that Leontes is unreasonable because Henry was unreasonable (as Walpole argues), but rather that the play's bizarre accumulation of details around Leontes's suspicions recapitulates the bizarre accusations of adultery, incest, and treason through which Henry and his counselors, in the wake of Anne's failure to bear him a son, tried to make retrospective sense of Henry's wrecked lineal ambitions. For example, Leontes's reading of Hermione's hospitable reception of Polixenes—"But to be paddling palms, and pinching fingers, / As now they are, and making practis'd smiles / As in a looking-glass; and then to sigh, as 'twere / The mort o' th' deer" (1.2.115-18)—reiterates Henry's *ex post facto* conversion of Anne's Petrarchan flirtations with male courtiers into sexual, rather than social, intercourse. Although the five men charged with committing adultery with Anne represented the whole gamut of male positions at court (one musician, two grooms of the privy chamber, one former page of the king, and Anne's own brother George Boleyn, Viscount Rochford), all of them had attempted to advance their ambitions by playing the queen's courtly lovers, subscribing to what Eric Ives calls "the common currency of courtly dalliance" by claiming to love their sovereign's wife (366).[11] In the context of Anne's indictment, however, these interchanges became described as her "inciting . . . five men to have sexual relations with her by the use of touches and kisses that involved thrusting her tongue into their mouths and theirs in hers" (Warnicke 203). At issue seemed to be Anne's initiation of many of these mock flirtations as a way of consolidating her command of the royal household: Ives describes a conversation between Anne and one of the men later accused, Henry Norris, as her eliciting his political loyalty in the guise of his pledge of love (366). The same technique of the courtly lady commanding, rather than passively accepting, her lovers' pledges would later be used to great effect by Anne's daughter Elizabeth; but in Anne's case, this inversion of gender hierarchy came to be interpreted as a prelude to sexual malfeasance. As with Hermione and Leontes, it is a short step from the queen declaring "a lady's Verily's / As potent as a lord's" (1.1.50-51) to the king surmising that she "arms her with the boldness of a wife / To her allowing husband!" (1.2.184-85).

Like Anne Boleyn, Hermione is accused of adultery, treason, and conspiracy to murder the king, but hovering around those charges is another, stranger imputation that also haunted Anne: the imputation of witchcraft. Retha Warnicke has recently argued, suggestively if not conclusively, that Henry's horror of witchcraft was the primary reason he initiated proceedings to rid himself of Anne. On 29 January 1536, Anne was delivered of a stillborn male fetus whom the midwives probably thought deformed (Warnicke 201–03); witches were believed to give birth to deformed children. This circumstance, Warnicke contends, explains the care taken in the indictments of Anne to describe her as preternaturally seductive of both Henry and her adulterous lovers, initiating those "mortally sinful" tongue-thrusting kisses (Warnicke 203). Leontes is similarly disturbed by what he perceives as "[k]issing with inside lip" (1.2.286); witchcraft statutes cite "the intent to provoke any person to unlawful love" as actionable (5 Eliz. c. 16, qtd. in Rosen 56). At issue was not only the witch's provocation of men to desire, an action of course not unique to witches, but her intent to engage them thereby in unlawful, unnatural sexual acts that might in turn bring down God's punishment of a monstrous child. As well, Henry's concern that he had been bewitched might have moved him to declare himself a cuckold not only once, but five times over, since if Henry had fathered a child stillborn through witchcraft, then he himself might have been tainted through sexual contact with the witch's womb. On the other hand, sexual concourse with a witch was commonly thought to induce male impotence, a malady from which Henry evidently suffered, according to evidence given by Anne's brother George at his trial. The fact that George Boleyn's evidence was allowed to stand in the record is taken by Warnicke as evidence that Henry wanted his impotence with Anne to be made known, so that he could not possibly have fathered her monstrous son (216). Paradoxically, then, Henry's conversion of himself into a cuckold, and an impotent cuckold at that, allowed him to inoculate his patrilineage against the witch's sexual influence.

We are not qualified to assess whether Warnicke is right to hinge Anne's downfall on Henry's belief in her witchcraft. However, the rumors of witchery that sprang up against Anne and that persisted in the popular literature do bear reading in connection with *The Winter's Tale*'s treatment of uncertain paternity. Although witchcraft is a charge leveled not against Hermione but rather against Paulina, as we will discuss below, witchcraft's presumed effects on paternity—presumptions that distill and warp a whole constellation of early modern phobias about women's sexuality and women's authority—nevertheless haunt the margins of Leontes's irrational suspicions about Mamillius's parentage. Janet Adelman has described Leontes's contradictory responses to his son as gyrating attempts to purge himself of contact with feminine sexuality; while at one moment Leontes envisions

Mamillius as his duplicate, a product of fantasized parthenogenesis, at another moment Mamillius's resemblance to Hermione ("Though he does bear some signs of me, yet you / Have too much blood in him" [2.1.57-58]) causes Leontes further to recoil from Hermione's sexual desire and his own acquiescence to it (Adelman 224-28). Leontes ignores similar evidence of resemblance in the case of his baby daughter ("Although the print be little, the whole matter / And copy of the father" [2.3.98-99]) in order to declare her a bastard; one assumes that he discounts this evidence because of its source, Paulina, whose own forthrightness brings on her the charge of witchcraft that had never been elucidated against Hermione. But once the word "witch" has been uttered in connection with Paulina's refusal to keep silence, then Hermione's eloquent defense of herself, too, carries the tinge of female witchery—not solely, as Karen Newman has noted, because the witch's speech is heard in public, but because her speech coopts vehicles of hegemonic language: for early modern witches, prayers and the liturgy (66-70); for Hermione, the Oracle. But Hermione's speech, like that of the early modern witches who came to trial, and like that of Anne Boleyn at her own trial, falls on ears not prone to be seduced again. Like Anne, who pleaded her innocence with "so wise and discreet answers to all things laid against her, excusing herself with her words so clearly as though she had never been faulty to the same" (Ives 387),[12] Hermione is nonetheless ignored by her accuser, as is the Oracle that affirms her case.

Ignored, that is, until Leontes receives news that his son, "with mere conceit and fear / Of the queen's speed" (3.2.144-45), is dead. Here, then, is where Leontes begins to part company from Henry VIII, and where we have to gauge the effects of the play's slippage from a strict reproduction of 1530s events. Mamillius's resemblance to his father, along with the fact that he is a well-formed boy, not a monstrous fetus, bars Leontes from Henry's strategy of declaring that his son could not possibly be his. Thus, whereas for Henry the death of his unborn son constituted evidence for condemning the witch and her offspring, for Leontes the death of his son is, at last, convincing evidence of his own tyranny (3.2.146-47). *The Winter's Tale* thus airs Henry's warped reasoning only to expose it as precisely that, warped: "I have too much believ'd mine own suspicion" (3.2.151). Unlike Henry, who at the time of Anne's trial had already made preparations to further his patrilineal ambitions with a new wife, Leontes admits the Oracle's judgment that "the king shall live without an heir, if that which is lost be not found" (3.2.134-36), and accepts Paulina's stricture that he not remarry. In this way *The Winter's Tale* shifts its topical perspective from a Henrician era to a Jacobean stance. In a post-Elizabethan light Leontes's family seems in fact to revise and reverse Henry's, so that Mamillius begins to resemble not Anne's malformed, stillborn son, but the lamented Edward VI, cut down in his youth; and the baby, presumed dead, whose recovery saves the nation, resembles Elizabeth herself, who underwent a kind of internal exile and near-martyrdom (as Foxe reminded his readers) in her years of waiting to assume the throne from her sister Mary Tudor.

This displacement of historical judgment forward in time, called attention to by Time's own displacement of events in act 4, accounts in part for the possibility of reading the play's treatment of queenly reputation in multiple layers: Hermione's plight is replicated and redeemed in her daughter's, just as Anne Boleyn's reputation came to be absorbed and recuperated in Elizabeth's, and subsequently shadowed in the next Elizabeth, the Stuart princess. We wish briefly to consider the consequences of reading the second half of *The Winter's Tale* in light of Elizabethan and Jacobean reconstructions of Anne's downfall, with the aim of suggesting that the play's refracted treatments of the case of the slandered queen eventually unmoor the play from concerns specific only to royal women.

At first blush, the sixteen-year-old Perdita seems to continue to recollect Elizabeth Tudor, this time as an adult seeking to reform her mother's reputation. Perdita's concern for her chastity—to whose loss she seems to be darkly alluding when she avers that, faced with the wrath of his father, Florizel "must change this purpose" of marrying her "[o]r I my life" (4.4.39–40)—coalesces with her hatred for the grafted flowers she calls "nature's bastards" (4.4.83); and her refusal to plant these artificed and hence whorelike flowers demonstrates her desire to mend, in her own childbearing, any hint of bastardy: "No more than, were I painted, I would wish / This youth should say 'twere well, and only therefore / Desire to breed by me" (4.4.101–03). In this fashion, Perdita recalls Queen Elizabeth's steadfast maintenance of her virginity, which, many historians surmise, may have been motivated in part by her wish to expunge the nation's memory of Anne Boleyn's disastrous childbearing career as well as her own sporadic illegitimacy. As Frye describes her, Elizabeth early in her reign in fact sounded a great deal like Perdita: her coronation entry symbolically promised a queen who would be both fertile and wise, while at the same time it emphasized Elizabeth as the legitimate product of a legitimate royal marriage (33–36).[13] Later, of course, as it became clear that Elizabeth would not marry, the prospect of her fertility was dropped in favor of her sexual purity—and that virginity became a figure, as Peter Stallybrass has argued, for an inviolable England, an island nation defending its embattled borders against all comers. In the years leading up to and following the 1588 threat of Spanish invasion, Elizabeth's chastity admonished England to preserve its Protestantism and its sovereignty; together, England's religion and England's nationhood substituted for a child of Elizabeth's body as Elizabeth's "issue" (Sandler 164). And that admonition includes reminiscences of Anne Boleyn, converted (largely by means of Foxe's widely read *Actes and Monuments*) into a Protestant saint.[14]

In this regard even a slight romance like Robert Greene's *Pandosto*, Shakespeare's source for the plot of *The Winter's Tale*, might be read as a recuperation of Anne's reputation, and in turn Elizabeth's. Indeed, *Pandosto* provides an interesting initial case for our suggestion that Anne's story might be revived and revised to fit changing historical circumstances. Published in 1588, the year of the Armada and one year after the execution of Mary Queen of Scots, *Pandosto* capitalized on a historical moment in which the sexual status of queens was under intense scrutiny: even while English propagandists continued to publish accounts of Mary Queen of Scots as not only treasonous but also licentious, Catholic propagandists responded by describing Elizabeth as positively wolfish in her sexual appetites. Moreover, these Catholic accounts hurry to refer to Anne Boleyn as a means of further muddying Elizabeth's reputation.[15] *Pandosto*'s plot, in this milieu, seems to gather up English anxiety about the possibility of a sexual queen only to clear the queen's name.[16]

Pandosto's continued popularity—it went through six editions before *The Winter's Tale*'s first recorded performance in 1611 (Greene, *Perymedes* xxx-xxxii)—might be attributable, at least in part, to the continued resonance of the issue of queenly sexuality even after Elizabeth's death. As Barry Weller and Margaret Ferguson have recently argued, in the second decade of the seventeenth century Anne Boleyn's reputation was still a matter of religious and literary controversy.[17] Catholic polemicist Nicholas Sander's *De origine et progressu schismatis Anglicani*, first published in 1585, had gone through its sixth European edition in 1610: this work promotes a perception of Anne as witchlike, detailing her prodigious promiscuity as well as her physical disfigurements (Warnicke 247). On the other hand, historian and Protestant apologist John Speed asserts in his 1611 *History of Great Britaine*—a work Shakespeare consulted before writing *Henry*

VIII circa 1611-13 (*Henry VIII* xxxv) and thus may have had to hand as he was writing or revising *The Winter's Tale*—that Anne Boleyn's "adulteries," like Hermione's, were merely a matter of misread queenly benevolence: "I haue heard it reported that [George Boleyn, Viscount] *Rochford* the Queenes brother comming to her bed side to solicite a suite, leaned there-upon to whisper her in the eare; which the Spials gaue forth that hee did so, to kisse the Queen" (771).[18] Placing *The Winter's Tale*'s plot in conjunction with a writer like Speed suggests a further displacement and revision of the slanderable queen in order to suit Jacobean circumstances. If the anticipated marriage of *The Winter's Tale*'s Perdita indeed refers, as David Bergeron has argued, to the 1613 wedding of Elizabeth Stuart to the Protestant Elector Palatine (*Shakespeare's Romances* 157, 160), then we might see Shakespeare's play as part of a national effort to recuperate Elizabeth Tudor as a new, less threatening Elizabeth, one who safeguards her chastity so that she may eventually deliver it into her husband's keep-ing.[19] This reading metamorphoses Perdita into James's daughter Elizabeth Stuart, and Hermione into an amalgamated and purified Anne Boleyn and Elizabeth Tudor. Hermione's reputation is so thoroughly cleared that her own sexuality, upon her revival, entirely disappears: like Elizabeth Tudor the Protestant martyr, her concern is only for the welfare of her daughter, the future of the nation.

In the end, though, *The Winter's Tale*'s centrifugal movement away from Anne Boleyn's historically limited case also moves the play beyond merely a study of queens' susceptibility to sexual slander. A focus solely on royal women past and present would allow *The Winter's Tale* to be a play more like *Henry VIII*—that is, a play whose final emphasis is on England's unsullied national lineage and national reputation, in which "when / The bird of wonder dies, the maiden phoenix, / Her ashes new create another heir / As great in admiration as herself" (5.4.39-42). And admittedly *Pandosto*, which contains all of the plot elements of *The Winter's Tale* that we have discussed so far, would be a sufficient text for our consideration of reputation in connection to queens. However, *The Winter's Tale* does not restrict its representation of slander and female criminality to a creative reworking of Anne's and Elizabeth's sexual and reproductive careers. As queens, these women experienced lives quite different from those of other women in the early modern period. Yet queens were also considered exemplary, just as the accusations that Hermione, Perdita, and even Paulina suffer are versions of those which many women had to face. *The Winter's*

Tale's two departures from *Pandosto's* plot—the voice of Paulina, and the revival of the queen—prove crucial to our consideration here. Particularly in the context of these two original additions to Greene, Shakespeare's play pointedly returns its female characters to circumstances familiar to slandered early modern women of all classes; in other words, the play departs from allegories of queens into fictions of law. But in the process, the play also radically reinvents early modern legal culture in order to reread positively the nexus of female sexuality and authority that is so troubling to the patriarchal order, both of the play and of early modern England.

David Underdown explores the "crisis of order" in early modern England in terms of gender strains resulting from women's economic independence, suggesting that public anxieties about scolds, witches, and physically or sexually rebellious women, increasingly expressed between 1560 and 1660, are different manifestations of a similar response to opportunities for female economic autonomy (121, 135-36). Interestingly, Underdown does not consider Elizabeth's rule as a potentially contributing factor to this phenomenon. As a woman authorized to rule over men, she is the scold *par excellence*, and capable of obliquely but emphatically asserting her superiority to a male Parliament, as in her 1566 speech on marriage and succession, where she twice exclaimed that "it is monstrous that the feet should direct the head" (Rice 79, 81). It was precisely this specter of female regiment that was punished when scolds were "enthroned" on cucking stools, or "cuckqueans," and ducked in water (Boose 190, 195). Lynda Boose's remarks on the scold's nexus of verbal and sexual transgression are useful to contrast with our current discussion:

. . . the talkative woman is frequently imagined as synonymous with the sexually available woman, her open mouth the signifier for invited entrance elsewhere. Hence the dictum that associates "silent" with "chaste" and stigmatizes women's public speech as a behavior fraught with cultural signs resonating with a distinctly sexual kind of shame. (196)

The Winter's Tale explicitly counters this nexus, within the context of a recuperation of Elizabeth's heritage and authority, by showing female outspokenness as compatible with and appropriate to female virtue and chastity, linking instead male speech with shame and the disruption of patriarchal succession.

Breaking the link between women's authority and their sexual malfeasance, however, requires *The Winter's Tale* to represent slanders against women, such as the imputation of scolding, as crimes with negative consequences for the social order, a representation that runs counter to most legal understandings of the problem in early modern England. First, it would be difficult to imagine that a king's accusations, regardless of their veracity or his motivations, could ever have been construed as constituting defamation. And even if this were possible, Leontes's words against Hermione would probably not have constituted defamation according to the ecclesiastical definition, because he believes the truth of his statements; he apparently does not speak them out of malice, and he pursues his allegations against her through legal channels (Ingram 295).[20] In only one limited and anomalous legal arena would sexual slanders against early modern Englishwomen have been understood as resulting in monetary loss or social unrest: the court of Star Chamber, in which a husband might complain that he, his wife, and the community at large were damaged by sexual slanders against her. Although the Star Chamber apparently takes cognizance only of a threat to a husband's reputation, it nevertheless registers that, since his reputation substantially depends on his wife's, sexual slander against her has a serious impact.[21] Only the court of Star Chamber, then, acknowledges the dilemma sexual slander poses for the patriarchy: even while it may circumscribe a woman's sexual behavior, it may also dismantle the family name.

The Winter's Tale raises this legal exception to the status of legal commonplace. In the world of the play, the horns of this patriarchal dilemma are exposed in the king's desire to protect his own honor while exposing the queen's dishonor. He asks Camillo,

> Dost think I am so muddy, so unsettled,
> To appoint myself in this vexation; sully
> The purity and whiteness of my sheets,
> (Which to preserve is sleep, which being spotted
> Is goads, thorns, nettles, tails of wasps)
> Give scandal to the blood o' th' prince, my son,
> . . . .
> Without ripe moving to 't?
>
> (1.2.325–32)

The answer to this question, given Leontes's dislike of his wife's persuasive power over Polixenes, is yes: his accusations against her immediately defuse her influence in court. But despite his status as king and his belief in his own allegations, Leontes's imputations against Hermione are clearly marked as slander causing widespread social damage. Paulina most evidently articulates the harm caused by threats to female reputation:

> . . . for he,
> The sacred honour of himself, his queen's,
> His hopeful son's, his babe's, betrays to slander,
> Whose sting is sharper than the sword's. . . .
>   (2.3.83–86)

Strikingly, she focuses on the fact that his accusations harm not only his wife and children, but his own honor. The slander against Hermione transforms into a self-slander: "this most cruel usage of your queen / . . . will ignoble make you, / Yea, scandalous to the world" (2.3.116, 119–20). Even the king acknowledges early in the proceedings, if for the wrong reasons, that his animus against Hermione and her alleged co-conspirators only serves to damage him: "The very thought of my revenges . . . / Recoil upon me" (2.3.19–20). Later, Leontes is indeed shown that his slanders have serious consequences for his own reputation, his happiness, and the stability of his rule (3.2.185–202). Similarly, the false imputation of sexual impropriety that Polixenes makes against Perdita, and that threatens to replay the tragedy of her mother, is shown to wreak damage on the speaker, not the victim. Responding to his father's violent rebuke and sexual slander of Perdita, Florizel resolves to himself,

> . . . then
> Let nature crush the sides o' th' earth together,
> And mar the seeds within! . . .
> From my succession wipe me, father. . . .
>   (4.4.478–81)

Polixenes will face the same loss of an heir and the same uncertain succession that Leontes is grappling with; in both cases, sexual slanders against women are shown to pose dangerous national consequences. But they also endanger, if on a higher social register, the legitimacy and respectability on which even middling classes depended for credit relations and for securing property transfer through inheritance.[22]

The play's rereading and transformation of the process of contemporary slander law for women is similarly employed in its representation of female criminality generally. Hermione, Paulina, and Perdita all are essentially defamed to the extent that they are falsely accused of a considerable number of transgressions; their manifest innocence serves not only to discredit the speakers of the imputations, but also to call into question the construction of commonly defined popular notions of women and crime. Paulina's role in particular broadens the play's scope to consider a number of slanders commonly directed toward women. Leontes consistently deploys the rhetoric used to describe scolds in his attempts to delegitimate and silence Paulina's speech. She is a "callat / Of boundless tongue, who late hath beat her husband, / And now baits me!" (2.3.90-92); her rebelliousness moves beyond her husband and threatens her king. He asks Antigonus, "canst not rule her?" (46), and charges he is "woman-tir'd, unroosted / By thy Dame Partlet here" (74-75), a "lozel, . . . worthy to be hang'd / That wilt not stay her tongue" (108-09). Antigonus, however, rejects the charges by responding in kind, but with a difference: "When she will take the rein I let her run; / But she'll not stumble" (51-52). The punishment of "bridling" was often imagined as a fit fate for early modern scolds (see Boose); Antigonus invokes this punishment only to demonstrate its inapplicability to the current circumstances. Paulina is also called a witch (67), a bawd (either a prostitute or a purveyor of prostitutes) (68), a traitor (81), and, by implication, a heretic (113-15); these, or similar charges of sexual or hierarchical transgression (including bastardy), are also laid at the feet of Hermione and/or Perdita. But these accusations are already defused before they are spoken, since not only the play's audience but also the other characters within the play are aware of their baselessness.

The irrationality of these imputations begins to put pressure on the logic of patriarchy itself. When Leontes remarks disparagingly that Antigonus "dreads his wife," again evoking the specter of the scold, Paulina retorts, "So I would you did; then 'twere past all doubt / You'd call your children yours" (2.3.79-81). The popular ideology that held women physically, intellectually, and morally inferior to men depends on the proposition that wives are more susceptible to sinning and cannot be trusted. In *The Winter's Tale*, in contrast, a husband who looks up to rather than down on his wife can trust that her integrity will keep her faithful to him. Paulina emphasizes the stupidity of Leontes's jealousy, by way of insisting on the legitimacy of his second child, in her catalogue of his similarities to his newborn daughter. She concludes:

> And thou, good goddess Nature, which hast made it
> So like to him that got it, if thou hast
> The ordering of the mind too, 'mongst all colours
> No yellow in 't, lest she suspect, as he does,
> Her children not her husband's!
>
> (2.3.103–07)

J. H. P. Pafford, the editor of the New Arden edition of the play, brings in a Leontesian note on these lines by suggesting that Paulina says the opposite of what she means here, "i.e., that it is the deliberate expression by Shakespeare of the kind of mistake which an excited woman might easily make" (49n106–07). But the absurdity here is not Paulina's, but Leontes's: as Pafford alternatively glosses, Perdita's doubting the fatherhood of her own children would be just as irrational as her father's baseless fears.

It is interesting to note that while slanders against women were relegated to the less powerful and the less lucrative jurisdiction of the ecclesiastical courts, slanders by women (often against men) were given the separate category of scolding that received disproportionate attention in popular literature and vigorous initiative in the means of communal punishment (see Boose, Underdown). Strikingly, the play also departs from social and legal practice in vindicating Paulina's "scolding." At the moment when her charges appear to cross the line dividing truth and slander, when she comes closest to fitting the stereotype of a scold, Leontes justifies her speech. "Go on, go on: / Thou canst not speak too much; I have deserv'd / All tongues to talk their bitt'rest" (3.2.214–16). In contrast to Henry VIII's licensing defamations against Anne and Elizabeth to deflect infamy from himself, here the king licenses, in effect, defamations against himself as punishment for the infamy he has brought on his wife. While a bystanding lord chastises Paulina, and she remorsefully berates herself for showing "too much / The rashness of a woman" (220–21), Leontes insists on the validity of her words: "Thou didst speak but well / When most the truth: which I receive much better / Than to be pitied of thee" (232–34). Paulina's speaking is recuperated at its most radical and potentially most criminal moment, suggesting the need to reevaluate the category of scolding and the motivations behind its punishment.

Similarly, the charges of witchcraft leveled at Paulina in act 2 are dismissed at the play's end precisely when they are most credible. Leontes invokes the dangerous discourse of witchcraft in remarking on the astonishingly lifelike figure of Hermione:

> . . . O royal piece!
> There's magic in thy majesty, which has
> My evils conjur'd to remembrance, and
> From thy admiring daughter took the spirits,
> Standing like stone with thee.
>
> (5.3.38–42)

All of the statutes legislated against witchcraft in the sixteenth century particularly forbid the invocation of evil spirits; here, in contrast, the conjuration is marvelous and cathartic, reminding Leontes of his past deeds and uniting the spirits of Perdita with those of her mother. Leontes's licensing of the magic that here commences is all the more remarkable considering that Paulina, again the focus of anxiety over female authority, again expresses that anxiety herself, anticipating that others will make the charge of witchcraft against her:

> I'll make the statue move indeed; descend,
> And take you by the hand: but then you'll think
> (Which I protest against) I am assisted
> By wicked powers.
>
> (5.3.88–91)

She refers twice more to the possibility that some will suspect "it is unlawful business / I am about" (96–97, 105), even while making use of language associated with witches' practices as she addresses the statue: "Come! / I'll fill your grave up . . . / Bequeath to death your numbness; for from him / Dear life redeems you" (100–103). The witchcraft act passed by Parliament in 1604 forbids anyone to

use practise or exercise any invocation or conjuration of any evil and wicked spirit . . . ; or take up any dead man, woman, or child out of his, her, or their grave, or any other place where the dead body resteth, . . . to be employed or used in any manner of witchcraft, sorcery, charm, or enchantment. (1 Jac. I c. 12, qtd. in Rosen 57)

With the threat of female transgression once more hanging in the air, Leontes steps in to validate the transgression itself: "If this be magic, let it be an art / Lawful as eating" (110–11). He is still not sure if magic is behind the revivification of his wife, but even so, he insists on the legitimacy of Paulina's actions.

The slanders spoken against Hermione, Perdita, and Paulina in the course of *The Winter's Tale* give a sense of how female criminality was understood at the time, but these accusations are shown, ultimately, to be constructs of male anxiety without basis in reality. The qualities associated with female transgression in early modern society are instead presented as valuable; rather than destabilizing the social order, Paulina's "offenses" serve, ultimately, to restore order and succession to Leontes's realm. This is not to say that disruptions to the social order do not occur in the play; damage is done, however, not by the women accused but by their male accusers. All three women suffer losses as a result of masculine defamations in the play, but perhaps the biggest loser, from a patriarchal perspective, is Leontes himself. If early modern patriarchal wisdom finds value in a less than vigorous redress of slanders against women, the play insists on the severity of those slanders' damages, not only to Hermione, Paulina, and Perdita, but especially to Leontes and his entire kingdom in the loss of a male heir.[23] The danger here lies not in female criminal behavior but in criminalizing female behavior.

We are suggesting that *The Winter's Tale* takes a feminist stance in relation to early modern law, though by "feminist" we do not mean the kind of thoroughgoing overthrow of patriarchal principles that would be indicated in a late twentieth-century use of the term. Rather, the play proposes women as integral and morally reliable caretakers of the patriarchal project of lineal inheritance; proposes that women's sexual reputations are to be treated as equal before the law to men's economic livelihoods; and, perhaps most audaciously, proposes that women have the authority to define those sexual reputations for themselves. However, Paulina's repeated, almost anxious iteration of the lawfulness of her actions serves as a reminder of women's tenuous stance before the law in early modern English society. After all, the radical claims that we argue *The Winter's Tale* advances are made within a play whose title suggests its very fictionality as well as its superannuation.[24] This improbability is further stressed by the play's disruption of the classical unities of action, place, and, most self-consciously, time. Time's choric appearance draws attention to the artificiality of his role, but also to its legality:

> I that please some, try all: both joy and terror
> Of good and bad, that makes and unfolds error,
> Now take upon me, in the name of Time,

> To use my wings. Impute it not a crime
> To me, or my swift passage, that I slide
> O'er sixteen years, and leave the growth untried
> Of that wide gap, since it is in my power
> To o'erthrow law, and in one self-born hour
> To plant and o'erwhelm custom.
>
> (4.1.1-9)

The strange self-referentiality of this speech (3-4) intensifies its implausibility even as Time authorizes his capacity to make or break law. His ability to judge (with the pun on "trial" in line 1) is indicated, yet he also expresses the fear of slander (4). He has the power to determine or dismiss law, but he must ask permission of the audience to skip these years and apologizes for the inconvenience (15, 29-32). The ambivalence Time voices in this speech articulates the difficult project of the play. Shakespeare stages a tale "stale [to] / The glistering of this present" (4.1.13-14), the bygone gender controversies embedded in the lives and deaths of Anne Boleyn and Elizabeth Tudor, as a vehicle for the very lively and disruptive current debates over women in early seventeenth-century England. In cautiously revivifying dead queens—and Time's appearance suggests that this recuperation is dependent on the hiatus—the play opens up a space, if an uncertain space, within which to begin a critique of current gender politics. Whether this fantastical tale found fertile ground in the legal culture of the seventeenth century is a question that future scholars of women's legal history will need to explore and answer.

Notes

The authors wish to thank Frances Dolan for her comments on an earlier draft of this essay; the members of Lindsay Kaplan's graduate and honors seminars in Women in Renaissance Law and Drama for their stimulating discussions of the essay's issues; and Laura Deal, Margaret Ferguson, Ralph Hexter, and Marjorie McIntosh for crucial scholarly advice.

1. As J. A. Sharpe notes, "Female crime, except for witchcraft, perhaps, is a subject which has so far attracted surprisingly little attention, one facet of the regrettably undeveloped nature of the study of women's history in the early modern period" (*Crime* 108); he cites Carol Wiener's and J. M. Beattie's articles as exceptions. Since the appearance of these essays, some important inroads have been made into this field, such as the work by Boose, Cioni, Dolan, Erickson, Ingram, and Spring, to mention just a few studies pertinent to the sixteenth and seventeenth centuries. For a consideration of defamation and gender that often parallels the views of our essay, see Jardine.

2. The content of the words spoken and their results also determined the jurisdiction for redress, as the common-law and ecclesiastical courts divided responsibility for remedying this wrong. For a rigorous account of the historical development of defamation in both the ecclesiastical and common-law courts in England, see Helmholz.

3. In her chapter "Finding What Has Been 'Lost': Representations of Infanticide and *The Winter's Tale*" Frances Dolan points out that this crime usually associated with mothers is linked in Shakespeare's play to a father, who is then excused of the crime (159-70). Because it is not explicitly linked with female criminality in the play, we omit consideration of infanticide in our essay.

4. Treatments of Elizabeth as successfully wielding a masculine persona depend upon unskeptically accepting that the legal doctrine of the King's Two Bodies served to expunge the monarch's political persona of all perceived weakness, including the weakness of being a woman. Such a belief has marred otherwise fine readings of, for example, Shakespeare's comedies (Marcus, "Shakespeare's Comic Heroines") and Spenser's *Faerie Queene* (Miller); for more complex analyses, see Marcus's revised account of Elizabeth's "composite" identity (*Puzzling* 51-105); Eggert, "Ravishment" (3-16); Frye (12-19); and especially Levin's chapter "Elizabeth as King and Queen" (121-48).

5. Such a representation of Elizabeth as defender of the faith could be used both for and against James I and Charles I; see Woolf.

6. *The Diary of Sir Simonds D'Ewes, 1622-1624*, ed. E. Bourcier (Paris, 1974), 142, qtd. in Woolf 179.

7. One of the defining "incidents" determining redress of defamation in an ecclesiastical court was that the suit be "merely 'for the soul's health': in no circumstances could cash damages be awarded" (Ingram 296). Although in special circumstances offenders could request that their penance be commuted to a fine, these monies were paid to "poor relief and other pious objects," not to the victims (Ingram 336-37). While women were allowed to sue in common law for defamation if they could prove damages (Ingram 296; see the case of Davyes v. Gardiner, in which the competing jurisdictions are discussed [Baker and Milsom 627-28]), the vast majority of common-law slander cases list male plaintiffs. It should, however, be pointed out that most married women in the period did not have separate legal and, therefore, financial identities from those of their husbands (Baker 550-57).

8. Gowing claims that defamers "twisted [these materials] towards other ends than the original intention" (10). However, we would argue that both unauthorized and authorized commentators on female behavior, both slanderers and tract-writers, share the common aim of circumscribing female sexual behavior. See Kaplan for an exploration of slander's employment in general as a tool for punishment and humiliation. While the punishment for defamation in the ecclesiastical courts called for a humiliating public penance, it is clear from the small percentage of final sentences that many slanderers did not endure the same public embarrassment experienced by their victims (Ingram 336-37, 317-18).

9. As Bruce Boehrer explains, the charges of incest leveled against Elizabeth's parentage were by no means consistent: the same Catholic polemicist might call Elizabeth both the product of Henry's and Anne's incestuous marriage, and the product of Anne's incest with her brother George (47-48).

10. Richard Wilson also briefly notes the analogies between Hermione and Anne Boleyn

in his discussion of early modern medical discourse and its shift toward male scrutiny and control of gynecological and obstetrical study and practice (134-35).

11. However, two of the five men charged were also suspected of sodomy. Buggery was also popularly implicated in early modern English discourses of incest and witchcraft, two of the charges against Anne (Warnicke 191-95). The homosexual transgression underlying accusations of the queen's "lovers" may be echoed by homoerotic tensions between Leontes and Polixenes in act 1 of *The Winter's Tale*.

12. The speaker is contemporary chronicler Charles Wriothesley, whose sympathy toward Anne is remarkable considering that he argued Catherine of Aragon's divorce to be unjust (Ives 387).

13. This was one emphasis made in Elizabeth's coronation procession through London; at Gracechurch, she was presented with "a stage of three tiers. . . . In the lowest were Henry VII and his Queen; in the next—happy sight after twenty-two years!—Henry VIII and Anne Boleyn; in the highest, Elizabeth" (Neale 61).

14. The 1587 edition of Holinshed's *Chronicles*, for example, after referring the reader to Foxe for a refutation of "the sinister iudgements, opinions and obiections of backebiters against that vertuous queene," digresses into Christopher Ocland's 1582 poem Ειρηναρχια Siue Elizabetha (miscited as another 1580s poem by Ocland, *Anglorum prælia*), which describes Anne as having a prophetic vision of her death and its ultimately triumphant Elizabethan consequences:

Anglorum prælia saith, that this good queene was forwarned of hir death in a dreame, wherein Morpheus the god of sleepe (in the likenesse of hir grandfather) appeared vnto hir, and after a long narration of the vanities of this world (how enuie reigneth in the courts of princes, maligning the fortunate estate of the vertuous, how king Henrie the eight and his issue should be the vtter ouerthrow and expulsion of poperie out of England, and that the gouernment of queene Elizabeth should be established in tranquillitie & peace) he saith vnto hir in conclusion by waie of prophesie, as our poet hath recorded:

> Forti sis animo, tristis si nuncius adsum,
> Insperata tuæ velox necis aduenit hora,
> Intra triginta spacium moriere dierum:
> Hoc magnum mortis solamen habeto futuræ,
> Elizabetha suis praeclarè filia gestis
> Nomen ad astra feret patris, matrísque, suúmque.
>
> (3: 797)

J. Sharrock's 1585 translation of Ocland's poem renders these lines as follows:

> Be not in minde dismayde, though mestiue message I foreshow,
> The houre vnlookt for of thine end, with swift course on doth draw,
> For within thirtie dayes, thou shalt outgasp thys vitall breath.
> Howbeit this solace great, of me receaue, before thy death:
> *Elizabeth* through wondrous actes, to starrs shall lift the name,
> Both of her selfe, and mightie Sier, and most renowmed dame.
>
> (B4v-C1r)

Anne's vision of Elizabeth's stellification of her parentage helps to carry out, in the 1580s, the cultural work of national self-defense: even as the Armada approaches England, Elizabeth's reign is imagined as one of "tranquillitie & peace." Small wonder that Ocland's poem was reprinted in 1589, just after the Armada year.

15. Adam Blackwood, in his 1587 *Martyre de la Royne d'Escosse,* declared that Anne "had buck teeth, six fingers on her left hand, and a large lump under her double chin; she was used as a whore by the principal courtiers of England and France, and was a Lutheran" (Phillips 174).

16. To our knowledge, *Pandosto* has not been given a topical reading in regard to events of the late 1580s, even though Greene was more than capable of capitalizing upon current events for the plots of his fiction: his *Spanish Masquerado,* for example, published the year after the Armada defeat, issues broadsides against the entire Spanish monarchy and military command, finally to conclude that England and its queen have been blest among nations. For Greene's canny expansion of his audience base for *Pandosto* via its combination of elite and popular literary forms, see Newcomb.

17. In their recent edition of Elizabeth Cary's *Tragedy of Mariam,* a play published in 1613 and probably composed at some time in the preceding decade, Weller and Ferguson argue that Anne Boleyn's story is a subtext both for Salome, the lascivious female villain of the piece, and Mariam, the virtuous and martyred second wife of the tyrant Herod (Cary 30-35); this refraction of the slandered queen into several personae is similar to the one we are describing in *The Winter's Tale.* The fact that a Jacobean writer like Cary, who eventually converted to Catholicism, might be ambivalent about Anne's moral status indicates, we think, the urgency of England's continuing cultural need to fix the queen's sexual reputation, even in the aftermath of queenship.

18. Suggestively, Speed marginally cites "Robert Greene" for his account of Anne's scaffold speech; however, we have been unable to discover a work in which Greene described Anne's death, or a speech from one of Greene's fictional imperiled women that would match the words Speed gives to Anne.

19. Katherine Eggert has argued the point of Hermione's desexualization of Elizabeth in an unpublished paper, " 'The Statue Is But Newly Fix'd': Remembering Queenship in *The Winter's Tale* (Or, the Queen's No Body)." Glynne Wickham suggests that Hermione's statue would have reminded the play's original audience of Elizabeth's and Mary Queen of Scots's recently installed effigies in Westminster Abbey; Bergeron further postulates that the statue would have evoked memories of both Elizabeth's funeral effigy of 1603 and Henry Stuart's of 1612 ("Restoration" 132).

20. It should be emphasized here that, in all likelihood, Henry VIII also believed the charges he leveled against Anne (Warnicke 235), and like Leontes, pursued his accusations through a court proceeding. But although Henry won his case, the sense of the potential similarity of his claims and the slanders spoken against Anne earlier in her marriage to him registers obliquely in the Second Succession Act quoted above.

21. A definition of criminal defamation or libel, usually a written detraction either of a prominent figure or of someone else whose slandering led to a breach of the peace, developed in Star Chamber in the sixteenth and seventeenth centuries; the court meted out damages and punishments in passing sentence (Holdsworth 5: 201-12; Baker 137). In a sampling of

Star Chamber defamation cases litigated around the turn of the sixteenth century, five of the twenty-four cases Lindsay Kaplan examined included men complaining about sexual slanders against wives: P.R.O. STAC 243/26, STAC 172/6, STAC 88/11, STAC 304/36, and STAC 5/18.

22. According to common law, a bastard could not inherit property from his parents (Baker 558). David Harris Sacks has remarked in conversation with Lindsay Kaplan that in early modern England, a man's reputation for controlling his wife was taken in the community as a measure of his ability to manage his household economy. If this reputation or credit suffered, it was difficult for him to convince tradespeople to extend the credit necessary to run that household.

23. For the intense love the people bear toward Mamillius, see Camillo's conversation with Archidamus (1.1.33-45). Oddly, the death of Mamillius suggests the enduring life of his subjects, who would desire to live until the king has another son, something that the conclusion of the play suggests is unlikely to happen.

24. Coleridge remarks that "on the whole, this play is exquisitely respondent to its title" (217). Several other uses of the phrase in Shakespeare's works help piece together a definition of the winter's tale. In *Macbeth* it is synonymous with an old wives' tale: "O! these flaws and starts / (Impostors to true fear), would well become / A woman's story at a winter's fire, / Authoris'd by her grandam" (3.4.62-65). Richard II sees it as a tragic story of bygone times: "In winter's tedious nights sit by the fire / With good old folks, and let them tell thee tales / Of woeful ages long ago betid; / And ere thou bid good night, to quite their griefs / Tell thou the lamentable tale of me, / And send the hearers weeping to their beds" (5.1.40-45). In *3 Henry VI*, Prince Edward dismisses the validity of Richard's taunting remarks about his parents by retorting: "Let Aesop fable in a winter's night; / His currish riddles sorts not with this place" (5.5.25-26). Mamillius offers his view on the matter in *The Winter's Tale*: "A sad tale's best for winter: I have one / Of sprites and goblins" (2.1.25-26). He proceeds to tell what promises to be a classic ghost story: "There was a man . . . / Dwelt by a churchyard" (29-30). The play itself incorporates all these elements in its tragedy, its suggestions of raising the dead, and its radical improbability.

Works Cited

Adelman, Janet. *Suffocating Mothers: Fantasies of Maternal Origin in Shakespeare's Plays*, Hamlet *to* The Tempest. New York: Routledge, 1992.

Allen, William. *An Admonition . . . Concerninge the Present Warres*. Antwerp, 1588.

Amussen, Susan Dwyer. *An Ordered Society: Gender and Class in Early Modern England*. Oxford: Blackwell, 1988.

Baker, J. H. *An Introduction to English Legal History*. 3rd ed. London: Butterworths, 1990.

Baker, J. H., and S. F. C. Milsom. *Sources of English Legal History: Private Law to 1750*. London: Butterworths, 1986.

Beattie, J. M. "The Criminality of Women in Eighteenth-Century England." *Journal of Social History* 8 (1975): 80-116.

Bergeron, David M. "The Restoration of Hermione in *The Winter's Tale*." *Shakespeare's Romances Reconsidered*. Ed. Carol McGinnis Kay and Henry E. Jacobs. Lincoln: U of Nebraska P, 1978. 125-33.

————. *Shakespeare's Romances and the Royal Family*. Lawrence: UP of Kansas, 1985.

Boehrer, Bruce Thomas. *Monarchy and Incest in Renaissance England: Literature, Culture, Kinship, and Kingship*. Philadelphia: U of Pennsylvania P, 1992.

Boose, Lynda E. "Scolding Brides and Bridling Scolds: Taming the Woman's Unruly Member." *Shakespeare Quarterly* 42 (1991): 179-213.

Cary, Elizabeth. *The Tragedy of Mariam, The Fair Queen of Jewry*. Ed. Barry Weller and Margaret W. Ferguson. Berkeley: U of California P, 1994.

Cioni, Maria L. *Women and Law in Elizabethan England, with Particular Reference to the Court of Chancery*. New York: Garland, 1985.

Coleridge, Samuel. *Coleridge's Literary Criticism*. London: Frowde, 1908.

Dolan, Frances E. *Dangerous Familiars: Representations of Domestic Crime in England, 1550-1700*. Ithaca: Cornell UP, 1994.

Eggert, Katherine. "Nostalgia and the Not Yet Late Queen: Refusing Female Rule in *Henry V*." *ELH* 61 (1994): 523-50.

————. "Ravishment and Remembrance: Responses to Female Authority in Spenser and Shakespeare." Diss. U of California, Berkeley, 1991.

Erickson, Amy Louise. *Women and Property in Early Modern England*. London: Routledge, 1993.

Foxe, John. *Actes and Monuments*. 8 vols. New York: AMS, 1965.

Frye, Susan. *Elizabeth I: The Competition for Representation*. New York: Oxford UP, 1993.

Gowing, Laura. "Gender and the Language of Insult in Early Modern London." *History Workshop* 35 (1993): 1-21.

Greene, Robert. Perymedes the Blacksmith *and* Pandosto *by Robert Greene: A Critical Edition*. Ed. Stanley Wells. New York: Garland, 1988.

————. *The Spanish Masquerado. The Life and Complete Works in Prose and Verse of Robert Greene*. Ed. Alexander B. Grosart. 15 vols. 1881-86. New York: Russell, 1964. 5: 235-88.

Helmholz, R. H., ed. *Select Cases on Defamation to 1600*. Selden Soc. 101. London: Selden Soc., 1985.

Holdsworth, W. S. *A History of English Law*. 16 vols. Boston: Little, Brown-Methuen, 1927-66.

Holinshed, Raphael. *Holinshed's Chronicles of England, Scotland, and Ireland*. Ed. Henry Ellis. 6 vols. 1807-08. New York: AMS, 1965.

Ingram, Martin. *Church Courts, Sex, and Marriage in England, 1570-1640*. Cambridge: Cambridge UP, 1990.

Ives, E. W. *Anne Boleyn*. Oxford: Blackwell, 1986.

Jardine, Lisa. " 'Why should he call her whore?': Defamation and Desdemona's Case." *Addressing Frank Kermode: Essays in Criticism and Interpretation*. Ed. Margaret Tudeau-Clayton and Martin Warner. Urbana: U of Illinois P, 1991. 124-53.

Jordan, Constance. *Renaissance Feminism: Literary Texts and Political Models*. Ithaca: Cornell UP, 1990.

Kaplan, M. Lindsay. "Slander for Slander in *Measure for Measure*." *Renaissance Drama* ns 21 (1990): 23-54.

Levin, Carole. *"The Heart and Stomach of a King": Elizabeth I and the Politics of Sex and Power*. Philadelphia: U of Pennsylvania P, 1994.

Marcus, Leah S. *Puzzling Shakespeare: Local Reading and Its Discontents*. Berkeley: U of California P, 1988.

———. "Shakespeare's Comic Heroines, Elizabeth I, and the Political Uses of Androgyny." *Women in the Middle Ages and the Renaissance: Literary and Historical Perspectives*. Ed. Mary Beth Rose. Syracuse: Syracuse UP, 1986. 135–53.

Miller, David Lee. *The Poem's Two Bodies: The Poetics of the 1590* Faerie Queene. Princeton: Princeton UP, 1988.

Neale, J. E. *Queen Elizabeth I: A Biography*. 1934. New York: Anchor-Doubleday, 1960.

Newcomb, Lori Humphrey. " 'Social Things': The Production of Popular Culture in the Reception of Robert Greene's *Pandosto*." *ELH* 61 (1994): 753–81.

Newman, Karen. *Fashioning Femininity and English Renaissance Drama*. Chicago: U of Chicago P, 1991.

Ocland, Christopher. Ειρηναρχια Siue Elizabetha. London, 1582.

———. *The Valiant Actes and victorious Battailes of the English nation. . . . Also, of the peaceable and quiet state of England*. Trans. J. Sharrock. London, 1585.

Phillips, James Emerson. *Images of a Queen: Mary Stuart in Sixteenth-Century Literature*. Berkeley: U of California P, 1964.

Rice, George P., Jr. *The Public Speaking of Queen Elizabeth: Selections from Her Official Addresses*. New York: Columbia UP, 1951.

Rosen, Barbara. *Witchcraft in England, 1558-1618*. Amherst: U of Massachusetts P, 1991.

Samaha, Joel. "Gleanings from Local Criminal-Court Records: Sedition amongst the 'Inarticulate' in Elizabethan Essex." *Journal of Social History* 8 (1975): 61–79.

Sandler, Florence. "*The Faerie Queene*: An Elizabethan Apocalypse." *The Apocalypse in English Renaissance Thought and Literature: Patterns, Antecedents, and Repercussions*. Ed. C. A. Patrides and Joseph Wittreich. Ithaca: Cornell UP, 1984. 148–74.

Shakespeare, William. *King Henry VI Part 3*. Ed. Andrew S. Cairncross. London: Methuen, 1964.

———. *King Henry VIII*. Ed. R. A. Foakes. London: Methuen, 1957.

———. *King Richard II*. Ed. Peter Ure. London: Methuen, 1961.

———. *Macbeth*. Ed. Kenneth Muir. London: Methuen, 1984.

———. *The Winter's Tale*. Ed. J. H. P. Pafford. London: Methuen, 1963.

Sharpe, J. A. *Crime in Early Modern England, 1550-1750*. London: Longman, 1984.

———. *Defamation and Sexual Slander in Early Modern England: The Church Courts at York*. Borthwick Papers 58. York: Borthwick Institute of Historical Research, 1980.

Speed, John. *The History of Great Britaine*. London, 1611.

Spring, Eileen. *Law, Land and Family: Aristocratic Inheritance in England, 1300 to 1800*. Chapel Hill: U of North Carolina P, 1993.

Stallybrass, Peter. "Patriarchal Territories: The Body Enclosed." *Rewriting the Renaissance: The Discourses of Sexual Difference in Early Modern Europe*. Ed. Margaret W. Ferguson, Maureen Quilligan, and Nancy J. Vickers. Chicago: U of Chicago P, 1986. 123–42.

Statutes of the Realm. London, 1587.

Underdown, David E. "The Taming of the Scold: The Enforcement of Patriarchal Authority in Early Modern England." *Order and Disorder in Early Modern England.* Ed. Anthony Fletcher and John Stevenson. Cambridge: Cambridge UP, 1985. 116-36.

Walpole, Horace. *Historic Doubts on the Life and Reign of King Richard III.* Ed. P. W. Hammond. Gloucester: Sutton, 1987.

Warnicke, Retha M. *The Rise and Fall of Anne Boleyn: Family Politics at the Court of Henry VIII.* Cambridge: Cambridge UP, 1989.

Wickham, Glynne. "Romance and Emblem: A Study in the Dramatic Structure of *The Winter's Tale.*" *Elizabethan Theatre III.* Ed. David Galloway. Toronto: Macmillan, 1973. 82-99.

Wiener, Carol Z. "Sex Roles and Crime in Late Elizabethan Hertfordshire." *Journal of Social History* 8 (1975): 38-60.

Wilson, Richard. "Observations on English Bodies: Licensing Maternity in Shakespeare's Late Plays." *Enclosure Acts: Sexuality, Property, and Culture in Early Modern England.* Ed. Richard Burt and John Archer. Ithaca: Cornell UP, 1994. 121-50.

Woolf, D. R. "Two Elizabeths? James I and the Late Queen's Famous Memory." *Canadian Journal of History* 20 (1985): 167-91.

Gender, Cant, and Cross-talking
in The Roaring Girl

JODI MIKALACHKI

OVER A DECADE AGO, Mary Beth Rose noted that Moll Frith, the cross-dressing heroine of Thomas Dekker and Thomas Middleton's *The Roaring Girl*, cannot be said to appear in disguise at any moment in the play.[1] In the decade since Rose's groundbreaking article on the social and sexual anxieties that Moll's "simply present[ing] herself in society as a woman wearing men's clothes" produce, Moll's apparel has become one of the more contested signs in discussions of early modern constructions of gender, sexuality, class, and the theater.[2] I join this debate, which has tended to focus on the degree to which Moll's cross-dressing is subversive or transgressive, to explore another crossing she effects, namely her translation in 5.1 of thieves' cant (or "pedlar's French") for the benefit of Lord Noland and several gentlemen. Like her cross-dressing, Moll's translating allows her a certain license to move between the rogues of the London suburbs and the gentlemen and lords who visit the City. Although it argues a familiarity with street culture that might put her on the wrong side of the law, Moll's "cross-talking," like her cross-dressing, paradoxically entrenches her yet further with gentlefolk and aristocrats. If class is (to modern readers) the less apparent *doppelgänger* of gender in the potential confusion of categories in cross-dressing, so gender plays an important if not immediately obvious role in Moll's "cross-talking" in this scene. With reference to other female "cross-talkers," both fictional and archival, I hope to explore the implications for gender and class in this other crossing Moll performs.

119

My primary concern will be to examine how Moll's "cross-talk"—and the play's staging of cant—relates to legal attempts at policing disorderly and criminal behavior in the period.

Speaking in thieves' cant was not in itself illegal in early modern England, as cross-dressing was.[3] Canting terms were associated with illicit behavior, however, acting as linguistic markers of criminality, almost in the way a brand or other bodily mutilation identified convicted criminals. While thieves, prostitutes, bawds, and the criminal underclass generally might be expected to use canting terms, thieves' cant as a developed sociolinguistic system was most strongly associated with vagrancy in early modern England. Vagrants, vagabonds, or simply "rogues" were popularly believed to constitute a carefree yet highly organized anti-society, whose criminal ranks and activities were codified in a canting language that became more byzantine with each new publication on the phenomenon. Dating from the early sixteenth century, word lists and descriptions of a vagrant anti-society became increasingly numerous in the second half of the century, culminating in the thriving trade of rogue pamphlets from the 1590s through 1610s, in which Dekker's own "Canting Dictionary" figures prominently.[4] Although recent historical studies of vagrancy have generally dismissed the anti-society and its language as the fictional inventions of this literature, at least some of these pamphlets were regarded as late as 1930 as useful contemporary accounts of a vagrant subculture, and even contemporary historians have drawn on them for evidence of *mentalité*.[5] More importantly, the pamphlets enjoyed currency in early modern England as both scandalous *reportage* on a criminal underworld, and as practical handbooks for the prosecution of rogues and the preservation of honest citizens from their wiles. The most influential of these pamphlets, Thomas Harman's *A Caveat or Warning for Common Cursitors, Vulgarly Called Vagabonds* (first published in 1566), was written by a justice of the peace who claimed to have compiled his information from hundreds of interviews with vagrants in Kent. Although Harman's pamphlet owes an extensive debt to earlier literature, it is not impossible that some of his information might indeed have been elicited from vagrant subjects.[6]

The complicated issues of how a person already in violation of the vagrancy laws responds to a justice of the peace clearly seeking a certain kind of information necessarily qualify any material Harman may have collected in this manner. What interests me more than the nature of Harman's evidence, however, is his self-presentation as an active officer of the law publishing professional records of criminal behavior, organization, and language. He begins his *Caveat* by invoking the distinction between the deserving and idle poor that was the backbone of Elizabethan poverty legislation, addressing himself to Elizabeth, countess of Shrewsbury, his "especial good lady" (and in her more popular persona of "Bess of Hardwick" herself something of an aristocratic analogue to Moll Cutpurse). Writing "for the utility and profit of his natural country" (i.e., Kent), Harman's first aim is to prevent the countess from being duped by false rogues and vagabonds into offering charity to the undeserving poor (61).[7] His initial stance, elaborated in the dedication's proto-euphuistic rhetoric, is that of a courtly adviser addressing a prince on the vexed question of almsgiving.

Yet Harman was not a courtier, but rather a justice of the peace whose twenty-year confinement by illness to his estate in Kent, he argued, had given him a large experience of vagabonds.[8] And his desired audience was not merely a noble patroness, but also his fellow officers of the law, whom he called on to carry out their legal mandate throughout the realm

to the confusion of their drowsy demeanour and unlawful language, pilfering picking, wily wandering, and liking lechery of all these rabblement of rascals that ranges about all the coasts of the same, so that their undecent, doleful dealing and execrable exercises may appear to all, as it were in a glass, that thereby the Justices and shrieves may in their circuits be more vigilant to punish these malefactors, and the constables, bailiffs and borsholders, setting aside all fear, sloth, and pity, may be more circumspect in executing the charge given them by the aforesaid Justices. (62)

Harman begins by emphasizing the criminal associations of cant. A justice wanting both to educate his peers ("Justices and shrieves") and to ensure the enforcement of his judgments by subordinates ("constables, bailiffs and borsholders"), he lists "unlawful language" alongside theft, wandering, and lechery as elements of criminal behavior. At the same time, however, he indulges himself in a spirited display of cant, his alliterative enumeration of disorderly behaviors in mid-sentence bearing as much weight as the catalogue of local officials that concludes this exercise in parataxis. Indeed, the passage's obsessive elaboration and parallelism suggest a rhetorical similarity between "unlawful language" and legal terminology. The concluding list of judicial officers that parallels the enumeration of roguish wiles not only replaces but also emerges rhetorically from the linguistic invention and energy of the canting catalogue. Like Moll in 5.1 of *The Roaring Girl*,

Harman displays his mastery of cant in the very context of warning an elite audience against those who use it.

This propagation of a fictional world of cant and roguery has been cited as an important element in the criminalization of the poor in early modern Europe.[9] The fascination with canting language that pervades the pamphlets and other popular representations of roguery is a recurrent motif in juridical investigations of criminal behavior. The oldest known example of an invented canting language, "*La langue de Coquille*," survives in a word list compiled as part of the record of a 1455 trial in Dijon. As in the canting dictionaries of the English rogue pamphlets, most of the terms in this list are titles of various criminal ranks or occupations.[10] Six canting ballades by François Villon, one of the accused in the trial, were published posthumously in 1489.[11] Norbert Schindler cites the terminology of early modern German rogue pamphlets in his study of nicknames and popular culture in the period, noting that roguish nicknames betokening illegal callings were often worn with pride by members of the lowest orders of society, who accepted these dangerous titles as occupational hazards (78-120). A fascination with "unlawful language" resurfaces in the nineteenth-century literature of criminality, from the canting pickpockets of *Oliver Twist* to the encyclopedic histories of roguery that provide the groundwork for the twentieth-century studies and collections on which we still draw.[12] The lure of cant seems endemic both to contemporary response and to the historical study of rogues, vagabonds, and criminal underworlds.[13]

Dekker and Middleton, of course, participated in the early modern fascination with a vagrant anti-society. Dekker in particular asserted and defended his knowledge of roguery and its canting language. His "Belman" pamphlets emphasize linguistic invention, charting the development of cant as a language and displaying mastery over it in translated word lists and songs. It was precisely on this point that he came under attack, however, both for plagiarizing Harman's *Caveat* and for supposed inaccuracies in the "Canting Dictionary" of *The Bellman of London* (1608). He responded with a full chapter on "Canting" in *Lantern and Candlelight* (1608), and finally with the "Canting Song" and its translation that conclude *O Per Se O* (1612), much as the rogues' "Song" and Moll's translation round out the canting episode in 5.1 of *The Roaring Girl*.[14] Around the probable composition period of *The Roaring Girl*, then, Dekker was not only engaged in producing cant, but also in defending his canting expertise.[15] Other Jacobean dramas include roguish characters who use canting expressions, from Shakespeare's Autolycus in *The Winter's Tale* (1610–11) to Beaumont and Fletcher's *Beggars' Bush* (1612–14?) and Jonson's *Gypsies Metamorphosed* (1621), but I have found no other dramatic examples of speeches or songs written entirely in cant and requiring onstage translation.[16] Moll's virtuoso display of canting in 5.1, her ability to pierce every roguish deceit and bring them all to light for her gentle audience, should also be understood as Dekker's self-vindication, his claim to the preeminent power to represent and interpret roguery.

Yet what does this power mean? The social history summarized above suggests that thieves' cant was yet another early modern marker of disorderliness, to be ranged alongside behaviors like scolding, vagrancy, and witchcraft in the "crisis of order" thesis developed by social historians in the 1980s. The revival of legal definitions and punishments for such behaviors helped redefine the role of the law in a period of perceived social disorder.[17] If an emphasis on cant does do some of the work of criminalizing the poor in early modern Europe, even as it celebrates the irreverent freedom of a supposed vagrant anti-society, one might take up Moll's deployment of cant in 5.1 in the familiar historicist terms of the 1980s' subversion/containment debate, exploring whether it creates or highlights a linguistic confusion comparable to the social effects some have argued for Moll's cross-dressing, or merely serves as a device of ultimate containment, offering the titillation of a brush with the colorful criminality of the rogue pamphlets to Lord Noland and the wider audience of the play.[18] Rather than reviving this debate, however, I would like to explore what the staging of cant and its translation suggests about the dramatization of the law in this period. How are we to understand a character like Moll, who both represents and reveals roguery? How much does her role in this regard depend on the double "cross-talking" of cant and translation? Moll is remarkable as a stage rogue in this period both for her canting fluency and her extended translations. She is also (to the best of my knowledge) one of only two female dramatic characters to speak in cant, although she does so cross-dressed as a man.[19] How does this complex character relate to the law in policing the play's "unlawful language"? And how does the play's staging of cant relate to the quasi-legal work of a pamphlet like Harman's, or to the official duties of the justices, shrieves, and petty officers he addresses?

In the play's long penultimate scene, Moll takes Lord Noland and a group of gentlemen on a rogues' tour of greater London, displaying her knowledge of the canting language of its denizens and her mastery of the crooked ways they both inhabit and enact. Contravening and enforcing the law at different moments, she engages throughout in what I shall call the paralegal activities of identifying rogues, explicating their language and behavior, and mediating between them and an elite audience. Her multiple roles as guide, interpreter, and intermediary structure both the language and the action of the scene. Confounded by the bombast, counterfeit Dutch, and "pedlar's French" of the arch-rogues Trapdoor and Tearcat, who are begging in disguise as wounded soldiers, Sir Beauteous Ganymede reaches for his purse in exasperation, exclaiming, "Here, here—let's be rid of their jobbering" (105-06). "Not a cross, Sir Beauteous," Moll cries as she intervenes between the openhanded gentleman and the "undeserving" rogues, enforcing the statutory proscription of casual charity even as she reveals her special knowledge of criminal language and deception.[20]

Moll's virtuoso display of canting—as a speaker, singer, and interpreter—follows this threat, as she uncovers all the roguish deceptions of dress and language, explicating Tearcat's name and rank in the "commonwealth of rogues" (131-38) so thoroughly that he confesses to having instructed Trapdoor "in the rudiments of roguery" (143-44). She then leads them through their canting catechism, beginning by saying, "I hope then you can cant" (150), later shifting to the challenge, "Come you rogue, cant with me" (182), to which Sir Thomas Long adds monetary encouragement—"Cant with her, sirrah, and you shall have money—else not a penny" (184-85)—and ultimately joining both rogues in a lusty rendition of the canting "Song" she later translates (214-27). When the canting trio finishes their song, the elite audience finally agrees to "give these soldiers their pay" (233). "Here, Moll," says Lord Noland, handing her the money, which she promptly distributes to Trapdoor and Tearcat with the words, "Now I see that you are stalled to the rogue and are not ashamed of your professions: look you, my Lord Noland here, and these gentlemen, bestows upon you two, two bords and a half: that's two shillings sixpence" (235-40). "Thanks to your lordship," responds Trapdoor, and "Thanks, heroical captain," says Tearcat to Moll (241-42).

Why does Moll prevent Sir Beauteous's first offer of alms, only to act later as distributor of the money collected among the gentlemen for the rogues? The latter have certainly not proved themselves to be among the "deserving poor" in the meantime, and Jack Dapper's ultimate assessment of their canting song echoes Sir Beauteous's initial response to their jobbering speech: "The grating of ten new cart-wheels, and the gruntling of five hundred hogs coming from Romford market cannot make a worse noise than this canting language does in my ears" (229-32). Moll's status when she reveals her canting expertise is difficult to determine. Her role as intermediary comprehends both linguistic and monetary transactions, so that she functions as the gatekeeper of economic and linguistic traffic between men of high and low status. With this role, she assumes the power of one who can both deny ("Not a cross, Sir Beauteous") and facilitate exchange by her expertise as a "cross-talker."

And yet the very knowledge that allows her to identify the rogues is potentially incriminating. Turning on Trapdoor after staying Sir Beauteous's hand, Moll threatens the rogues on their own terms: "You base rogues, I have taken measure of you better than a tailor can, and I'll fit you as you—monster with one eye—have fitted me" (107-09). The dangerous reflexivity of a canting revenge in which Moll does indeed "fit" Trapdoor in word and deed implies her membership among the rogues even as she routs them. Lord Noland ultimately sanctions this display of "unlawful language" by paying the rogues with Moll as his agent. Her subsequent canting encounter with the unnamed cutpurses, however, moves him to wonder at her knowledge of the criminal underclass and its language, and provokes her only confession of unruly if not illegal behavior. Moll's cross-talking in 5.1 thus bears the double edge of associating her with a criminal underworld even as it ingratiates her with an elite audience. Before elaborating her role in this scene, I would like to turn to an earlier paralegal episode where she easily dismisses both gentle and roguish incriminations.

A similarly extended scene at the center of the play, 3.1, also provides Moll with a series of encounters and challenges. Like the streets of 5.1, its setting of Gray's Inn Fields also stages a public, outdoor venue frequented by a variety of persons on all sides of the law. Much of the action in the play's second act anticipates this setting, proposing it repeatedly as the site for assignations in both the gentle and city plots. Having contracted to meet characters from both plots between three and four o'clock, Moll arrives to keep these assignations in 3.1, cross-dressed as a man for the first time in the play. This is one of the few moments in which she momentarily deceives other characters (but not the audience) as to her identity and gender, being taken initially for a barrister or student of the Inns of Court by both Laxton and Trapdoor. This repeated error, coupled with the reiteration of the scene's setting, suggests some association with the legal institution of the Inns of Court. Indeed, I would suggest that at the center of *The Roaring*

Girl, in the long scene where she metes out rough justice to would-be seducers and assassins, the cross-dressed Moll acts under the implied aegis of London's central institution of legal justice and education.

Moll's justice in 3.1 depends on the imposition of legal process. Laxton, whose initial address rejects any connection with legal business—"You seem to be some young barrister; / I have no suit in law" (3.1.49-50)—soon finds himself begging for a hearing after Moll's speech in defense of honest womanhood—"Hear me!" (113)—and ends by confessing his guilt—"I do confess I have wronged thee, Moll" (118). Moving from Laxton's assumption of Moll's easy virtue to her counter-accusation, to Laxton's plea for a hearing, their fight, and his confession, 3.1 brings Laxton's illicit seduction plot into the realm of law, transforming it into a trial by combat on the ground of Gray's Inn Fields.

That ground becomes a kind of extramural court where Moll both reigns and tries her assignees. Trapdoor's entrance after Laxton's departure provokes her comment, "Here comes my man that would be; 'tis his hour" (141), suggesting that Trapdoor, too, has arrived at his appointed time for judgment. In this second encounter, Moll develops a more complicated relation to the law, as she both impersonates one of its students and denies the specificity of its language. Trapdoor's hopeful appeal after being jostled by the apparent lawyer who will shortly reveal herself as his mistress—"I hope there's law for you, sir!"—sets off a series of puns that demonstrate how difficult it is to determine his interlocutor's relationship to that institution:

TRAPDOOR
Heart, this is no good dealing. Pray let me know what house you're of.
MOLL
One of the Temple, sir.   *Fillips him.*
TRAPDOOR
    Mass, so methinks.
MOLL
And yet, sometime I lie about Chick Lane.
TRAPDOOR
I like you the worse because you shift your lodging so often; I'll not meddle with you for that trick, sir.
MOLL
A good shift, but it shall not serve your turn.
TRAPDOOR
You'll give me leave to pass about my business, sir?
MOLL
    Your business?—I'll make you wait on me
    Before I ha' done, and glad to serve me too!

TRAPDOOR

How sir, serve you? Not if there were no more men in England!

MOLL

But if there were no more women in England,
I hope you'd wait upon your mistress then.

(159-72)

Punningly spinning dialogue out of a vocabulary of housing, lying, shifting, and serving until she has trapped the would-be trapper in her own net of cross-talk, Moll demonstrates how she eludes any simple relation to the law. She is rather a "shifter" in language, dress, and gender as well as house, Temple, or "legal address," celebrating the unhoused freedom and wit of the rogue even as she draws on the topographical specificity of the courts.

Indeed, although they were adjacent to several of the Inns, Gray's Inn Fields were also associated with illicit activity in the period. Edward H. Sugden notes that the open fields north of Gray's Inn Gardens were "frequented by footpads and other undesirable characters" after the day's activities, and Thomas Nashe describes in *Christ's Tears over Jerusalem* (1593) how people stricken with plague were conveyed from their households and abandoned in Gray's Inn Fields, which he portrays as a kind of no-man's-land outside the normal bonds of kinship and service.[21] The plurality of "Fields" in this place-name suggests how it evades univocal definition. The haunt of vagrants as well as students and barristers at law, a place where a cross-dressing female "cutpurse" could be mistaken for the men of law who might prosecute her, Moll's chosen place of justice is a mixed one, invoking both the law and lawlessness.

This peripatetic resistance to any fixed relation to the law works to Moll's advantage in 3.1, where she manages her encounters without an onstage audience. In the suburban streets of 5.1, however, her freedom of movement becomes increasingly limited even as it risks incriminating her. Real criminals—as opposed to the hapless Trapdoor—make their only appearance here, forcing Moll to define her relation to the law more explicitly. And in Lord Noland a new rank—the aristocracy—enters the play, putting to the test her social mobility. All three episodes of this long scene—Moll's entrance with the young gallants; her canting dialogue with Trapdoor and Tearcat; and her encounter with the cutpurses and its aftermath—constitute trials of her legal and social status. Where the complex character of Moll presided over the paralegal rituals of Gray's Inn Fields, eluding any simple relation to the law, that very complexity puts her at risk in the streets of 5.1.

She enters the scene in the exclusive company of gentlemen, once again cross-dressed as a man, and congratulating herself on the rescue of Jack Dapper. Jack complains of how his own father sent the sheriff's men after him, giving Moll's rescue action all the festive glamor of an assault on the dual authority figures of the law and the father. Moll explains her similar grievance against Sir Alexander Wengrave early in the scene, describing him as "a justice in this town, that speaks nothing but 'Make a mittimus, away with him to Newgate' " (11-13). She returns to this grievance when she attempts to secure Trapdoor as a witness later in the scene: "You'll maintain, sirrah, the old justice's plot to his face?" (246-47). The "old justice" becomes the scapegoat for anti-judicial sentiment in this scene, just as he represents the classic comic blocking figure in the courtship plot. Frustrated by Moll in his attempts to "find law to hang her up!" (1.2.233), Sir Alexander ends by confessing his own guilt and begging her forgiveness (5.2.243-50). His humiliations in the play's last scene include Sir Guy's withholding of pity in the very terms addressed by Harman to the countess of Shrewsbury: "Who'd place his charity so unworthily, / Like one that gives alms to a cursing beggar?" (5.2.31-32). Wholly unsuccessful in his attempts to thwart his son and prosecute Moll, the "old justice" is himself reduced to the status of a canting beggar.

The humiliation of Sir Alexander and Moll's general resistance to the paternal imposition of law suggest the kind of festive inversion that facilitates comic endings rather than social change. Moll's rescue of Jack Dapper produces just such a reversal as she and the gentlemen prepare to "walk and talk" their way about London:

SIR BEAUTEOUS
Come, come, walk and talk, walk and talk.
JACK DAPPER
Moll and I'll be i' the midst.
MOLL
These knights shall have squires' places, belike then.
(5.1.32-34)

Imagining herself and Jack Dapper as knights between the "squires" Sir Beauteous and Sir Thomas Long, Moll is at the height of her powers as 5.1 opens. Less than fifty lines into this long scene, however, the gentlemen regroup to accommodate the entrance of Lord Noland. Although all characters greet Noland at his entry, he responds only to the gentlemen, addressing them first by their shared status, and then individually by name and title: "Well met, gentlemen all: good Sir Beauteous Ganymede, Sir Thomas Long—and how does Master Dapper?" (50-52). When Moll steps forward to offer him tobacco, Noland dismisses her with a curt, "No, faith, Jack" (55). As the gentlemen form plans to go to Pimlico, Moll is noticeably silent, to the point where one wonders whether the (original) stage direction "*They walk*" includes her (63). Initially "i' the midst" of the gentlemen as they "walk and talk," Moll risks being excluded from both activities as Noland upstages and silences her. Only the providential entrance of the rogues allows her to begin to reestablish herself by calling on Jack Dapper to give the "maimed soldiers" money.

This appeal is puzzling in light of Moll's later restraint of Sir Beauteous's bounty. Even her exclamation, "I love a soldier with my soul" (80-81), does not explain it, for posing as wounded veterans of the nation's wars was one of the deceptions most commonly attributed to rogues, and Moll goes on to demonstrate her knowledge of all such wiles. The staging of this moment must be difficult, requiring a decision as to whether Moll is indeed duped by the rogues at their first appearance, and if not, then some motivation for why she chooses to play along with them initially. In social terms, however, Moll's appeal to Jack Dapper is merely the flip side of her intervention between Sir Beauteous and the rogues. Once Lord Noland upstages her, Moll's only hope of regaining a place in the scene's walking and talking is to act as an intermediary who both promotes and controls the exchange between the gentlemen and the rogues. Her actions in this scene should not be read so much in terms of personal motivation or even self-promotion. Rather, they develop within a set of restrictions where her character's only dramatic possibilities lie in the mediation of exchange between gentlemen and rogues.

Moll's uncharacteristic struggle for Lord Noland's attention recalls the dependency of other female rogues or vagrants on the goodwill of the gentlemen they entertained with roguish stories and cant. Not only in pamphlets like Harman's and Dekker's, but also in the occasional court record, women provide information about a vagrant anti-society, including canting dialogue. In one of these archival examples, a woman who was vagrant and disciplined over a period of four years for a variety of petty crimes associated with female rogues—theft, prostitution, bearing of bastards—provides a long and colorful account of nocturnal revelry in a secluded alehouse on Christmas and New Year's. The holiday license of the rogue pamphlets runs through this account, in which tinkers and "gents" share stolen meats, keep rendezvous with their sweethearts, and conclude one of their gatherings with an ale-throwing brawl.[22] The most prominent "roguish" feature in this classic account of misrule is the citation of cant. "A poxe confound the Rum Cove of the next ken for he did wrong," cries one reveller, invoking one of the generic titles of rogues and their grouping into "kens." "Yea and the Devil Glimmer him for he is a foresworne knave," replies the keeper, using the canting term "glimmer" for fire, and then asking another patron about his vagrant mistress or "mort."[23]

This vivid deposition was recorded in the case book of a justice of the peace roughly seventy years after the first publication of Harman's *Caveat*. It does not seem to have had any legal issue, for the woman who made it was not bound over to give evidence at the next assizes. Despite her presence at gatherings where everything from illicit sexual encounters, poaching, and possible highway robbery was chargeable, the justice's female informant seems only to have been called on to depose. Her story may have been so obviously influenced by the pamphlet literature that he chose not to pursue it. Her deposition nevertheless takes up a full page in the case book, more space than all but a handful of other depositions therein. And in distinction to every other entry in what seems to have been a working notebook, it has been recorded in fair copy, neatly filling the entire page, with even margins on three sides.[24]

I describe this document at such length to suggest the possibility that this magistrate, like Harman seventy years earlier, had a quasi-professional interest in cant that moved him to make an exceptionally long and de- tailed record of this deposition. Like Harman, he may have encouraged his informant to provide a sensationalist account in keeping with literary stereotypes popularized in pamphlets like Dekker's and performances like *The Roaring Girl*. What is striking about the few archival examples of thieves' cant in this regard is that they are all in depositions given by women.[25] As in 5.1 of *The Roaring Girl*, women seem to be the chief purveyors of cant to a gentle male audience. Why should this be so? The sample is very small for the court records, but reading it against supposed interviews of female vagrants in the pamphlet literature and Moll's role in 5.1 of *The Roaring Girl*, I would suggest that the main interest in these female testimonies, both fictional and archival, may lie in the titillation of eliciting cant and other information about a supposed vagrant underworld from *women*.[26]

Sexual prurience certainly informs Harman's study of the ranks of female vagrants. The account he gives of interviewing a "walking mort," one of the supposed female orders of vagrancy, begins with his condemnation of "her lewd life and beastly behaviour," to which she responds, "God help! . . . how should I live? None will take me into service. But I labour in harvest-time honestly." Harman's rejoinder of "I think but a while with honesty" plays on the sexual senses of labor and honesty, especially as applied to women (100). Here, indeed, the role of language in the criminalization of the poor emerges, as Harman punningly turns his subject's statement of economic distress into a lewd joke. His insistence on discovering an illicit sexuality in his female examinants runs throughout this section of the *Caveat*. His record of an interview with a "doxy," the most sexualized order of female vagrants, reveals most clearly the prurient line of his questioning. Thinking her "a necessary instrument to attain some knowledge by," Harman first offers her food and drink, as well as the promise of money, "if she would open and discover to me such questions as I would demand of her." In closing this account of how he approached his informant, Harman produces a telling articulation of juridical prurience vis-à-vis female vagrants. All this, he writes, he does "before I would grope her mind" (106).

And yet the justice's insistence on producing sexual titillation from his female examinants does not necessarily consign them to passive victimization in a patriarchal legal establishment. The woman whose labor and honesty Harman explicates as "lewd life and beastly behaviour" responds to this prompting with a fabliau-like tale of how she triumphed over an adulterous employer's attempts at sexual coercion. Joining forces with the man's wife to punish his illicit desires and past behavior, she sets him up for a sexual rendezvous in his barn. In place of the expected sexual encounter, her employer finds himself blindfolded, stripped naked, and beaten by this woman, his wife, and several neighbor women (100–05). Something of Moll's triumphant self-vindications against Laxton and Trapdoor in 3.1 of *The Roaring Girl* emerges in this exchange between the scholar-magistrate and his female subject. Like Laxton, the adulterous husband and coercive employer is punished for his unchaste and illicit desires at the very moment he thinks to achieve his object. One might extend the analogy to include Harman himself, whose prurient assumptions about his examinant's sexuality receive an implied reprimand in the recounted fate of her employer. At the same time, the concluding spectacle of a naked man duped and beaten by women offers its own titillation in the fabliau tradition.[27]

In contrast to Harman's persistence in lecherous double entendres, sexual prurience is notably lacking in Noland's and Long's questions to Moll about how she acquired her knowledge of the vagrant underworld. Indeed, Moll censors the sexual references in her canting "bout" with Trapdoor in 5.1. Challenged by Moll and promised payment by Sir Thomas Long, Trapdoor produces several lines of "pure" cant requiring translation. Instead of a linguistic response, however, Moll strikes him with hands and feet, provoking Lord Noland's question, "Nay, nay, Moll, why art thou angry? What was his gibberish?" (193–95). Moll obediently translates the bulk of Trapdoor's canting invitation to robbery, cutting purses, and sleeping under hedges, but declines to render his closing words:

MOLL
"And there you shall wap with me, and I'll niggle with you,"—and that's all.
SIR BEAUTEOUS
Nay, nay, Moll, what's that wap?
JACK DAPPER
Nay, teach me what niggling is; I'd fain be niggling.
MOLL
Wapping and niggling is all one: the rogue my man can tell you.
TRAPDOOR
'Tis fadoodling, if it please you.
SIR BEAUTEOUS
This is excellent; one fit more, good Moll.

(204–11)

Moll refuses to engage in the sexual wordplay Harman insists on producing in his exchanges with female rogues. Cross-dressed as a man, she invites Trapdoor to a canting contest between male rogues—"Come you rogue, cant with me"—to which he responds, "I'll have a bout if she please," after Long's promise of payment (183–85). When Trapdoor concludes with a sexual invitation properly addressed to a female rogue, Moll beats him as she does all men who question her chastity. Although one might argue that Moll successfully distinguishes herself from the pamphlet stereotype of the female rogue, here, as in Harman's fabliau, the dialogue continues to pander to the gentlemen's desire for sexual titillation. Moll's angry refusal to translate emphasizes the sexual cant, causing the gentlemen to repeat the offending terms and ultimately producing Trapdoor's euphemism "fadoodling." This makes for good stage humor both in the heat of Moll's response and the elaborate teasing out of Trapdoor's meaning, providing "excellent" entertainment for the play's wider audience as well as Sir Beauteous. I would argue that the excellence of this entertainment depends on the female role of displaying cant for the entertainment of gentlemen. The low status of the female canting informants seems particularly important, anticipating Freud's observation that "men of a higher class are at once induced, when they are in the company of girls of an inferior class, to reduce their smutty jokes to the level of simple smut" (101). In her dual role as informant and interpreter, Moll resembles Harman's female subjects even when she violently rejects Trapdoor's canting invitation. Even if not especially in her angry response to Trapdoor, Moll's resistance both instructs and delights her gentle, male audience.

Her subsequent encounter with the cutpurses is more difficult. Unlike the hapless Trapdoor and Tearcat, easily unmasked and willing to share all their recently acquired knowledge of roguery, the cutpurses pose a genuine criminal threat in *The Roaring Girl.* Their grand entrance—*"Enter a* Cutpurse *very gallant, with four or five* Men *after him, one with a wand"*—deceives Noland and Long into thinking them of their own status, and the cutpurses' plan to rob the gentlemen is only averted by Moll's recognition of their leader (268–80). Although all the non-elite characters are in some way disguised in this scene—Trapdoor and Tearcat as wounded soldiers and Moll as a man—the cutpurses' assumption of elite dress is the only potentially dangerous form of deception. Indeed, it is the only legally proscribed form of cross-dressing in the play. Their entrance marks a shift from the stage roguery of Trapdoor and Tearcat to a genuine criminality, almost as though real thieves had wandered off the street and onto the stage.

The historical Moll Cutpurse, of course, was charged with having taken the stage at the Fortune Theatre after a performance of *The Roaring Girl,* as well as with having "vsually associated her selfe with Ruffinly swaggering & lewd company as namely with cut purses blasphemous drunkardes & others of bad note."[28] How does the cutpurses' entrance affect the position of her stage double? Having identified their leader, Moll proceeds to explicate the canting terminology of the cutpurses' trade. And yet the cutpurses themselves hardly use cant at all, including only scattered terms like "silver shells" for money or "smoked" and "boiled" for being discovered, expressions easily understood in context. It is Moll, in fact, who requires translation for her long, canting commentary on the ranks and offices of "the figging-law," and Moll, of course, who provides it (279–92). Other than this additional display of her canting fluency and knowledge of criminal behavior, the brief encounter with the cutpurses near the end of this long scene seems rather pointless.

I would argue that the point of this encounter is precisely to distinguish real criminality from the canting entertainment provided by Moll, Trapdoor, and Tearcat and sanctioned by Lord Noland and the gentlemen. Historians of early modern England and sociologists of contemporary vagrancy agree that developed canting languages for vagrants are largely fictional. They do, however, allow that a few canting terms may have a limited currency (Beier 123–26; Phillimore; Pound 97–99). The cutpurses' dialogue, intelligible even with its occasional canting terms, may be closer to the actual speech of rogues in this period. And yet, far from distinguishing Moll from real criminals, her interaction with the cutpurses provokes Noland's "I wonder how thou camest to the knowledge of these nasty villains" and Long's animadversions on her own epithet of Cutpurse, "A name, methinks, damned and odious" (311–14). Here, for the only time in the play, Moll struggles to justify herself, explaining how she studied roguery in her youth. She prefaces this part of her speech with the words "I must confess," hitherto wrung from her adversaries' lips rather than her own (315–16). And despite a brief return to her characteristic language of self-sufficiency when she claims, "I please myself, and care not else who loves me" (349), Moll ends this long scene still pleading for the good opinion of Lord Noland: "Good my lord, let not my name condemn me to you or to the world" (353–54). Here, on the heels of her encounter with serious criminals, the double edge of Moll's cross-talking becomes most evident.

It is at this moment, I would argue, that Dekker's identification with his cross-talking heroine and the anxieties she provokes emerges. While the celebration of a joyously unfettered anti-society of rogues brought him fame as a popular writer, the claim to firsthand knowledge of criminal life on which that fame rested was potentially incriminating. In Moll's equivocal relation to the law in 5.1, Dekker dramatized his marginal existence as a playwright and pamphleteer specializing in London's criminal underclass.[29] The onstage audience of elite men allows itself to be diverted into countenancing the roguery of Trapdoor and Tearcat. Moll's role as a linguistic and financial intermediary in this regard only works to her advantage, bringing her back into the circle of gentlemen from which Noland's entrance threatened to banish her. Even in her violent response to Trapdoor's sexual invitation, she continues to facilitate an encounter that offers the gentlemen the titillation of a brush with roguery while preserving them from any of its dangers. Like the rogue pamphlets from which much of its dialogue is taken, this interlude provides a diverting and harmless fiction of criminal language and wiles.

In contrast to the easy transactions she negotiates between Trapdoor and Tearcat and their elite audience, however, Moll's encounter with the cutpurses suggests a more intractable vision of criminality and the law. As though struggling to return to the earlier moment when she displayed her canting knowledge without censure, Moll draws on all the rhetorical strategies of the pamphlets in explaining her knowledge of roguery:

> When next, my lord, you spy any one of those—
> So he be in his art a scholar—question him,
> Tempt him with gold to open the large book
> Of his close villainies; and you yourself shall cant
> Better than poor Moll can, and know more laws
> Of cheaters, lifters, nips, foists, puggards, curbers,
> With all the devil's blackguard, than it is fit
> Should be discovered to a noble wit.
> I know they have their orders, offices,
> Circuits, and circles, unto which they are bound,
> To raise their own damnation in.
>
> (322–32)

Although other speeches by Moll recycle actual passages from Dekker's pamphlets, her confession speech most clearly displays the rhetorical strategies of the pamphlets. Drawing on their catalogues or word lists of canting terms and orders, she encourages Noland to adopt the investigative stance from which Harman derived his authority in the device of "interviewing" roguish informants.[30] And her conceit of the scholar tempting the rogue "to open the large book / Of his close villainies" recalls Harman's claim to educate both legal professionals and the ruling elite.

Neither Dekker nor Moll could claim Harman's social and legal status as a gentleman and a magistrate. When Moll concludes her confession by insisting that rogues "have their orders, offices, / Circuits, and circles," Jack Dapper returns to the vexed question of how she has acquired her knowledge. "How dost thou know it?" he asks, to which she responds, "As you do: I show it you, they to me show it" (330–33). The rhyming couplet formed by Dapper's half-line and Moll's response emphasizes the interrelation of knowing and showing. The popular representation of roguery claimed its authority precisely on the basis of firsthand knowledge of criminals and their behavior. Moll elaborates this claim in an international analogy, where she compares her instruction of the gentlemen to their own possible warnings to a friend about to travel in a foreign country of which they have knowledge. "Must you have / A black ill name because ill things you know?" she asks. "Good troth, my lord, I am made Moll Cutpurse so" (334–43).

The cutpurses are indeed genuinely foreign to Noland and the gentlemen in a way that the "stage rogues" Trapdoor and Tearcat are not. Moll's "cross-talk" mediates between this elite audience and a criminal underclass they do not understand, yet which they must identify and discipline. Paradoxically, the sign of the cutpurses' foreignness is their very intelligibility, that relative freedom from the literary stereotype of cant Moll deploys in this scene. Moll's "cross-talk" and the staging of cant in *The Roaring Girl* thus bear a complex relation to legal attempts to police disorderly and criminal behavior in early modern England. If a popular fascination with roguery is indeed one of the signs of the criminalization of the poor in this period, the staging of cant in 5.1 carries out the larger cultural work of the law. By identifying and explicating rogues and their language, Moll assumes a paralegal role in this cultural process. Yet it is a role that risks incriminating her even as she does the work of the law. As a dramatic character who speaks, encourages, and translates cant, Moll both produces and embodies criminality on the stage. Her complex relation to the law in this regard comes to a head after her encounter with the cutpurses, when she develops an apology for the whole enterprise of representing roguery, the "knowing" and "showing" from which the pamphlets and the play derive their authority. This literary enterprise underwrote legal attempts to police poverty and disorder in the period. When Moll enacts its titillating instruction with Trapdoor and Tearcat, Noland and the other gentlemen sanction the display of "unlawful language," rewarding their entertainers with money and the illusion of social intimacy. Yet when the threat of real criminality enters with the oddly intelligible cutpurses, Moll's cross-talking expertise makes her the object of elite suspicion.

How does this complex dramatic character stand in relation to the law at the play's conclusion? I would argue that 5.1 prepares the way for the play's comic conclusion by staging two versions of criminality. The first, consistent with what the pamphlet stereotypes might lead an audience to expect from a play entitled *The Roaring Girl*, produces the requisite sexual titillation from Moll's canting cross-talk, confining all violence to blows exchanged among the rogues for the excellent entertainment and instruction of the gentlemen. Like the pamphlet literature that serves as its model, it transforms the poverty and social upheaval of vagrancy into a literary stereotype of freedom. The economic, sexual, and linguistic license of this stereotype delights even as it informs honest citizens about the roguish wiles of a criminal underclass. The second version of criminality, staged briefly in the cutpurse encounter and its aftermath, reveals the social fears disguised by the literary stereotype. As more people fell through the bottom of early modern English society, these fears of an increasingly unruly order of disenfranchised persons, independent of any rule of law, contributed to the criminalization of the poor.

Both these versions of criminality inform the canting literature of roguery. Their consecutive staging in 5.1 focuses and to some extent exorcises anxieties about criminality and the role of criminal fictions inherent in the project of staging London's "roaring girl." Notorious traveler between fact and fiction, this complex dramatic character takes form in relation to both versions of criminality and the law. Caught between them, both profiting from her cross-talking expertise and risking the very criminalization she helps to enforce, the roaring girl is indeed "made Moll Cutpurse so."

Notes

I am grateful to Philip J. Finkelpearl for reading and commenting on an earlier draft of this essay.

1. "It should be stressed that Moll is not in disguise: she is neither a disguised player, a man pretending to be a woman; nor is she a disguised character, whose role requires a woman pretending to be a man. . . . Although certain of the *Dramatis Personae* in *The Roaring Girl* occasionally fail to recognize her immediately, the fact that Moll is a woman is well known to every character in the play. She simply presents herself in society as a woman wearing men's clothes" (Rose 367).

2. In addition to Rose, see Howard, "Sex and Social Conflict"; Orgel; Garber; Howard, "Crossdressing"; Dollimore; and Cheney.

3. Although status rather than gender was the explicitly protected category in the sumptuary laws, which prohibited the assumption of higher forms of dress by those of lower social status, the assumption of dress appropriate to the opposite gender was also troubling, if not illegal, in the period. For the interrelations of class and gender transgression in cross-dressing see especially Rose; Howard, "Crossdressing"; and Orgel.

4. A. V. Judges reprints a selection of the pamphlets with notes and a sociohistorical introduction.

5. For discussions of the rogue pamphlets before Judges, see the more literary studies of Chandler (1907); Aydelotte (1913); and their Victorian forerunner, Ribton-Turner (first pub.

1887), chs. 4–6. Judges showed most caution in dealing with rogue pamphlets, emphasizing the severity and often rigorous enforcement of statutory punishments for vagrancy, which included whipping, stocking, branding, and ear-boring. Two works from the early 1970s are Pound and Salgado. For sociohistorical work that dismisses the pamphlets as evidence, see Clark; Slack, "Poverty and Politics" and "Vagrants and Vagrancy"; and Beier, which synthesizes this and related work, as well as presenting additional research to allow for a national discussion of vagrancy in the period. See also Samaha for a more general discussion of crime, which also concludes that the vagrant anti-society was a myth.

6. Judges praises Harman for having "all the deftness of the trained sociologist" (495). Harman's debt to Awdeley's *Fraternity of Vagabonds*, first published in 1561, compromises his proto-sociological claims. Unless otherwise noted, I use Judges's edition for all pamphlet references.

7. John Pound notes the consistent linking of poverty and vagrancy in Tudor legislation, which began to address poor relief and vagrancy only after the economic depression of the 1520s. He cites the Act of 1531 as the first to distinguish between the impotent and able-bodied poor, and summarizes the sixteenth-century statutes addressing poverty and vagrancy (39–57).

8. Harman's house at Crayford was near the ancient highway of Watling Street, one of the most traveled thoroughfares in England (Judges 495).

9. Sharpe 194–95. Florike Egmond notes the increasing uniformity imposed by Nether-landish authorities on suspects for a variety of crimes as officials "tried to fit them into a homogeneous category of marginal and dangerous people" (192–99). Norbert Schindler, in a study of nicknames as markers of "outsiderhood" or marginality, describes their function in a growing economy of the poor in early modern Germany (101–08).

10. Derived from local dialects and drawing heavily on archaisms, "*la langue de Coquille*" seems to have been an elite clerical invention for writing about illicit activity within a secret fraternity whose members were believed to engage in highway robbery, counterfeiting, and murder. The extent to which such a fraternity existed and pursued these activities is not known; the surviving trial record that preserves the word list, however, "*les Archives du Procès des Coquillards*," indicates that the judiciary took them seriously at the time, and probably had the list compiled to decipher "evidence" and to gain greater knowledge of the fraternity's membership and operations. In addition to elaborating the fraternity's internal hierarchy, the terms in the word list refer to types of deception and their victims, judicial officers and proceedings, and gambling. English canting "dictionaries" emphasize these same topoi. For an account of the trial and the word list, see Guiraud 274–83. I am grateful to the late Michel Grimaud for drawing my attention to the Villon material and to Guiraud's work on *jargon*.

11. Pierre Guiraud (7) claims to be the first to have deciphered these, drawing on the word list from the trial record and his own linguistic model for the derivation of cant (*jargon*). In this respect, Villon's posthumously published ballades differ from canting songs or speeches in English plays or pamphlets, which were generally accompanied by English "translations."

12. See especially Ribton-Turner, who devoted three chapters to the Elizabethan and Jacobean rogue pamphlets, providing the groundwork for Aydelotte, Chandler, Judges, and Salgado. In German, see Friedrich Christian Benedict Avé-Lallemant, *Das Deutsche Gauner-tum* (Wiesbaden, n.d.), published in English in 1858 as *German Rogues & Vagabonds* (qtd.

in Mosse 134). Avé-Lallemant was a police officer whose multivolume study of roguery set out, like Harman's *Caveat*, to help officials and law-abiding citizens distinguish rogues from honest folk.

13. Cant is still an area of inquiry in studies of contemporary vagrancy. A recent sociological collection includes an essay exploring the use of slang terms for vagrancy by vagrants. Its findings are that such terminology is extremely limited, and that although vagrants may use its most exclusive terms for other vagrants, they never use them in reference to themselves (Phillimore 29-48). I am grateful to Susan Silbey for bringing this collection to my attention.

14. Chapter 1, "Of Canting," of *Lantern and Candlelight* also concludes with "A Canting Song" and its "Englished" version (189-204). Judges includes a portion of Middleton's *The Black Book* (1604), as well as nearly complete selections from Dekker's Bellman pamphlets: *The Bellman of London* (1608), which includes the "Canting Dictionary"; *Lantern and Candlelight* (1608), where he defends himself against charges of plagiarism from his new rival, the author of the "Martin Markall" pamphlets; and *O Per Se O* (1612) (attributed to Dekker), reprinted in its entirety, including the closing "Canting Song" with its accompanying translation, "for satisfaction of the readers, Englished," recalling Moll's "Song" and her subsequent "translation" of it in 5.1 of *The Roaring Girl*. See Judges 510-15 for Samuel Rid's probable authorship of the "Martin Markall" pamphlets, and his challenge to Dekker's knowledge of cant in particular. For full versions of *The Black Book* and the excerpted Dekker pamphlets, see Bullen's edition (1-46) and Grosart's edition (61-170, 171-304), respectively.

15. I use Paul A. Mulholland's dating of composition and first performance to the first half of 1611 (18-31). While noting the possibility of some contributions or revisions by Middleton, Mulholland largely confirms Dekker's authorship of 5.1 in his introduction to the Revels edition (11). I use this edition for all citations.

16. Shakespeare 4.3; Beaumont and Fletcher 2.1, 5.1.100-09, 5.2.226; Jonson *passim*. I am grateful to Philip J. Finkelpearl for referring me to *Beggars' Bush* and *The Gypsies Metamorphosed*. Richard Brome's *A Jovial Crew* (1641), written a generation later than these plays but drawing on the same pamphlet sources (and perhaps the earlier plays themselves), also stages canting songs and dialogue, but again without translation. On the eve of the closing of the theaters, *The Roaring Girl* remained singular in its close attention to the linguistic details of cant and its translation on the stage.

17. For the crisis of order in early modern England, see Amussen; Clark and Slack, eds.; Fletcher and Stevenson, eds.; Underdown; and Wiltenburg.

18. Indeed, Stephen Greenblatt added a discussion of the rogue pamphlets and their display of cant to "Invisible Bullets," the essay that in its original publication in *Glyph* 8 (1981) and revised versions in the mid- and late 1980s set the terms of the subversion-containment debate. See Greenblatt 49-52.

19. An "Autem Mort" is brought on stage briefly to sing an untranslated canting song in *A Jovial Crew* 2.2.251-62. Ancient, drunk, and of no further importance, she provides none of the sexual titillation otherwise associated with canting women in the period. (I explore this association and its implications below.)

20. Keith Thomas describes how the introduction of this prohibition to sixteenth-century legislation, combined with mandatory provision for the impotent poor, exacerbated contemporary uncertainty about the moral status of the poor and the individual's responsibility toward them (560-69).

21. Sugden 232. Sugden also cites *The Roaring Girl* 2.1. Nashe 160: "In Grayes-Inne, Clarkenwell, Finsbury, and Moore-fieldes, wyth myne owne eyes haue I seene halfe a dozen of such lamentable out-casts. Theyr Bretheren & their Kinsfolkes haue offered large summes of money, to gette them conueied / into any out-house, and no man would earne it, no man would receiue them. Cursing and rauing by the High-way side haue they expired, & theyr Maisters neuer sent to them, nor succourd them."

22. The misrule of holiday is also invoked in *The Roaring Girl*, whose action takes place largely on what Gallipot calls "Of all the year . . . the sportful'st day"(2.1.418). This reference is not elaborated (Mulholland speculates that Shrove Tuesday or May Day may be meant), and seems to function as a general invitation to festive inversion and escape from the workaday world.

23. This deposition is recorded in the manuscript case book of Sir Francis Ashley in the British Library, Harley MS 6715 67. The case book has been published with some calendaring. I draw on a microfilm of the original throughout. I am grateful to David Underdown for bringing the Balstone material in the Ashley case book to my attention and for lending me his microfilm of the manuscript.

24. In addition to its unusually careful arrangement on the page, the deposition also includes quotation marks around the canting expressions. Manuscript quotation marks are generally rare in the period, and this is the only example I have encountered in manuscript court records. For a discussion of the hands and probable recording practices of Ashley's case book, see J. H. Bettey's Introduction to the printed edition (v).

25. Two female vagrants examined in Essex in 1580 had been overheard speaking "Pedlar's French" (Hunt 49-54); and another Dorset woman used canting terms in a deposition of 1613 (Beier 123-26).

26. The narrator's first informant in *The Bellman of London* is "an old nymble-tongd beldam" whom he bribes to hide him in a cottage frequented by rogues that he might "be a *Spectator* of the comedy in hand, and in a priuate gallery behold all the Actors" (ed. Grosart, 79-80). Robert Greene also draws on supposed female informants in *A Disputation between a He-cony-catcher and a She-cony-catcher* (1592), both in the "disputation" proper and in the confessional "Conversion of an English Courtezan" that concludes it (Judges 206-47). Stephen Orgel notes the "continuing fascination for a variety of male inquisitors, formal and informal" of the historical Mary Frith (12).

27. Although I allow for some possibility of Harman's having incorporated terms and information from actual interviews with vagrants, I consider this story, like most of his *Caveat*, to be a literary borrowing or invention of his own. For accounts of women whose testimony was shaped by popular literary genres, however, see Davis 77-110.

28. For a transcript of the charges against Mary Frith dated 27 January 1612 in the *Consistory of London Correction Book*, see "Appendix E" to the Revels edition (262-63).

29. For the contemporary reputation of Dekker's rogue pamphlets, as well as his obscure origins, chronic indebtedness, possible imprisonment, and condemnation as a "Rogue" by Ben Jonson, see Bentley 241-45.

30. For Dekker's more blatant self-borrowings from *The Bellman of London* and *Lantern and Candlelight* in 5.1, see Mulholland's introduction (14).

Works Cited

Amussen, Susan Dwyer. *An Ordered Society: Gender and Class in Early Modern England.* Oxford: Blackwell, 1988.

Ashley, Francis. *Case Book.* British Library, Harley MS 6715.

———. *The Case Book of Sir Francis Ashley J.P., Recorder of Dorchester 1614-1635.* Ed. J. H. Bettey. Dorchester: Dorset Record Soc., 1981.

Aydelotte, Frank. *Elizabethan Rogues and Vagabonds.* Oxford: Clarendon, 1913.

Beaumont, Francis, and John Fletcher. "Beggars' Bush." *The Dramatic Works in the Beaumont and Fletcher Canon.* Ed. Fredson Bowers. Vol. 3. Cambridge: Cambridge UP, 1976. 225-362.

Beier, A. L. *Masterless Men: The Vagrancy Problem in England 1560-1640.* London: Methuen, 1985.

Bentley, Gerald Eades. "Thomas Dekker." *The Jacobean and Caroline Stage.* 5 vols. 1941-56. Vol. 3: *Plays and Playwrights.* Oxford: Clarendon, 1956. 241-75.

Brome, Richard. *A Jovial Crew.* Ed. Ann Haaker. Lincoln: U of Nebraska P, 1968.

Chandler, Frank Wadleigh. *The Literature of Roguery.* Boston: Houghton, 1907.

Cheney, Patrick. "Moll Cutpurse as Hermaphrodite in Dekker and Middleton's *The Roaring Girl.*" *Renaissance and Reformation* ns 7 (1983): 120-34.

Clark, Peter. "The Migrant in Kentish Towns 1580-1640." Clark and Slack 117-63.

Clark, Peter, and Paul Slack, eds. *Crisis and Order in English Towns, 1500-1700.* London: Routledge, 1972.

Davis, Natalie Zemon. *Fiction in the Archives: Pardon Tales and Their Tellers in Sixteenth-Century France.* Stanford: Stanford UP, 1988.

Dekker, Thomas. "The Belman of London." *The Non-Dramatic Works of Thomas Dekker.* Ed. Alexander B. Grosart. Vol. 3. London: Hazell, Watson, and Viney, 1884. 61-169.

———. "Lanthorne and Candle-light; or, The Bell-Mans Second Nights-Walke." *The Non-Dramatic Works of Thomas Dekker.* Ed. Alexander B. Grosart. Vol. 3. London: Hazell, Watson, and Viney, 1884. 171-303.

Dollimore, Jonathan. "Subjectivity, Sexuality, and Transgression: The Jacobean Connection." *Renaissance Drama* ns 17 (1986): 53-81.

Egmond, Florike. *Underworlds: Organized Crime in the Netherlands 1650-1800.* Cambridge: Polity, 1993.

Fletcher, Anthony, and John Stevenson, eds. *Order and Disorder in Early Modern England.* Cambridge: Cambridge UP, 1985.

Freud, Sigmund. *Jokes and Their Relation to the Unconscious.* Trans. and ed. James Strachey. New York: Norton, 1963.

Garber, Marjorie. "The Logic of the Transvestite: *The Roaring Girl* (1608)." *Staging the Renaissance: Reinterpretations of Elizabethan and Jacobean Drama.* Ed. David Scott Kastan and Peter Stallybrass. New York: Routledge, 1991. 221-34.

Greenblatt, Stephen. "Invisible Bullets." *Shakespearean Negotiations: The Circulation of Social Energy in Renaissance England.* Berkeley: U of California P, 1988. 21-65.

Guiraud, Pierre. *Le Jargon de Villon ou le Gai Savoir de la Coquille.* Paris: Gallimard, 1968.

Harman, Thomas. "A Caveat or Warning for Common Cursitors, Vulgarly Called Vagabonds." Judges 61-118.

Howard, Jean E. "Crossdressing, The Theatre, and Gender Struggle in Early Modern England." *Shakespeare Quarterly* 39 (1988): 418-40.

———. "Sex and Social Conflict: The Erotics of *The Roaring Girl*." *Erotic Politics: Desire on the Renaissance Stage*. Ed. Susan Zimmerman. New York: Routledge, 1992. 170-90.

Hunt, William. *The Puritan Moment: The Coming of Revolution in an English County*. Cambridge: Harvard UP, 1983.

Jonson, Ben. "The Gypsies Metamorphosed." *Ben Jonson*. Ed. C. H. Herford, Percy and Evelyn Simpson. Vol. 7. Oxford: Clarendon, 1941. 565-615.

Judges, A. V., ed. *The Elizabethan Underworld*. London: Routledge, 1930.

Middleton, Thomas. "The Black Book." *The Works of Thomas Middleton*. Ed. A. H. Bullen. 8 vols. 1885-86. Boston: Houghton, 1886. 8: 1-46.

Middleton, Thomas, and Thomas Dekker. *The Roaring Girl*. Ed. Paul A. Mulholland. Manchester: Manchester UP, 1987.

Mosse, George L. *Nationalism and Sexuality: Respectability and Abnormal Sexuality in Modern Europe*. New York: Fertig, 1985.

Mulholland, P. A. "The Date of *The Roaring Girl*." *Review of English Studies* ns 28 (1977): 18-31.

Nashe, Thomas. "Christs Teares over Iervsalem." *The Works of Thomas Nashe*. Ed. Ronald B. McKerrow. 5 vols. Oxford: Blackwell, 1958. 2: 1-175.

Orgel, Stephen. "The Subtexts of *The Roaring Girl*." *Erotic Politics: Desire on the Renaissance Stage*. Ed. Susan Zimmerman. New York: Routledge, 1992. 12-26.

Phillimore, Peter. "Dossers and Jake Drinkers: The View from One End of Skid Row." *Vagrancy: Some New Perspectives*. Ed. Tim Cook. London: Academic, 1979. 29-48.

Pound, John. *Poverty and Vagrancy in Tudor England*. London: Longman, 1971.

Ribton-Turner, C. J. *A History of Vagrants and Vagrancy, and Beggars and Begging*. 1887. Montclair, NJ: Patterson Smith, 1972.

Rose, Mary Beth. "Women in Men's Clothing: Apparel and Social Stability in *The Roaring Girl*." *English Literary Renaissance* 14 (1984): 367-91.

Salgado, Gamini, ed. *Cony-Catchers and Bawdy Baskets: An Anthology of Elizabethan Low Life*. Harmondsworth: Penguin, 1972.

Samaha, Joel. "Gleanings from Local Criminal-Court Records: Sedition amongst the 'Inarticulate' in Elizabethan Essex." *Journal of Social History* 8 (1975): 61-79.

Schindler, Norbert. *Widerspenstige Leute: Studien zur Volkskultur in der frühen Neuzeit*. Frankfurt am Main: Fischer, 1992.

Shakespeare, William. *The Winter's Tale*. Ed. Frank Kermode. New York: Signet, 1963.

Sharpe, J. A. "The History of Crime in Late Medieval and Early Modern England: A Review of the Field." *Social History* 7 (1982): 187-203.

Slack, Paul. "Poverty and Politics in Salisbury 1597-1666." Clark and Slack 164-203.

———. "Vagrants and Vagrancy in England, 1598-1664." *Economic History Review* 2nd ser. 27 (1974): 360-79.

Sugden, Edward H. *A Topographical Dictionary to the Works of Shakespeare and His Fellow Dramatists*. Manchester: Manchester UP, 1925.

Thomas, Keith. *Religion and the Decline of Magic.* New York: Scribner, 1971.

Underdown, David. *Revel, Riot and Rebellion: Popular Politics and Culture in England, 1603-1660.* Oxford: Oxford UP, 1987.

Wiltenburg, Joy. *Disorderly Women and Female Power in the Street Literature of Early Modern England and Germany.* Charlottesville: UP of Virginia, 1992.

Shakespeare's Merry Wives *and the*
Law of Fraudulent Conveyance

CHARLES STANLEY ROSS

SEVERAL FORMS OF fraudulent conveyance characterize Shakespeare's *Merry Wives of Windsor*.[1] Fraudulent conveyance may be defined as "putting realizable assets beyond [a] creditor's process, whatever form that process might take" (Glenn 2). Laws against such transfers of assets occur in every society that recognizes the obligation to pay debts. The flip side is that civil societies have a certain tolerance for people who devise means to avoid the clutches of creditors.

The concept of fraudulent conveyance was found in Roman law;[2] it arose in canon law, where the pauper status of clerics complicated the collection of debts;[3] and it had a noble history in England, where complex legal mechanisms were constantly devised to frustrate judicial processes that sought to take property for the benefit of creditors. From the time of the Magna Carta, the Parliament of England regularly protected royal interests against fraudulent conveyances. A series of statutes provided remedies against mortmain, subinfeudation,[4] conveyances to defeat a lord of his wardship,[5] the seeking of sanctuary to escape financial liabilities,[6] fraudulent deeds used by those accused of treason to protect family property, as well as other devices, some still being invented in Shakespeare's day.[7] For legal historians the most significant of these statutes is 13 Eliz. 5 (1571), because Sir Edward Coke, the queen's attorney general, gave the statute two readings, in Twyne's case (3 Co. Rep. 80b [1601]) and Packman's case

(6 Co. Rep. 18b [1585]).[8] The language of the statute—still present in the law of many states—forbids

fraudulent feoffements, Giftes, Grantes, Alienationes, Conveyances, Bondes, Suites, Judgements and Executions as well of Landes and Tenements, as of goods and Cattells [sic] . . . devised and contrived of malice, fraud, covin, collusion or guile, to the end, purpose and intent, to delay, hinder or defraud, creditors and others of their iust and lawfull Actions, Suites, Debts. (13 Eliz. 5)

Garrard Glenn characterizes the statute as purely political and punitive, designed to protect the interest of the Crown in land.[9] That it was not aimed at creditors can be deduced from the fact that a bankruptcy statute passed the same year did not mention fraudulent conveyance. The political purpose of similar statues explains why Spenser frequently mentions fraudulent conveyance in his *View of the Present State of Ireland* (1596), written but not published within a few years of Shakespeare's composition of *The Merry Wives*.[10] Just beginning a tenure as sheriff of Cork, the Protestant poet complains, through the medium of the *View*, that the Irish practice fraudulent conveyance when they deed their property to a relative before going into rebellion. According to English law, a dead rebel had to forfeit his property to the queen. If the man no longer had title to his land, the queen was deprived of her "escheat" (the reversion of land to the Crown). Spenser warns the authorities in London that much land has been conveyed secretly for this purpose.

A few modern instances should suggest the range and moral ambiguity of fraudulent transfers that make them a perennial concern. First, a man or woman facing bankruptcy may seek to put assets in the name of a spouse or child. The law will generally void such transfers as an attempt to defraud creditors. (Most states provide certain exemptions as a matter of policy to preserve the family unit.) Second, some forms of Medicaid provide free care for the indigent. Is it fraudulent to give your lifetime savings to your children to prevent their depletion by nursing-home expenses that Medicaid will cover? One view regards the practice as mere "asset planning"; another regards those who transfer for less than full value as lacking a "modicum of decency."[11] The classic American standoff between farmers and bankers provides a third example.[12] Midwest farmers routinely ship grain to distant elevators to keep their product out of the hands of bankers in case they default on crop loans.[13] This example suggests that the form of the conveyance is of marginal importance. (Narrowly defined, a conveyance is a means for transferring estates in land.) Although it might make all the difference whether one must only send a truck for hidden grain rather than tracing property that may have been sold several times to a series of *bona fide* purchasers, morally the issue is simply whether society will allow certain practices to defeat creditors.

Shakespeare's composition and revision of a play that echoes such practices coincided with the first important appearance of the concept of fraudulent conveyance in the debtor law of England. Twyne's case (1601) also records the first instance in which Justice Coke spelled out the "badges of fraud" that determined whether a conveyance was fraudulent or not. A creditor sought to attach the sheep of a man named Pierce in payment for debt, but Pierce "conveyed" them to a man named Twyne by deed. Because Pierce conveyed the sheep to Twyne to avoid his debt, the English court declared the deed void and allowed the creditor to obtain possession of the animals. Coke defended his belief that the conveyance was meant to defraud by pointing to several indicators: the gift was made in secret, the sheep retained the original owner's mark, Pierce had no other assets, and the deed unnecessarily proclaimed itself *bona fide*. The prominence of the case suggests that the courts were moving to protect creditors' rights in new ways. Coke believed he could guess Pierce's intentions.[14] Understanding Falstaff's conveyancings in *The Merry Wives* proves more difficult.

I

A law and literature analysis typically considers what a legal perspective can tell us about a work of art, or what a literary understanding reveals about the law, or the regulation of literature by law. Although Shakespeare's play may open our eyes to the acceptance of fraud (or near fraud) in the law of conveyancing, this essay concentrates on the first approach for the most part.

The plot of *The Merry Wives* involves many legal themes: Justice Shallow's suit against Falstaff for a deer poached by the fat knight, Falstaff's attempts to avoid debt, the several marriage negotiations concerning Anne Page, the clever ways the wives avoid adultery by fending off Falstaff's advances, the rules of the duel, and the theft of horses. There is even a hint of the issue of same-sex marriage at the end of the play when two suitors find they have carried away boys instead of Anne Page. The element of fraud these adversarial situations share raises what Richard Posner calls the "fundamental problems of law, which is how to control human behavior effectively by means of rules" (105). Fraud becomes socially acceptable when laws no longer reflect the mores of a society. The colonial context in which Spenser operated, as an English agent in Ireland, reminds us that what looks fraudulent from the creditor's perspective often seems, from the debtor's angle, to be a legitimate way to protect a family inheritance from an antagonistic political power or impersonal creditor

The link between law and literature is rarely literal. Law as a subject matter is usually "just a metaphor for something else" (Posner 15). Anthony Trollope is a rare exception, as is a certain passage in Vladimir Nabokov's *Lolita*, in which Humbert Humbert brilliantly parodies a legal memo on the issue of interstate travel with an underage companion for immoral purposes.[15] The literary use of the law is usually much less exact: Portia's trial of Shylock in *The Merchant of Venice* is a legal farce and—to take another well-known example from the law and literature field—Melville probably did not have his eye on naval law when he wrote *Billy Budd* (Posner 162). In the same way, the law of fraudulent conveyance forms an interesting and necessary background to *The Merry Wives of Windsor*, but the play is not about legal technicalities.

Yet Shakespeare's play has long been recognized for the legal language that distinguishes the Folio from the Quarto text: characters use words and phrases such as quorum, Star Chamber, Justice of the Peace, *custalorum*, "bill, warrant, quittance, or obligation,"[16] "the register" (of follies), "fee'd every slight occasion," "exhibit a bill in the parliament,"[17] building on another man's ground, fee simple, fine and recovery,[18] waste, cheaters,[19] exchequers, egress and regress, suits and oyers.[20] An earlier generation of critics used this language to argue that Shakespeare was a trained lawyer; more sober reflection has shown that these words and phrases were readily available and rarely employed with technical exactness.[21] Nowhere do we find a "conveyance" in the narrow sense of a transfer of title by deed, but the recent work of Patricia Parker has revealed a "discursive network" that "links the transporting or translating of words with the transfer, conveying, or stealing of property" in the play.[22]

It is the possibility and practice, not the legal technicality, of the law of fraudulent conveyance that enters the comedy. As Parker has shown, conveying plays a large metaphoric role in *The Merry Wives*, introducing not merely signs of the law (the legalisms pursued by earlier scholars) but subversive practices that inspired the law, such as fraud. For this reason, conveyance operates as a paradigm for actions that illustrate a relationship between law and literature: a parody or parallel more productive than the illusion of legal substance, the representation of the adversarial process, or the use of legal terminology.

A true theory of law and literature requires a conception of the jurisprudence that underpins the ways an author employs legal materials, by which I mean the author's assessment of the source and function of law in society. A creative writer need not be bound by a single jurisprudence, but if sensitive to the operation of law, he or she may create a dramatic interaction between different ways of understanding society's formal rules. As analysts of law and literature, our task begins with the identification of traditional categories of jurisprudence, such as natural, customary, and positive law, as well as the fields where law functions: property, family, commerce, administration, torts, procedure, contracts. The story told will either be one of conflict or transition: a clash between fundamental values, or changing conceptions of law based on our historical assessment of a given society. A competition between legal and literary modes of dispute resolution will naturally recur from work to work, providing the possibility of a sustained approach to literary history.

If, as Richard Weisberg claims, "literature provides unique insights into the underpinnings of law" (*Poethics* 3), and if Shakespeare's *Merry Wives* provides such insight into the practice of fraudulent conveyance, nonetheless Posner rightly warns us about a fundamental incompatibility of the outward structures of the law and a play. This incompatibility requires us to make three critical assumptions that separate *The Merry Wives* from the law. First, we presume organic unity in a work of art—that the various actions that comprise the plot express a single theme—in contrast to a series of separable issues that compose legal thinking. Second, we regard *The Merry Wives* not as a brief about fraudulent conveyance but as a dramatic presentation of what lawyers today call the "public policy" to which laws eventually conform. Third, we recognize that the bourgeois characters of *The Merry Wives* use mercantile and legal language even when the matter is not mercantile and legal, so sometimes they talk literally and other times metaphorically. These characters serve as foils to Falstaff, who sometimes seems out of touch with, but sometimes is perceptive about, certain matters of fraud.

II

Shakespeare's *Merry Wives* finds Falstaff financially embarrassed and involved in a number of carryings on to obtain money. Early in the play he plans to seduce two wives of Windsor, Mistress Page and Mistress Ford, not for love but to gain access to the moneybags of their rich husbands. Much of the drama's humor derives from Falstaff's failure to dissimulate his intentions effectively.

The wives learn of Falstaff's plot when he sends them each an identical love letter. Falstaff's men, Pistol and Nym, then reveal his game to the wives' husbands. The result is a series of humiliations: most famously, Mistress Ford's servants secretly "convey" Falstaff in a buck-basket of dirty laundry from Mistress Ford's house to the Thames for a dunking. The conveyance saves Falstaff from the wrath of a jealous husband while punishing him at the same time. But Falstaff's conveyance in a buck-basket is only the most spectacular of several imitations of legal deception in the play.

In *2 Henry IV* Falstaff recalls his time as a law student at Clement's Inn (3.2.308). Although Mistress Page, as a woman, would not have attended the Inns of Court, she often sounds more like a lawyer than Falstaff. Traditionally the first act of fraud was Jacob's deception of Isaac to win Esau's birthright (Parker, *Literary* 74). Mistress Page cites it when she compares her letter from Falstaff to Mistress Ford's: "heere's the twyn-brother of thy Letter: but let thine inherit first, for I protest mine never shall" (Folio 2.1). Later, after Falstaff is beaten as a woman, Mistress Page produces the densest legalism in the play: "if the divell have him not in fee-simple, with fine and recovery, he will never (I thinke) in the way of waste, attempt us againe" (4.2). Mistress Page compares Falstaff's beating to an exorcism of the devil, who has surely been driven out unless he has undisputed possession of Falstaff ("fee simple"), a fee often obtained, in the late sixteenth century, by the legal maneuver of "fine and recovery."[23] Mistress Page not only uses legal language; she is also alert to fraud and deception.

For the second part of Mistress Page's sentence compares Falstaff's attempts on the ladies' virtue to a dispute over rights to exploit real estate. Paul S. Clarkson and Clyde T. Warren correctly gloss "waste" as "the unauthorized use of land," "the spoil or destruction done, or permitted, to houses, lands, trees, or other corporeal hereditaments by the tenant in possession to the prejudice of the reversioner or remainderman in fee simple or fee tail," noting the objection that "Falstaff was certainly no tenant (metaphorically, of course)" (166–67). But this account misses the point that such waste was a recognized form of fraudulent conveyance.[24] In 1601 Elizabeth's Parliament passed a statue that reflects the wider association of fraud and waste: 43 Eliz. 8, "an act against fraudulent administration of Intestates goods," targeted estate administrators who managed to give away goods before creditors could be paid because the creditors, "for lack of knowledge of the place of habitation of the Administrator, cannot arrest him," or if they find him and sue him, learn he is unable to pay "the value of that he hath conveyed away of the intestates goods, or released of his debts, *by way of wasting*" (*Anno xliii*; emphasis added). Mistress Page identifies *herself* as one with the potential to *waste* and understands that waste is a form of fraudulent conveyance.

Besides making a legal pun on *waste* and *waist*, Mistress Page also plots. She vows revenge when she receives Falstaff's letter; she enlists Mistress Quickly; she suggests disguising Falstaff as a woman when he will not enter the basket a second time; and she invents Falstaff's third humiliation, the Herne the Hunter scenario.[25] Most spectacularly, she instigates Mistress Ford to convey Falstaff in a buck-basket when Ford, like a judgment creditor, demands that his wife hand over Falstaff.

Finally, Mistress Page associates legal language with the plans she conceives. For example, the Folio assigns Mistress Page a significant use of the word "convey" in the play, one of several legalisms by which Shakespeare's revisions find legal language to catch up with and recognize the nature and complexity of the plot.[26] In the Quarto Falstaff first uses the word "convey" in reference to his concealed transport in Mistress Ford's buck-basket ("convey me hence" [3.3]), but his usage seems to be accounted for by the presence of the word in *Tarlton's News out of Purgatorie*, a probable source (Bullough 31). By contrast, when Mistress Page says "convey" in the Folio, one first feels that the word signals a character's awareness of its legal and ethical associations: "If you have a friend here, convey, convey him out," she tells Mistress Ford. "Bethinke you of some conveyance. . . . Looke, heere is a basket" (3.3). Something similar happens when Richard II shouts "Conveyers are you all!" at Bullingbroke after he orders his men to "convey" Richard to the Tower (*Richard II* 4.1).

The exquisite humor of the buck-basket parody lies in the double sense of conveyance as both the means of transferring title and the property itself. Where real property is at issue, a "conveyance" is always metaphorical (even when livery of seisin is confirmed by dropping a clod of earth). A deed may be "conveyed," but it or another document has value only through what it represents. A marriage debt is similarly metaphorical, even though it may entail physical activity. Falstaff expects the wives to betray their husbands, to whom they owe their loyalty, by loving him instead. Mistress Ford and Mistress Page, however, protect their reputations and chastity by secretly conveying Falstaff out of Ford's house. The buck-basket parody works because it inverts the literal and metaphorical aspects of a fraudulent conveyance. The "conveyancing" of Falstaff actually takes place, and Falstaff becomes, literally, the conveyance.

III

An overlooked element of fraud also lies concealed in another well-known legalism, Ford's reference to building on another man's land. Having learned Falstaff intends to seduce his wife, Ford disguises himself as a stranger named Brooke (Broome in the Folio). He meets Falstaff at the Garter Inn, claiming he loves Mistress Ford and offering to pay Falstaff to seduce her on the theory that, having once fallen, she will then favorably receive his entreaties. Amazed at Brooke's profession of love and confession of failure that drives him to this extreme, Falstaff asks him, "Of what quality was your love then?" Ford responds with a legal metaphor, comparing his love of Mistress Ford "to a fair house, built on another mans ground, so that I have lost my edifice, by mistaking the place, where I erected it" (2.2.215). Clarkson and Warren echo earlier legal scruntinists, that "at common law if a man by mistake erected a house upon another man's land it became a part of the land and the property of the landowner" (164). The rule is that whatever is affixed to the soil belongs to the soil (*"quicquid plantatur solo solo cedit"; "aedificium solo cedit"*).[27] The idea occurs in Shakespeare's sonnet 146: "Why so large cost, having so short a lease, / Dost thou upon thy fading mansion spend?" (Dunbar Barton 114). The rule was a commonplace of the law.

Criticism of *The Merry Wives* has not noticed, however, the opportunity the rule provided for mischief. Consider a tenant who seeks a twenty-year lease knowing that he wants to construct a building. The tenant will naturally bargain for a lease price discounted to reflect the future value of the building that will belong to the landlord once the lease expires. Yet if the landlord can manage to accelerate the lease—perhaps by demanding payment when the tenant blunders into insolvency, or even by driving the tenant into financial trouble—the landlord will effect a conveyance to himself. Modern lawyers describe a similar situation as a *constructive* fraudulent conveyance (meaning the effect against other creditors is the same, although strictly speaking there is no *conveyance*) (Kennedy). Such a situation occurs when a landlord terminates a lease, leaving the lessee/debtor with no income to pay his creditors, thereby causing the tenant to forfeit his building or premises.

Exactly this process occurred in Shakespeare's circle in the 1597, when the twenty-year lease that James Burbage had taken from Gyles Allen for land on which to build the Theatre expired. Allen had the law on his side. He owned the land, and when the lease was up he owned the building.[28] And yet, to the Burbages and their resident theater company, including Shakespeare, it doubtless seemed that Allen was morally or contractually obligated to renew the lease. When Allen refused, and Burbage's plans to cover himself by moving into Blackfriars ran into trouble, Shakespeare's company reacted as if Allen had effected a constructive fraudulent conveyance, and they took measures to void it. They literally disassembled the Theatre from Allen's property on 28 December 1598, and then floated the timbers across the Thames to construct the new Globe Theatre.

Like the conveyance of an entire theater—a gesture initiated by actors alert to maintaining their assets—the buck-basket that carries Falstaff humorously suggests a theatrical representation of statutes on fraudulent conveyance. As Posner writes, law functions best in literature not as "a complex of rules and institutions" but as a "practice" that can be "imitated" in the Aristotelian sense (79). The practice at which the statutes aimed was amazingly widespread. A. W .B. Simpson has called the late sixteenth and early seventeenth centuries "the age of fantastic conveyances," as lawyers manipulated legal estates to outwit the Statute of Uses and the Statute of Enrollments passed under Henry VIII: "The chaotic state of the land law on points such as these was all the more lamentable during a period of social upheaval marked by an increase in the prosperity and social status of the lesser landowners, which, in its turn, brought an accompanying desire to 'found families' and ensure that the family estate should not be alienated out of the family in the future" (Simpson 186). This common topic was readily available to Shakespeare and his circle in popular and indexed epitomes, such as those of Robert Brook, William Rastell, Fernando Pulton, William West, and Edmund Plowden, many published by Richard Tottel.[29]

We do not know if Shakespeare read these works, but we do know his friends (if not he himself) practiced the deceptions these books describe. For not only did Shakespeare's acquaintances take a dim view of the termination of Burbage's lease, but, in a related gesture, they themselves readily conveyed property to avoid creditors. For example, before he died, John Brayne had been James Burbage's partner in constructing the Theatre. In 1591 an attorney named Henry Bett mentioned in a deposition that Brayne habitually prepared deeds of gift whenever he anticipated being imprisoned for debt. Bett implied that Brayne acted to defraud creditors, commenting, "That yt was a Common thinge, wth the said John Braine, to make deedes of gifte of his goodes and Chattelles, the reason was . . . to prevent his Credito[rs] aswell before buildinge of the Theatre, as since, for he beinge redie to be imprisoned for debt he would prepare sutch safetie for his goodes, as he could / by those deedes" (Wallace 86). At the time he wrote, Bett was an ally of the Burbages in defending their interests against Brayne's widow, who acted at the instigation of a man named Robert Miles. Later he witnessed the assignment of the lease of the Theatre to Cuthbert Burbage.

Another legally ambiguous conveyance occurred in 1596, when James Burbage protected his estate "by making a deed of gift to Cuthbert of all his personal property, and another deed of gift of the Blackfriars to his second son, Richard" (Shakespeare's acting partner) (Wallace 23–24). As a result of this gift, Robert Miles filed suit in 1597 against Cuthbert, Richard, and Ellen Burbage. Miles charged that James Burbage fraudulently conveyed his estate to defeat Miles and other creditors of their due. Perhaps because the law was still unsettled, Miles lost his legal action, as did Gyles Allen, who raised the same issue in 1599 when he sued the Burbages for the value of his lost building.

The prevalence and uncertainty of the practice of fraudulent conveyancing gives layers of meaning to Ford's speech to Falstaff. We have seen, for example, that an unscrupulous landlord might let someone who was ignorant of his title build on his land. Ford, disguised as Brooke, similarly encourages Falstaff to "build" on his "ground" (his wife). The metaphor works at least two ways: first, "Brooke" builds false hope upon another man's ground; second, Ford suspects someone has made "shrewd construction" on his wife's "enlarged mirth." In the latter case the "building" is not vain desire but a sexual erection: Mistress Quickly unknowingly blunders onto the truth a few lines later. Falstaff catches her meaning, but he is remarkably unaware of the risk he takes of being defrauded by Brooke, since he himself will be "building" on another man's (Ford's) "ground." Instead, Falstaff's mind conjures a law that arises from the works of nature (nature to which his mind compares woman), when he says that he has mistakenly built upon a "woman's promise" (3.5.41). Ford's "building" image refers to a form of fraudulent conveyance under a lease, but Falstaff (fresh from a dunking in the Thames) thinks, rather quaintly, in terms of riparian rights. Land is stable, but a riverbank can shift in flood, and the changing course of a stream may eliminate one's property interest.[30] A "woman's promise," Falstaff suggests, shifts like a shoreline, and one's possessions may be washed away.

IV

Like Mistress Page and Ford—and in contrast to Falstaff's somewhat retrograde activity—the Host also thinks like a contemporary lawyer. He is eager to use the legal terminology of "egress and regress" ("said I well?"),[31] and he worries that "Brooke" has a "shute [suit] against my knight." He somewhat suspiciously keeps a room for Falstaff even when the Garter has been taken over by Germans ("They have had my [house] a week at command. I have turn'd away my other guests" [4.3.8]).[32] He also seems to have a precocious sense of what in later contract law will be called "mutual mistake" when he assigns Caius and Evans to different locations for their duel, effectively preventing their encounter. (A contract is void when a broker makes a sale by describing a different article to each party; cf. Tiffany 3.) The result is good comedy.

The Host also connives with Falstaff with regard to the employment of Bardolphe. The dismissal of a servant to evade debt is a very old legal trick. Justinian mentions fraudulent manumission and gives an example: "A grant of freedom amounts to fraud on creditors when the grantor is already insolvent at the time of the manumission or will become so by freeing the slaves" (Justinian, *Institutes* 41 [1.6.3]). Bardolphe is not a Roman slave, of course, but in *2 Henry IV,* Falstaff says he "bought" him at St. Paul's. When Falstaff follows his announcement that he needs to "turn away" some of his followers by saying "I sit at ten pounds a weeke" (1.3), the Host of the Garter is not slow to realize that he receives most of that expense. (The tavern bill found on Falstaff in *1 Henry IV* suggests that Falstaff spends thirteen shillings a day for food and drink, which with half a crown or so for rent, comes to about ten pounds a week.) Mine Host picks up Bardolphe's hire because he values a good customer. He is the beneficiary of Falstaff's transfer of Bardolphe, and the transfer verges on fraud because of a trust relationship between Falstaff and the Host to the detriment of other creditors (although it was legitimate to *prefer* one creditor over another). As a tapster, Bardolphe will spend much of his time doing what he would do anyway, fetching sack for Falstaff.

Falstaff's show of concern for finding new employment for Bardolphe conceals the fact that a transfer of assets is taking place. Openly, Falstaff defends letting Bardolphe go by claiming he has lost his skill in filching. Pistol—who has just heard Falstaff rationalize his dismissal of Bardolphe by claiming that he stole not in time—perhaps puts a right name to what has happened. Shakespeare's characters usually base their puns and wordplay on something someone else has just said or done. Pistol has heard Nym use the word "steal" a moment before, but he may have come up with the word "convey" in response to the way Falstaff engineers Bardolphe's new occupation when he offers a synonym for theft: "Convay, the wise it call. Steal? foh: a fico for the phrase!"

Falstaff has told his followers he needs to practice deceit—"to shuffle, to hedge, and to lurch"—thus coloring even his inadvertent actions with a degree of intentionality. Pistol's suspicion of Falstaff's secret dealings helps account for his and then Nym's refusal to carry Falstaff's love letters. The distaste for pimping that they express seems like a sudden attack of virtue, but their possible suspicion is borne out when Falstaff seizes his chance to cashier his two remaining followers. Whatever his true motive, and whether or not the Host connives with him (as Twyne did with Pierce), Falstaff gets a kind of fresh start by releasing Bardolphe. He reduces his expenses, and he may also make money if Bardolphe, Pistol, and Nym are receiving a military salary that Falstaff can pocket. We remain uncertain as to whether Falstaff makes a sly reference to the deceptive practice of fraudulent conveyance when he refers to Bardolphe's new occupation as a "good trade," but others, including the perspicacious Host, seem well aware of what is happening.

Ford, Mistress Page, and the Host constitute a pattern of legal think- ing that reflects the increasingly mercantile world of turn-of-the-century England. Their values contrast with those of the knightly class to which Falstaff belongs. England's gentry and aristocracy embraced a romantic ideology of exploration and commercial adventure that also colors Falstaff's language.[33] As an apologist for empire, or like an old aristocrat, the knight believes that fortunes are made by wooing women for their wealth.[34] Falstaff is certain the wives of Windsor will yield riches: he declares that Mistress Ford and Mistress Page are lands of "gold, and bountie: I will be Cheaters to them both, and they shall be Exchequers to mee: they shall be my East and West Indies, and I will trade to them both" (1.3.29ff.). He means, "I will deceive them; they will be my source of wealth. I will take money first from one, then the other." But Falstaff's language undercuts him by echoing a commercial world to which he seems a stranger. In real life, "cheaters" were tax collectors, and they were capable of fraud. The situation at Cadiz in 1596 shows such a corrupt representative of the Exchequer at work, as J. E. Neale tells the story:

Both Howard and Essex were under promise and orders to save the plunder of the voyage for the Queen: they gave it with a bountiful hand to their men. An official had been attached to them to see the order carried out: he plundered with the rest. (346)

Whether or not Shakespeare knew about Cadiz, the problem of repossessing property that such embezzlers bought with the king or queen's money is typical of a series of cases in James Dyer's *Reports* on fraudulent conveyance.[35] This close connection between "escheators" for the Crown and fraud suggests the limited range of Falstaff's ideas on trading and cheating: he maintains an epic attitude of bravado and lying in a world where economic activity was increasingly seen as a technically sophisticated adventure.

The problem of Falstaff's legal knowledge surfaces most acutely in the final act, when Ford announces that Falstaff owes "Brooke" (the name that Ford assumes in disguise) the sum of twenty pounds, money that Falstaff has accepted in exchange for his promise to Brooke to seduce Mistress Ford. In the Quarto version of the play Ford mentions "a further matter" to Falstaff: "There's 20 pound you borrowed of M. Brooke Sir John, /And it must be paid to M. Ford Sir John" (5.5.117). Mistress Ford tells her husband to forgive his debtor, thereby effecting a reconciliation appropriate to the comedy's conclusion: "Nay husband let that go to make amends, / Forgive that sum, and so weele all be friends."

In the Folio, however, Mistress Ford says nothing about forgiving Falstaff, while Ford announces that Falstaff's "horses are arrested" to ensure repayment of the debt. Lewis Theobald retained the Quarto reading, noting, in a quasi-judicial manner, that "Sir John Falstaff is sufficiently punished, in being disappointed and exposed. The expectation of his being prosecuted for the twenty pounds, gives the conclusion too tragical a turn. Besides it is *poetical justice* that Ford should sustain his loss, as a fine for his unreasonable jealously" (216). I believe Theobald overreacts. For one thing, Ford's legal move may have been merely practical: in *1 Henry IV*, when Prince Hal hides Falstaff's horse before the Gadshill robbery, he knows that the fat knight is not likely to move far unmounted.

If Ford has not taken Falstaff's horses as a joke, then the term "arrest" may be a legalism. Falstaff may have been compelled to give horses to the sheriff as pledges that he will appear in court. His horses would have been "arrested" because the writ that forced Falstaff to pledge the horses was the *capias ad respondendum,* a common writ used to start a case.[36] But nothing indicates Falstaff knows what has happened. John Cowell's *Interpreter* (1601) offers another possible gloss in the writ of *arrestandis bonis ne dissipentur,* "which lyeth for him, whose catell or goods are taken by another, that, during the controversie, doth, or is like to make them away, and will be hardly able to make satisfaction for them afterward."[37] Yet this writ fits the facts of the case imperfectly, since Falstaff did not take horses from Ford.[38]

It is tempting to suggest that perhaps old Falstaff knows a thing or two about fraudulent conveyances and that Ford is merely blustering when he claims to have arrested Falstaff's horses. Falstaff seems unperturbed by the news, and it may be that Ford sent the bailiff too late. I am not the first to think that those horses of the Host stolen by the "Germans" may well have been Falstaff's, doubtless on their way to a place beyond the reach of creditors.[39]

Falstaff's conveyance of his horses would be fraudulent if he had no other assets with which to repay his debt. He has clothes, and his room at the Garter counts as an asset if he has paid for it in advance. He may have an income either from an inheritance or as a military captain. Falstaff also has an uncertain number of horses—say four, one each for himself and his men—whose value we may estimate at about five pounds apiece, suggesting that "Brooke" knew his man if he purposely limited his lending to twenty pounds.[40]

Falstaff's notable failure to convey his horses beyond the reach of his creditor—which Ford's action presumes—illustrates how conveyancing suits comic drama. In Plautus and Terence, the creditor often takes the form of a distant father or husband or brothel owner to whom a girl owes a duty that she seeks to convey to a young man, whom she will marry.[41] Indeed, so suited is conveyancing, like revenge, to literary treatment that Erich Segal observes how young men typically court bankruptcy in the Roman comedies.[42] The lovers' insolvency—like Falstaff's (who therefore symbolically stands in for Anne Page's suitor Fenton, who has money enough but lacks the goodwill of Anne's parents)—allows comedy to represent the "breaking of restrictions" that is the "'heart' of the genre" (Segal 17-18). Like fraudulent conveyance, comedy can take many forms. In Moliere's *Le Festin de pierre,* for example, Don Juan gets rid of his creditor Monsieur Dimanche by professing such warm friendship and sharing such solicitude for him that the creditor never gets to demand his money (Olson 59). Shakespeare's comedies typically turn on sudden shifts in affection, as when a young man like Proteus in *The Two Gentlemen of Verona* claims to give one woman his heart (the title) but conveys his affection (the use) elsewhere. As Elder Olson observes, comedy contrasts to the narrow genre of tragedy, because comedy has an enormous range of plots.

The comic form of *The Merry Wives of Windsor* remains intact, despite what Theobald thought, if we follow the text and assume Ford did manage to arrest Falstaff's horses. Falstaff has traditionally been regarded as a *miles gloriosus* figure, the alazon or braggart of Roman comedy, or as a derivative of vice in the old morality plays. Recent critics, seeking to interpret the final pageant of *The Merry Wives,* see him as a carnival figure, a victim of folk ritual, or a scapegoat who bears the vices of misplaced sexuality and deception "shared by the very citizens who taunt him" (Hinely; Foley; Parten). I believe he is an effigy of fraud as well. The original Twelve Tables of Rome allowed creditors to divide the body of a debtor among them.[43] Falstaff therefore echoes the old Roman law when, reveling with the wives at Herne the Hunter's oak tree, he offers to divide himself up for their benefit, a haunch to each. Falstaff's symbolic role as a figure of fraud helps explain why Falstaff invites Brooke to Herne's oak to watch him give himself to Mistress Ford and also why Falstaff is ultimately forgiven his trespasses by the townspeople who mock him.

The reconciliation of Falstaff with the citizens of Windsor mirrors the general acceptance of this form of fraud by Shakespeare's society. Mistress Page's legal language suggests that she is an astute woman who recognizes the delightful way Falstaff's carriage in a buck-basket parodies the practice

of fraudulent conveyance. Mr. Ford conjures a form of "constructive" fraudulent conveyance when he compares making love to someone else's wife
with building on another man's land. The Host of the Garter also thinks like
a lawyer. He takes over Bardolphe's employment to help Falstaff manage his
affairs. Compared to these characters, Falstaff appears curiously retrograde
in his awareness of legal matters: the end of the Folio version holds up the
possibility that Falstaff, said to owe Ford twenty pounds, has missed an
opportunity to fraudulently convey his horses. In each case the play draws
on a common issue in the legal thinking of sixteenth-century England.

The moral ambivalence of fraudulent conveyance unifies the play and
explains its legal metaphors. Although there have been recent defenses of
Falstaff's role in the comedy, he has generally been taken to be a lesser
wit than the knight of the history plays. A. C. Bradley called Falstaff's
degradation "horrible."[44] Samuel Johnson said that the danger of Falstaff's
vice is its attractiveness to others.[45] I believe Bradley's view is misguided
and that Johnson's observation applies to *The Merry Wives* as well the
history plays. Falstaff reflects a society in which fraud is endemic and social
rules, including legal forms of conveyance, are in flux.

As a figure of the shifting ethics of conveyancing, Falstaff operates both
openly and secretly, intentionally and perhaps instinctually. Jill Levenson
observes that the narrative movement of comedy is often accompanied, in
the Renaissance, by "a series of debates" or *dianoia:* "that ongoing process
of reasoning and problem-solving which the commentators suggest is the
action of comedy" (268, citing Altman 139, 157–61). In Shakespeare's
history plays, Falstaff's illegal behavior threatens to mislead Prince Hal
and derange society (Kornstein 134–42). Shakespeare's comedy, however,
absorbs Falstaff's deceptive stratagems because the mores of the society
represented in the play show the same ambiguity that characterizes Falstaff.

Falstaff's simultaneous punishment and escape reflects the moral ambiguity of fraudulent conveyancing. The terms debtor and creditor are
like the image of a vase that becomes the profile of two women as we
stare at it. Depending on our situation, we will sympathize with one or
the other. Fraudulent conveyance operates in this shifting moral sphere,
where power blurs the line between right and wrong. Anyone, including
Falstaff, who appears unfairly oppressed by circumstances or misfortune
will arouse sympathy.

Notes

This essay was first presented at the Indiana College English Association, 30 October 1992, and at the Shakespeare and Law section, organized by Constance Jordan, of the 1994 meeting of the Shakespeare Association of America. I would like to thank David Bevington, Michael Murrin, the anonymous reader for *Renaissance Drama,* and Frances Dolan for providing written comments on previous versions. Thanks also to Patricia Parker, Seth Weiner, and Slaney Ross, who made several editorial suggestions.

1. Quotations are taken from the facsimile editions listed in the Works Cited. The editors of the Quarto facsimile give line numbers that correspond roughly to those of the Globe edition based on the Folio. Leah S. Marcus ("Levelling") comments on the different versions: *The Merry Wives of Windsor* "exists in a Quarto of 1602 with an urban setting strongly suggesting London or some provincial city, and the standard copytext, the 1623 Folio version, which sets the play in and around the town of Windsor and includes numerous topographical references to the area, its palace, park, and surrounding villages" (173). "Both versions of *Merry Wives* are teeming with folk rituals, but the way we interpret them will depend on which version we choose" (175). This essay suggests that what Marcus says extends to legal rituals as well.

2. Radin; Glenn 82.

3. Helmholz 8, 12; Martines 176; Simpson 174 (comparing the medieval use to modern tax evasion, as when the Franciscans, to maintain poverty, "found it convenient that property should be held by others to their use").

4. 9 Hen. III 35 was a statute against mortmain and subinfeudation (conveyance of lands to a religious house in order "to take the same land again to hold of the same house"). "A tenant might convey land to a church with the understanding that the church would subinfeudate him for lesser services. The result was that the superior lord now had the church for a tenant, with the resulting loss of feudal dues, but the erstwhile tenant still had the benefit of the land with his obligations considerably reduced" (Kempin 146).

5. 52 Hen. III 6.

6. 50 Edw. III 6 was aimed at those who, to avoid creditors, give their tenements and chattels to friends, who agree to pass on the profits, and then seek sanctuary in "the Franchise of Westminster, of S. Martin le graund of London, or other such priviledged places." The Parliament of Henry VII repeated the injunction of 50 Edw. III 6 against deeds of gift made to defraud creditors by those who seek "Sanctuary, or other places privileged" (3 Hen. VII c. 4).

7. A series of statutes under Richard II (11 Ricc. II 1–6) was aimed at five specific peers of the realm, accused of high treason, to void the "fraudulent conveyances of their goods to deceive the King." One bill under Henry VIII forced a single man, Sir John Shelton, to repeal fraudulent deeds and conveyances made to defeat the king and others of wardship, primer seisin, and relief, and to make clear that he, condemned to die, did so while seised of those lands, which the king could then reach (33 Hen. VIII 26). Later laws were aimed at recusants who sought by "convenous conveyance" "to defraud any interest, right, or title, that may or ought to grow to the Queen" or anyone else (23 Eliz. 2 and 29 Eliz. 6). Another statute (27 Eliz. 4, passed in 1585 and made perpetual in 1597 by 39 Eliz. 18) prohibited

fraudulent conveyances to defeat purchasers (in other words, it gave statutory form to the obvious notion that you should not sell the same thing to two people at the same time). In 1603, between the Quarto and Folio versions of *Merry Wives,* King James's first Parliament made fraudulent conveyance an act of bankruptcy (the law applied only to merchants). The issue in Elizabethan times was the *trade rule* in bankruptcy, which was added to the 1543 statute in 1571. After 1571, courts gradually clarified what manufacturers of tangible goods could be covered by bankruptcy law: shoemakers in 1592, drapers in 1610, dyers in 1621, bakers in 1623, carpenters in 1688 (Weisberg, "Commercial" 22-24). (Much later the issue would become discharge or the modern "fresh start.") The next act of this legal history occurred in 1623 when James's new bankruptcy bill (21 Jac. 19) incorporated the specific language of 13 Eliz. 5 and Twyne's case, which survives to this day in many states ("to delay, defraud, or hinder" creditors and others). The bill also uncannily echoes Falstaff's debt, since the fraudulent conveyancing provision only applies to amounts of twenty pounds or more. Another threshold in the bill is that the debtor's obligations must be one hundred pounds, the amount Fenton offers the Host to help him convey away Anne Page.

8. "Our notion of the fraudulent conveyance traces to a statute of Elizabeth . . . due to the restatement of the law which was made by Sir Edward Coke. . . . Later, no one cared to go back further; and so our law of fraudulent conveyances may be ascribed to Coke" (Glenn 79).

9. Glenn observes that the first Elizabethan statute against fraudulent conveyance had less to do with creditor's rights than with providing the queen with a legal means to enrich the royal treasury. The statute of 13 Eliz. 5 provided that, in Glenn's summary, " 'all and every the parties' to a fraudulent conveyance, 'being privy and knowing of the same,' shall forfeit one year's value of the land, if land was the subject, and 'the whole value of the goods and chattels,' one half to the Queen and the other half to any party who may be aggrieved" (92).

10. In addition, *A Briefe Note of Ireland,* if Spenser's, refers to fraudulent conveyancing in the last words the poet wrote: "Whereas manie of the lords of the Countrie not longe before the confederating of his rebellion procured there freeholders to take there lands of them selues by lease manie of which are since gone into rebellion / That provision may be made for the avoyding of such fraudulent conveyances made onelie to defeat hir Maiestie of the benefitt of theire attainder" (245).

11. See Carlson. See also (for convenience I cite in law-review style): Dobris, *Medicaid Asset Planning by the Elderly,* 24 REAL PPTJ 1 (cloud of fraudulent conveyance law creates no safe haven for divestment planning); *cf* Randall v. Lukhard, 729 F.2d 966, at 969 (4th Cir. 1984) (dissent said anyone who transfers for less than full value and then applies for Medicaid lacks even a "modicum of decency" and has sunk to "immoral depths"); State v. Goggins, 546 A.2d 250 (Conn. 1988) (allegation that transfer of Medicaid patient's property was fraudulent conveyance).

12. David Ray Papke reveals how American agrarian law valorized debtors ("Rhetoric").

13. This suspicion reflects the opinion of rural bankers I spoke with during a visit to the federal Bankruptcy Court in Lafayette, Indiana.

14. Coke, the queen's attorney general, paid no attention to the Crown's rights or interests "but he put life into the Statute by applying it to the rights of the citizen who has been cozened" (Glenn 99).

If Shakespeare knew the case, he would have read legal French, of which I give a sample:

"[I]n camera Stellata, pur contriver et publication dun fraudulent done des byens; Le case sur lestatute de 13 Eliz. cap. 5, fuit tiel: Pierce fuit endebt al Twyne en 400.li." Pierce had "byens et chateux al value de 300.li. en secret fait general done per fait, de touts ses byens et chateux reals & personals quecunque al Twyne." Twyne resisted "ad *Fieri facias* direct al Vicont de South." When he came to execute the brief, it was found that "cest done fuit fraudulent" under the statute because the gift had "les ensignes et markes de fraude": the gift was general without exception for clothing ("son apparel ou ascun chose de necessitie"). Also, the gift said it was done "honestly, truely, & bona fide," a phrase that aroused suspicion because "secrecie est un marke de fraude." Coke objects to the abundance and the growth of fraud "pluis que en former temps"; therefore the court must read the statute broadly and presume fraud: "tout Statutes faits encounter fraud serra liberalment & beneficialment expounde a suppresser fraud" (Coke, *Le Tierce Part* 80-82).

15. Anthony Trollope provides a brilliant legal analysis of intent in a charge of murder in *The McDermots of Ballycloran* (1847). The passage I have in mind in *Lolita* begins "Query: is the stepfather . . ." (Nabokov 174).

16. These first terms occur in the opening conversation of Justice Shallow and Slender, whose legal knowledge finds its image, a little later, in his apparent preference for Richard Tottel's *Songs and Sonnets* instead of that publisher's legal tomes.

17. The last three examples are cited by H. J. Oliver, who declares the significance of the legalisms hard to detect (lxxviii). When Mrs. Page says she will "exhibit a bill in the parliament for the putting down of men" (2.1.27), she sounds like Beatrice.

18. For an explanation of a simple fine, see note 23.

19. "Shakespeare used the word *'cheater,'* either in its original sense of escheator or officer who enforced escheats or forfeitures to the Crown, or in its derivative sense of a 'swindler' or 'cheat' " (Dunbar Barton 154-55).

20. "[T]he commencement of the mock trial of Falstaff at Herne the Hunter's Oak in Windsor Park at midnight . . . is shortly followed by a parody of ordeal by fire" (Phillips 89). Shakespeare "compares the starting of a fairy revel to the opening of a Court of Assize. The fairy Hobgoblin figures as Crier of the Courts; and is ordered to open the revels as if it were an Assize: 'Crier Hobgoblin make the fairy o-yes' " (Dunbar Barton 84).

21. Dunbar Barton 7, 159; Underhill 381; Keeton 301.

22. See Parker's *"The Merry Wives"* 236. I am indebted to her *Literary Fat Ladies* for the original inspiration of the first draft of this essay, which I rewrote after she kindly referred me to her article. Neither she nor Sandra K. Fischer (*Econolingua* 59), however, catches the legal sense of "conveyance," nor does William Carroll, who also comes near my topic, list it among the forms of transgression in the play (206). Otherwise my thesis finds a parallel but not overlapping path in Fischer's contrast between King Henry's use of new terms of contract and exchange in contrast to Richard's obtuseness in *Richard II* and her remarks on how Hal learns "which debts to keep and when and how to pay" from Falstaff and his father ("He means" 159).

23. "The conveyancers quickly developed ways of breaking entails, for the benefit of tenants-in-tail who wanted to alienate the land that came to them. The conveyancers' cleverest invention was the *common recovery.* It was known that a tenant for life or a term of years sometimes fraudulently conveyed away the fee simple of the land he occupied by means

of a collusive action: the purchaser claimed the land in court, and the tenant made only a gesture of defense, so that the purchaser 'recovered' the land by a legal judgment" (Harding 91). For the more complex "fine and recovery," see Clarkson and Warren 127; Underhill 405; Kempin 157.

24. William Rastell lists the rule that one who sustains damage can have a "writ of waste out of the Chancery against the escheator for his act" (522).

25. The moral ambiguity of fraudulent conveyance colors Mistress Page's behavior in the play. It can be argued that adultery has some attraction for her, just as fraudulent conveyance appeals to debtors. She is clever enough to put Mistress Ford at risk by arranging for Falstaff to come to her friend's house, although once there she plays a separate game by accusing Falstaff (who has sent two love letters) of two-timing her. Also, Anne's seven hundred-pound income (Folio 1.1.50) may have been assured by Mrs. Page's father as easily as by Mr. Page's side of the family (there is no textual way to choose), skipping a generation, perhaps creating some bitterness and giving Mistress Page reason to think hard about the transfer of property.

26. The Folio seems to me to be a later version of the play: Grace Ioppolo argues it was probably revised several times for "several Garter feasts" (120).

27. Dunbar Barton 122. William Rushton traces the maxim to Justinian and gives a variation in George Chapman's *May Day* (23-25). Clarkson and Warren (166) cite Dekker's *Shoemaker's Holiday* for a similar sexual metaphor: "hee / that sowes in another mans ground forfeits / his harvest."

28. Burbage knew his lease would expire and spent six hundred pounds on the Blackfriars, but a neighborhood petition drove him out. Shakespeare's company played at the Rose and the Swan for an interim year, then made plans to build the Globe: it was to finance this project that the Burbages allowed Shakespeare and five or so others to invest and thereby become part owners. "[B]y 1597 [the Theatre] was empty because of trouble with the lease of the land on which it stood" (Gurr, *Stage* 130).

In a private communication, Andrew Gurr expressed certainty that the law was not on the side of Shakespeare's confederates. He restated his position on the date of the play: if *The Merry Wives* was composed in 1597, then the reference "Brooke" makes would have been innocent; if composed in 1599, then it becomes a topical reference to Shakepeare's own situation. I believe this answers Elizabeth Schafer's objections to Gurr, "Intertextuality," that a 1597 date for the Folio, based on the lease reference, is only "speculation" (58).

29. W. F. Bolton counts over 225 editions of such law books and reports between 1553 and 1591, including works by Thomas Fortescue, Thomas de Littleton's *Tenures,* and James Dyer's *Reports* (54).

30. Spenser draws on a similar law of the sea in the tale of the two sons of Milesio, owners of eroding islands, when Artegall convinces them that they must be content with what the sea delivers them and what it takes away (*Faerie Queene* 5.4.4-20).

31. 2.1. Clarkson and Warren gloss "egress and regress" as derivative of words of leases that signify departure and return to some part of land (69-70).

32. English bankruptcy laws, like those of Rome, generally created some form of sanctuary, a place where a debtor could be free from arrest while he reorganized. See Thornley 183-86; Marcus, *Puzzling* 165-66; 32 Hen. VIII c. 12 ("places of priviledge and tuition for terme" included Welles in Somerset, Westminster, Manchester, Northampton, Norwich, York, and Darby). Usually a church or abbey lands served as a sanctuary, but as Bacon recognized in

his *Learned Reading upon the Statute of Uses,* debtors desired to find a retreat to live in after conveying their assets to a friend (412). They could then negotiate with their creditors, who would be willing to settle their claims at a discount because they would otherwise be unable to reach property held in trust for the debtors (Glenn 84). The Garter Inn operates symbolically in this way—rather like a "homestead" in modern law—for Falstaff lives there uninterruptedly, giving him time to effect the transfer of Bardolphe's employment to the Host of the Garter and to send love letters to Mistress Ford and Mistress Page, wooing them for their money.

33. David Quint notes that although plunder is "the normal means for an epic hero to acquire portable property," there was a tradition of debased heroes who ventured among the merchants (ancient critics called Ulysses a hording merchant, and Juvenal referred to Jason as "mercator Jason") (259). The old categories were breaking down by 1600 when Elizabeth gave a charter to the East India Company to trade wool cloth in the Indian Sea: "Commerce was the motive of exploration as well as warfare, and all three were combined in some of the greatest deeds of that generation. Romance and money-making, desperate daring and dividends, were closely associated in the minds and hearts of men" (Trevelyan 346–47).

34. Falstaff represents what Immanuel Wallerstein calls the old view of the world of trade as a trade in luxuries (food and handicraft production), not "bulk" goods (18).

35. Dyer's *Reports* cites a cluster of cases based on debt, sanctuary, and fraudulent conveyance, including the case of a man who purchased land with the money of the king: "Walter de Chyrton Customer al Roy esteant graunde dettour a luy, purchase terre ove le money le Roy, et prist lestate del terre a ses amyes a defrauder le Roy, mes il mesme prist les profits, ceux terres fueront extende al Roy in *Scaccario*" (295). The court of Exchequer voided the conveyances and gave the land to the king.

36. Normally the creditor would enlist a bailiff to execute the debt "against the body" of the debtor: this is the language used in 1582, for example, when the bailiff of the Manor and Liberties of Stebneth executed a debt of one hundred pounds against John Brayne (Wallace 91).

37. Dr. Cowell was Reader in Civil Law at the University of Cambridge; he published *The Interpreter* in 1601 (Keeton 342).

38. Notice that Ford arrests Falstaff's horses, not Falstaff. George W. Keeton observes that Antipholus threatens Angelo with a suit for wrong arrest in *The Comedy of Errors* (114). Other methods of distraint would be available *after* a judgment in court, which we may presume Ford has not yet sought. At that point a judgment creditor in the king's court could send a sheriff to levy on the debtor's animals by a writ of *fieri faciat,* employing a legal process that went back at least to 3 Edward I 18; *elegit* (a transfer of the debtor's personal property to his creditor at an appraised price); and *capias ad satisfaciendum* (where a local sheriff arrests the judgment debtor, who stayed in prison until he paid his fine) (Epstein 66; Dunbar Barton 85 and 92).

39. Geoffrey Bullough condemns the horse-stealing episode: "As it stands in both Q and F this is surely the worst-handled episode in all Shakespeare's plays" (11). W. W. Greg calls it "curiously fragmentary" (336); Robert S. Miola "badly garbled" (374).

40. Indictments involving the theft of horses often included the value of the animal. J. S. Cockburn lists prices in 1600: six pounds each for a black and a sorrel gelding (#2973); fifty shillings for a gray mare (#2975); three pounds for a gray gelding; five pounds for bright-bay

horse; three pounds for a sorrel horse (#3011): five pounds for a gray gelding, but twenty-six shillings for a white gelding (#3011). I owe this information on prices to Shawn Smith, my former student at Purdue who is currently completing a Ph.D. at Yale University.

41. In *The Ghost,* for example, Philematium is in debt to Philolaches for buying her freedom with his own money, so she pays back her debt by loving him exclusively, despite the advice of Scapha, who argues that Philematium overpays her debt, since Philolaches will certainly leave her. In other dramas of Plautus, slave girls are typically conveyed from house to house or given sanctuary to protect them from brothel keepers.

42. The theme also occurs in *Astrophil and Stella* 18, where Sidney wants only to lose "more" of what heaven "hath lent":

> With what sharpe checkes I in my self am shent,
> When into Reason's audite I do go:
> And by just counts my selfe a banckrout know
> Of all those goods, which heav'n to me hath lent:
> . . . .
> I see and yet no greater sorrow take,
> Then that I lose no more for *Stella's* sake.

43. See Sandars xv; Posner 93.

44. Other have defended Falstaff's role in the comedy. Brian Vickers complains that the plot requires that Falstaff by "easily duped" (141). But Oliver denies that there is a "gap" between the Falstaff who "loses the battle of wits over the Gadshill robbery and is not allowed to forget it" and "the one who can so easily be made to look foolish by the kind of honest women of whom he has little experience, or between the Falstaff who is frightened of being found by a jealous husband and the one who ran away at Gadshill." Like others, he observes that Falstaff's defeat is necessary to the comic drama (lxvii). Anne Barton concludes that Falstaff is a "lesser creature" because his character is "not . . . an end in itself" but an expression of the play's comic plot (287), a point made also by E. K. Chambers, cited by G. R. Hibbard (55).

45. "The moral to be drawn from this representation is, that no man is more dangerous than he that with a will to corrupt, hath the power to please; and that neither wit nor honesty ought to think themselves safe with such a companion when they see *Henry* seduced by Falstaff" (Johnson 356 [the last note to *2 Henry IV*]). Falstaff's double nature seems similar to Justinian's observation that fraud may be admirable: "[T]he old lawyers described even malice or fraud as good and held this expression to stand for ingenuity, especially where something was devised against an enemy or robber," and so they "added the world 'evil' " (Non fuit autem contentus praetor dolum dicere, sec adiecit malum, quoniam veteres dolum etiam bonum dicebant) (Justinian, *Digest* 119).

Works Cited

Altman, Joel B. *The Tudor Play of Mind: Rhetorical Inquiry and the Development of Elizabethan Drama.* Berkeley: U of California P, 1978.

Bacon, Francis. *Learned Reading upon the Statute of Uses. The Works of Francis Bacon.* Ed.

James Spedding, Robert Leslie Ellis, and Douglas Denon Heath. 14 vols. London: Longman, 1861. New York: Garrett, 1968. 7: 389-450.

Barton, Anne. Introduction. *The Merry Wives of Windsor. The Riverside Shakespeare.* Ed. G. Blakemore Evans. Boston: Houghton, 1974. 286-89.

Barton, Dunbar Plunket. *Shakespeare and the Law.* 1929. New York: Blom, 1971.

Bolton, W. F. "Ricardian Law Reports and *Richard II.*" *Shakespeare Studies* 20 (1988): 53-65.

Bradley, A. C. "The Rejection of Falstaff." *Oxford Lectures on Poetry.* London: Macmillan, 1909. 247-75.

Brook, Robert. *Auscun novel cases de les anz et tempz le roy H. 8 Edw. 6. & la roigne Mary le I.* London (?), 1576.

Bullough, Geoffrey. "Tarltons Newes out of Purgatorie." *Narrative and Dramatic Sources of Shakespeare.* 8 vols. 1957-75. Vol. 2: *The Comedies, 1597-1603.* London: Routledge, 1958. 26-34.

Carlson, David Gray. "Is Fraudulent Conveyance Law Efficient?" *Cardozo Law Review* 9 (1987): 643-83.

Carroll, William. " 'A Received Belief': Imagination in *The Merry Wives of Windsor.*" *Studies in Philology* 74 (1977): 186-215.

Clarkson, Paul S., and Clyde T. Warren. *The Law of Property in Shakespeare and the Elizabethan Drama.* Baltimore: Johns Hopkins UP, 1942.

Cockburn, J. S. *Calendar of Assize Records. Essex Indictments: Elizabeth I.* London: HMSO, 1978.

Coke, Edward. *Exact Abridgement.* London, 1651. Newberry Library Case SA 1877.

———. *Le Tierce Part des Reportes del Edward Coke Lattorney generall le Roigne.* London, 1602.

Cowell, John. *The Interpreter.* 1601. London, 1607.

Dyer, James. [*Reports.*] *Cy ensuant ascuns novel cases.* London, 1601.

[England-Statutes.] *Anno xliii. Reginae Elizabethae. At the Parliament . . . 1601.* STC 9495.

———. *A Collection in English, of the Statutes now in force, continue from the beginning of the Magna Charta.* London, 1598. STC 9321.

Epstein, David G. *Debtor-Creditor Law.* Nutshell Series. 4th ed. St. Paul: West, 1991.

Fischer, Sandra K. *Econolingua: A Glossary of Coins and Economic Language in Renaissance Drama.* Newark: U of Delaware P, 1985.

———. " 'He means to pay': Value and Metaphor in the Lancastrian Tetralogy." *Shakespeare Quarterly* 40 (1989): 149-64.

Foley, Stephen. "Falstaff in Love and Other Stories from Tudor England." *Exemplaria* 1 (1989): 227-46.

Glenn, Garrard. *Fraudulent Conveyances and Preferences.* 2 vols. Rev. ed. New York: Baker, Vorrhis, 1940. Vol. 1.

Greg, W. W. *The Shakespeare First Folio.* Oxford: Clarendon, 1955.

Gurr, Andrew. "Intertextuality at Windsor." *Shakespeare Quarterly* 38 (1987): 189-200.

———. *The Shakespearean Stage, 1574-1642.* 2nd ed. Cambridge: Cambridge UP, 1980.

Harding, Alan. *A Social History of English Law.* 1966. Gloucester, MA: Smith, 1973.

Helmholz, R. H. *Canon Law and English Common Law: Selden Society Lecture Delivered in the Old Hall of Lincoln's Inn, July 5th, 1982.* London: Selden Soc., 1983.

Hibbard, G. R. Introduction. *The Merry Wives of Windsor.* 1973. Harmondsworth: Penguin, 1981.

Hinely, Jan Lawson. "Comic Scapegoats and the Falstaff of *The Merry Wives of Windsor.*" *Shakespeare Studies* 15 (1982): 37-54.

Ioppolo, Grace. *Revising Shakespeare.* Cambridge: Harvard UP, 1991.

Johnson, Samuel, ed. *The Plays of William Shakespeare.* 7 vols. 1765. New York: AMS, 1968. Vol. 4.

Justinian. *The Digest of Justinian.* Ed. Theodor Mommsen, Paul Kreuger, and Alan Watson. 4 vols. Philadelphia: U of Pennsylvania P, 1985. Vol. 1.

————. *Justinian's Institutes.* Trans. Peter Burks and Grant McLeod. Ithaca: Cornell UP, 1987.

Keeton, George W. *Shakespeare's Legal and Political Background.* New York: Barnes & Noble, 1968.

Kempin, Frederick G., Jr. *Historical Introduction to Anglo-American Law.* Nutshell Series. 3rd ed. St. Paul: West, 1990.

Kennedy, Frank R. "Involuntary Fraudulent Transfers." *Cardozo Law Review* 9 (1987): 531-80.

Kornstein, Daniel J. *Kill All the Lawyers?: Shakespeare's Legal Appeal.* Princeton: Princeton UP, 1994.

Levenson, Jill. "Comedy." *The Cambridge Companion to English Renaissance Drama.* Ed. A. R. Braunmuller and Michael Hattaway. Cambridge: Cambridge UP, 1990. 263-300.

Marcus, Leah S. "Levelling Shakespeare: Local Customs and Local Texts." *Shakespeare Quarterly* 42 (1991): 168-78.

————. *Puzzling Shakespeare: Local Reading and Its Discontents.* Berkeley: U of California P, 1988.

Martines, Lauro. *Lawyers and Statecraft in Renaissance Florence.* Princeton: Princeton UP, 1968.

Miola, Robert S. "*The Merry Wives of Windsor:* Classical and Italian Intertexts." *Comparative Drama* 27 (1993): 364-76.

Nabokov, Vladimir. *Lolita.* New York: Putnam's, 1955.

Neale, J. E. *Queen Elizabeth I.* 1934. Harmondsworth: Penguin, 1973.

Oliver, H. J., ed. *The Merry Wives of Windsor.* The Arden Shakespeare. 1971. London: Routledge, 1993.

Olson, Elder. *The Theory of Comedy.* Bloomington: Indiana UP, 1968.

Papke, David Ray. "Discharge as Denouement: Appreciating the Storytelling of Appellate Opinions." *Journal of Legal Education* 40 (1990): 145-59.

————. "Rhetoric and Retrenchment: Agrarian Ideology and American Bankruptcy Law." *Missouri Law Review* 54 (1989): 871-98.

Parker, Patricia. *Literary Fat Ladies: Rhetoric, Gender, Property.* London: Methuen, 1987.

————. "*The Merry Wives of Windsor* and Shakespearean Translation." *Modern Language Quarterly* 52 (1991): 225-62.

Parten, Anne. "Falstaff's Horns: Masculine Inadequacy and Feminine Mirth in *The Merry Wives of Windsor.*" *Studies in Philology* 82 (1985): 184-99.

Phillips, O. Hood. *Shakespeare and the Lawyers.* London: Methuen, 1972.

Plowden, Edmund. *Les Comentaries, ou les Reportes.* London, 1571 (pt. 1), 1578 (pt. 2).

Posner, Richard. *Law and Literature: A Misunderstood Relation.* Cambridge: Harvard UP, 1988.

Pulton, Fernando. *De Pace regis et regni, viz. A Treatise declaring which be the great and generall offenses of the Realme.* London, 1608. STC 9548.

Quint, David. *Epic and Empire: Politics and Generic Form from Virgil to Milton.* Princeton: Princeton UP, 1993.

Radin, Max. "Fraudulent Conveyances at Roman Law." *Virginia Law Review* 18 (1931): 109-30.

Rastell, William. "To the Gentle Reader." *A Collection in English, of the Statutes now in force, continue from the beginning of Magna Charta.* London, 1598. STC 9321.

Rushton, William Lowes. *Shakespeare's Legal Maxims.* 1907. New York: AMS, 1973.

Sandars, Thomas Collett, ed. *The Institutes of Justinian.* 7th ed. London: Longman, 1952.

Schafer, Elizabeth. "The Date of *The Merry Wives of Windsor.*" *Notes and Queries* ns 38 (1991): 57-60.

Segal, Erich. *Roman Laughter: The Comedy of Plautus.* 2nd ed. New York: Oxford UP, 1987.

Shakespeare, William. *The Merry Wives of Windsor* (1602). Shakespeare Quarto Facsimiles, No. 3. Oxford: Clarendon, 1963.

———. *Mr. William Shakespeares Comedies, Histories, & Tragedies.* A facsimile edition of the First Folio prepared by Helge Kökeritz. Intro. Charles Tyler Prouty. New Haven: Yale UP, 1954.

Simpson. A. W. B. *A History of the Land Law.* 1961. 2nd ed. Oxford: Clarendon, 1986.

Spenser, Edmund. *A Briefe Note of Ireland. The Prose Works.* 233-45.

———. *A View of the Present State of Ireland. The Prose Works.* 39-232.

———. *The Works of Edmund Spenser: A Variorum Edition.* 11 vols. 1932-49. Ed. Edwin Greenlaw et al. Vol 9: *The Prose Works.* Ed. Rudolf Gottfried. Baltimore: Johns Hopkins UP, 1949.

Theobald, Lewis L. Cited in *The Plays of William Shakespeare.* 21 vols. Ed. George Steevens. London, 1803. Vol. 5.

Thornley, Isobel D. "The Destruction of Sanctuary." *Tudor Studies Presented.* Ed. R. W. Seton-Watson. London: Longmans, 1924. 182-207.

Tiffany, Francis B. *Handbook of the Law of Sales.* 2nd ed. St. Paul: West, 1908.

Trevelyan, G. M. *Illustrated History of England.* 1926. London: Longmans, 1956.

Underhill, Arthur. "Law." *Shakespeare's England.* 2 vols. 1916. Oxford: Clarendon, 1950. 1: 381-412.

Vickers, Brian. *The Artistry of Shakespeare's Prose.* London: Methuen, 1968.

Wallace, Charles William. *The First London Theatre.* 1913. New York: Blom, 1969.

Wallerstein, Immanuel. *The Modern World-System: Capitalist Agriculture and the Origins of the European World-Economy in the Sixteenth Century.* New York: Academic, 1976.

Weisberg, Richard. *Poethics, and Other Strategies of Law and Literature.* New York: Columbia UP, 1992.

Weisberg, Robert. "Commercial Morality, the Merchant Character, and the History of the Voidable Preference." *Stanford Law Review* 39 (1986): 3-138.

West, William. *Symbolaeographia.* London (?): Tottel, 1590.

Order and Justice in
Early Tudor Drama

PAT McCUNE

MOST DRAMA in England prior to the end of the fifteenth century had an eschatological focus, playing out the story either of Scripture or of the soul's salvation after a struggle between personified vices and virtues.[1] But by the early sixteenth century that focus had changed from judgment in the next world to judgment in this one, and from the welfare of the individual soul to the welfare of king and commonwealth. These plays are populated with divine and secular judges, rulers, their counselors, representatives of the governing estates, and of England itself. The structure of the morality play seized the interest of writers and their patrons in the late fifteenth century, and through much of the sixteenth century they were engaged in crafting this traditional form into new vehicles to convey their interests. There are more than fifty moral interludes known to have survived from the century before the advent of public theaters in 1576 (Lancashire; Houle). Early Tudor political culture transformed the old struggle of vices and virtues for the soul of mankind into a discourse about the balance of powers in secular authority.

Central to this exchange was the development of a distinct ideology of justice which valued retribution over reconciliation. The emergence of this ideology bears witness to the changing nature of English polity under the first two Tudors. We see it clearly in a prominent theme in early Tudor drama, the salvation of the body politic. That body is threatened by corruption among its members and healed through the administration

171

of royal justice. These morality plays are part of the culmination of a centuries-old convention, reflecting the final stage of development in the literature of complaint and counsel that flourished in England during the late Middle Ages (Coleman; Ferguson; Scattergood). Such works typically criticize generic moral faults, condemning the failure of those at every social rank to meet the obligations appropriate to their estates. Ordinarily the course of amendment centered on returning to customary virtuous practices that fulfilled duties in this life, and so earned salvation in the next. These traditional complaints about vice recommend their redress through a corresponding virtue. However, a significant exception is evident when the topic is mercy. The misgovernance resulting from the corruption of the virtue of generosity—and so of forgiveness—is cited frequently in this literature as the root of lawlessness.

We find complaints about the uses of generosity particularly in relation to the king and those responsible for administering his justice. Complaint literature reveals a growing conviction that abuses of royal mercy in the courts aggravated the prevailing disorder. There are extensive debates about appropriate recipients of the king's largesse; about who was entitled to counsel the king; about how corrupt favorites might be ousted; about how degenerate officials could be disciplined. These complaints were not new to the sixteenth century. Beginning in the late fourteenth century, writers increasingly articulated doubts that the king's prerogative of mercy was being used in a way that benefited society. In 1485, after nearly a century of factional strife, what the governing estates had in common— from the king and his favorites down to office-holders in the hundred—was an interest in maintaining order. The demand for punishment to replace pardon was clear by the early sixteenth century.

This ideology of justice was worked out and shared among the elites whose interests dominated. They articulated it in drama, just as they did in legal treatises, sermons, and chronicles. The ideology of justice turned on the threat of severe retribution for crimes committed by the lower orders, and of discipline of the elites by others who governed. The desire was to limit not only common felonies but—perhaps more significantly—also to curb the abuse of noble counsel and royal largesse. It was the king's obligation to keep the peace with the aid of his subjects by punishing felons and resolving disputes. Whether the Crown succeeded and how that end was sought are questions which have received extensive treatment from historians of late medieval and early modern England.[2] The role of punishment is a pivotal issue in the essentially opposing theories about how the law was used in governance and by whom.[3] Some claim that under the Tudors the Crown unilaterally directed the machinery of justice, enforcing its will through Parliament and the bench. Others insist that the Crown, either intentionally or inevitably, incorporated the values and objectives of those who served in the courts as officials and jurors.

Much has been written about practice as revealed through legal records, but little on the social values informing the law. We can begin to reconstruct the ideals and objectives of those who administered the law by examining representations of justice in the literature familiar to members of the governing estates, for they were the producers and consumers of literature in the fifteenth and sixteenth centuries. Just as popular verse and other genres earlier had been used in the literature of complaint and counsel, under the Tudors writers employed morality plays to voice their concerns about the changing nature of lordship and its perceived weaknesses, particularly as they affected the political community on a national level. The changes rung on the pattern of punishment and forgiveness are evident in the transformation of an ancient tale, referred to both as the Four Daughters of God and as the Parliament of Heaven. This allegorical representation of the trial and judgment of the faithless servant before his king was one of the most popular in the art and literature of medieval Europe. It continued to exert an influence in England well into the seventeenth century. Centered on the debate between sisters—Mercy and Peace on one side and Justice and Truth in opposition—this trope proved a fertile source of the arguments, settings, and symbols with which to explore the uses of judgment as dramatic representations of Parliament were moved from heaven to earth.

There have been excellent studies of what is said in early Tudor drama (Bevington; Fox; Walker). However, we need to move beyond the language of familiar texts and consider how plays were adapted self-consciously to convey the values of the creators and sponsors. Surprisingly little attention has been given to the metamorphoses in traditional figures and plots of early English drama. An analysis of these features in plays that draw on this allegory of judgment shows more than the internal development of a genre. It reveals the manipulation of ludic as well as literary traditions in the effort to promote an understanding of the way in which secular justice could serve the interests of the governing estates.

Patronage and Social Comment

Morality plays flourished for much of the sixteenth century, as the genre became a preferred form of social comment. This vitality is notable in light of sixteenth-century efforts to control religious drama (Lancashire xvii-xxxi; *Revels* 7–37). Until the 1530s little was done to oversee such productions in London or the counties. But during that decade, as Protestant reform began to disturb political and social life, the Crown first assumed control over the presentation of drama. Initially this only took the form of royal pressure on local authorities. The Crown wanted to suppress Robin Hood and kings plays, mystery cycles, Catholic pageants, saints plays, and the like, and instead promote antipapal propaganda. Under Cromwell this was done by underwriting politically acceptable moral interludes created by men such as Thomas Heywood, John Bale, and Nicholas Udall. By 1541, however, attacks were made on pieces featuring religious propaganda deemed insufficiently reformed. In 1543 a statute was passed prohibiting unorthodox plays, though it allowed interludes about vices and virtues that did not concern the interpretation of Scripture.

Henry's heirs took differing approaches. The 1543 statute was repealed in 1547, and Edward VI made no attempt to control works or companies sympathetic to his cause. Yet when some of those involved in Kett's rebellion took advantage of a public play to incite revolt, the Council temporarily prohibited all plays in the realm. Then in 1551 a proclamation required a license for all professional acting companies, and the Crown tried to devise controls over performance to guard against sedition. Mary turned the tables: a warning was issued about the performance of Protestant interludes, and licensing requirements were restated. During Elizabeth's reign, drama continued to thrive on social comment but blatant religious propaganda diminished as a result of proclamations early in her rule intended to reinforce the control over content begun under Edward and Mary (Collinson).

The source of patronage is an important factor in determining the social function of drama during this period. Certain forms of drama were associated with particular types of patronage; sponsorship, in turn, often was determined by the requirements of production. The mystery cycles, with their elaborate sets and many roles, called for extensive resources in terms of actors, craftspeople, and finances. These resources were found in towns and parishes, and so religious pageants were usually civic productions, with guilds presenting different parts of the cycle. Those plays that could be performed by small troupes and needed little in the way of staging were more likely to be realized through the support of an individual patron. By the late fifteenth century, morality plays were written by clerics and laymen. They were performed for religious instruction on feast days, or as evening entertainment for nobles. Their production might involve elaborate sets and many parts, or four men and a few props; they were acted by traveling players for townspeople, or by students for their fellows at college. It is the flexibility of the morality play that made it a popular form of entertainment for much of the sixteenth century, for its adaptable nature made it a valuable tool in the political wrangling and social advancement so necessary for the governing estates.

As the elaborate civic productions went into decline as a result of the efforts to control public religious propaganda, the streamlined moral interludes flourished. Tudor patrons had the resources to commission works, underwrite productions, and support small troupes of players. Such works, presented at the patron's court or as entertainment in other private and public venues, reflected values and positions pleasing to the patron and conveyed his or her views on current political, religious, and social issues. Moral interludes provided a vehicle for social comment unrestricted by financial concerns because of patronage, and they were less subject to regulation because performances were usually private and the players had powerful protectors.

Those who objected to uses of royal largesse such as the pardon were the same ones who sought it so assiduously. The literature of counsel and complaint was produced by men from the governing estates. England was ruled through the intersection of overlapping networks formed by the affinities of lordship and the Crown's administrative apparatus. Its governance was accomplished though a system of royal and public courts which required the participation of leading members of the community on local, county, and national levels in order to function (Given-Wilson; Rawcliffe and Flower; Gunn). Members of the nobility, gentry, yeomen, and artisans served in Parliament as justices, jurors, and the host of officials involved in the administration of the law. John Lydgate, John Fortescue, and George Ashby are typical of the fifteenth-century clerics, lawyers, and bureaucrats who criticized how the kingdom was governed and were actively engaged in its political life (Griffiths). William Cornyshe, Jr., William Dunbar, David Lindsey, John Skelton, Henry Medwall, and Nicholas Udall are just a few of the better-known playwrights from the early sixteenth century associated with the English and Scottish courts (Lancashire 409–28). The men who produced these plays were inextricably engaged in the very social processes they subjected to critique and sought to change.

Moral interludes, therefore, were themselves the product of an important form of largesse (Westfall; Walker; Anglo). The plays were presented in a bid for patronage or were commissioned, often for a particular event; they were performed to entertain, influence, and educate (Lancashire 373–408). There is a tendency to read these plays as didactic only in religious terms, yet they were intended to be politically and socially instructive as well (Bushnell; Walker 13–28). The patron exercised control over his or her production in terms of financial support and the subject of the play. The patron was also, in a significant sense, the object of the play: it was intended to reflect his or her values and magnificence. Public display and private entertainment provided ideal vehicles for presenting criticism and conveying political opinion. In short, the governing estates that were so dependent upon patronage were at the same time depended upon to be social critics.

An Allegorical Archetype of Judgment

Moralities were attractive to so many sixteenth-century writers as a form that values didacticism over narrative development. The morality provided a pattern within which one could fashion arguments on religious issues—and on political, economic, and social ones as well. Although influenced by the *psychomachia,* its origins were in the traditions of sermons and penitential works, literature urging repentance and teaching about God's pardon for sin. The earliest English moralities evoke a world in which man must sin and also must be saved; the necessity of the fall is unavoidable, but always amendable through repentance. The protagonist is never allowed truly to despair or be damned because the theological emphasis on divine mercy requires salvation. The salvation available through Christ's atonement is dramatized in allegory. Mankind is corrupted by vices but in the end seeks mercy, is repentant, and is saved through the assistance of virtues. These moralities teach how to rule the individual soul, and where to obtain aid when overwhelmed by corruption (Potter; Wickham 3–23). *Everyman* (1480–1500), a translation of a Dutch work, may now be the best known of these early English moralities. Perhaps more typical, in its content at least, is the play known as *Wisdom* (1461-85). Also representative of the late medieval morality are *Mankind* (1461-85), *Hickscorner* (1513-16), *Mundus et Infans* (1500-1520), and the fragmentary *Pride of Life* (1400-1425).

This conventional morality was transformed in the first half of the sixteenth century. A comparison of two plays that feature the Parliament of Heaven, *The Castle of Perseverance* (1400-1425) and Udall's *Respublica* (1553), reveals the striking metamorphosis of the traditional allegory and delineates the emerging ideology of justice. *The Castle of Perseverance* contains one of the best-known appearances of the Four Daughters of God in English literature. This play exemplifies the typical structure of moralities and attitudes about judgment commonly expressed in late medieval England. The dramatis personae include Deus Pater, Humanum Genus, and a panoply of Vices and Virtues struggling over the latter's soul. Although Humanum Genus is in a state of sin at the time of his death, because he dies while praying for forgiveness the play concludes with its central theme—the place of mercy in judgment. There is a debate about whether the soul of this faithless servant should be sent to heaven or hell. Each side of the argument is presented by a pair of advocates before the heavenly king acting as judge; these are the daughters of the king, Misericordia, Pax, Justicia, and Veritas. Justicia and Veritas demand that the letter of the law be met and the wicked soul damned, but Misericordia and Pax plead for clemency and salvation. Each Virtue is anxious to maintain her status in the kingdom: if there is always strict justice, Misericordia must flee; if pardon is available to all there is no place for Justicia. In the end it is the argument made by Pax that prevails and saves Humanum Genus. The Father, seated in his throne, announces, "Ego cogito cogitaciones pacis, non affliccionis. . . . To make my blysse perfyth / I menge wyth my most myth / Alle pes, sum treuthe, and sum ryth, / And most of my mercy" (lines 3562, 3570-74).

Respublica is the last literary work in England to use the Four Daughters in their usual roles, yet its similarity to the medieval allegory is largely superficial. In fact, the use of these familiar personifications indicates the extent of change in the value accorded by society to justice as punishment in strict fulfillment of the law. The play ordinarily is discussed in terms of Counter-Reformation propaganda because it was written for Mary and performed for her court. The prologue states that better times are coming for England now that Mary reigns. The widow Respublica, a figure for

England, becomes impoverished because she heeds the corrupt counselors masquerading as virtuous advisers. She is delivered from her wretched state only at the end, when the Four Daughters unmask the false counselors and restore harmony. These Virtues participate in rectifying the damage wrought on a once-innocent figure, but this is where the similarity to the medieval allegory ends. For there is barely a word of dissent among the sisters concerning the fate of the wrongdoers, and the divine king has been replaced by Nemesis, the goddess of redress. Peace does little besides complete the traditional quartet. Mercy is limited to bringing hope to Respublica and fetching Truth, who shows the widow the cause of her downfall and unmasks the culprits. Truth insists punishment must be executed by Nemesis, and Justice demands prosecution: "Severitee muste putt men in feare to transgresse; / Iustice muste geve eche manne that he dothe deserve" (lines 1863-64). Nemesis decides that Justice shall judge the Vices according to the law.

Transposing the primary action of the play and the scene of judgment in *Respublica* to a secular context affected not only the personifications used in the morality but also its very intent. Beneath the direct political satire of current events—the usual concern of literary historians—resides a more fundamental message about the role of royal justice in governance. This allegory is about the restoration of order to the community, but not through forgiveness and atonement. Employment of the familiar Four Daughters cannot conceal this radical departure from tradition. *Respublica* is concerned with the health of the English commonwealth and the maintenance of order through judgment. Though Mercy's first speech has portions usually associated with her traditional role, at heart it is about God's concern for the kingdom of England. Mercy and Peace surrender their active roles to Truth and Justice. The latter pair bring the corrupt counselors to the proper authority, a judge who combines secular and ecclesiastical jurisdiction. Justice no longer is a personification of theological concepts. Instead she has been transferred to the temporal sphere, and is one of a number of characters representing the reformation of government through England's courts.

Respublica is typical of the ways in which ludic traditions were manipulated as the role of justice in governance became the focus of political discourse. The figure of an archetypal mankind does not last, giving way instead to individuals with more fully developed characters. In general terms, there was a tendency for the soul to become a ruler, for the divine father to become a judge, and for Vices and Virtues to become counselors. And there are new figures that represent particular estates or the kingdom as a whole. The loss of eschatological concentration and an increased emphasis on mortal life and prudential ethics qualified virtue for reward and left transgression open to penalty in this life. So long as the central figure was mankind, a happy ending was the only possibility, but once dramatists bifurcated and then individualized the protagonists they created tragic moralities, too (Potter 117). Long before Portia asked for mercy, English writers were exploiting traditional literary and dramatic forms as they invented new venues for debating, threatening, and sometimes fulfilling the demands of justice. The moral interlude was an ideal vehicle for polemic, with its didactic focus and flexible structure. The subject of dramatic dispute expanded. Many of these plays were concerned not with the soul, but with the kingdom; not with repentance, but with discipline. They explore how the commonweal is secured, maintained, or regained through good governance, and more specifically through the administration of justice.

Dramatic Justice and English Governance

A review of this allegory in its varied sixteenth-century permutations demonstrates how a familiar form was overlaid with new meanings for contemporaries. Although these plays still treat the means of the soul's salvation, they now also express a sharp anxiety about civil order, authority, and control. This is evident in the use of justice figures, in the setting—in legal and royal courts—and in the use of legal terminology. The dominant subject shifts from divine judgment to the administration of English justice.

Consider first the "careers" of the Four Daughters. Three of the four continue to appear, but in a markedly diminished capacity compared to the medieval personifications. Peace's sharply truncated role in *Respublica* is indicative of her fate in sixteenth-century drama as a whole. Peace appears briefly in two moralities, *Albion, Knight* (1537-65) and *Impatient Poverty* (1547-58). Truth similarly recedes into the background. In *Horestes* (c. 1567) she is brought in with Duty at the end to discuss the right way to rule the kingdom. Truth, along with Chastity and Good Counsel, helps the king in Lindsey's *Ane Satire of the Thrie Estaitis* (1535-40) to overcome the influence of the vices. A female figure, Verity, appears in Bale's *King Johan* (1530-36), representing religious truth or the reformation spirit.

A male figure, Conscience, along with Justice, attempts to reform the wicked king in *Appius and Virginia* (1559-68). Conscience also has a small role, similar to that usually played by Truth, in *Impatient Poverty*. Mercy appeared in drama more frequently than Peace and Truth, albeit as particular aspects of the fuller medieval understanding of the virtue.[4] Mercy is recognizable through its relationships to the protagonist and other virtue and vice figures. For example, we find Good Deeds in *Everyman*, Pity in *Hickscorner*, Charity in *King Darius* (1559-65) and *Youth* (1513-29), Good Hope in Skelton's *Magnyfycence* (1513-16), Mercy in *Mankind*, God's Merciful Promises in *Lusty Juventus* (1547-53), and Charity and Humility in Thomas Lupton's *All for Money* (1559-77).

Justice is the daughter who triumphs, and justice is the virtue that is given precedence: to a greater extent than the other three Virtues, she remains a full character. The names by which this figure is known in the plays signal what was valued, and the fact that some plays feature multiple personifications of justice indicate its significance for the theme and resolution of the play. Justice appears under that name in *Albion, Knight* and *Appius and Virginia*. There is Redress in *Magnyfycence*, Equity in *King Darius*, Imperial Majesty in *King Johan*, Divine Correction in *Ane Satire of Thrie Estaitis*, Trial, Proof, and Execution in Thomas Preston's *Cambises* (1558-69), and Conscience and Reward in *Appius and Virginia*. The frequent presence of judges and magistrates in the plays also signals the importance of legal administration. So we find Old Christmas judging rebels in the fragmentary *Good Order* (1500-1533), the Judge in *The Contention between Liberality and Prodigality* (1567-68), Authority and Correction in George Wapull's *Tide Tarrieth No Man* (1576), Jupiter in Heywood's *Weather* (1500-1533), Judge Daniel in *Nice Wanton*, Good Remedy in *Wealth and Health* (1553-57), Judge Severity in Ulpian Fulwell's *Like Will to Like* (1562-68), the Margrave Severus in George Gascoigne's *The Glasse of Governement* (1575), and Judex in *The Most Virtuous and Godly Susanna* (1568-69). There are even corrupt judges: All for Money in the play of that name, Sisamnes in *Cambises*, and Appius in *Appius and Virginia*.[5]

Judgment scenes were common in moral interludes enjoying popularity in the century before the opening of public theaters. Audiences continued to have an appetite for the portrayal of divine justice, yet there was a taste for enacting it in a secular context. Writers often used classical or biblical stories to provide the examples; so we have *Appius and Virginia, Cam-*

bises, Godly Queen Hester (1525-29), and *The Most Virtuous and Godly Susanna.* Many plays feature English courts and their personnel bringing charges against and trying evil counselors and petty criminals—characters who in earlier centuries would have been simple Vices. So, for example, in addition to the judges mentioned above, *Nice Wanton* includes Clerk, Jury, and Bailiff, *Liberality and Prodigality* Constable, Tipstaves, Clerk, and Cryer, and *The Most Virtuous and Godly Susanna* Cryer and Bailiff. Literary enactment of judgment, particularly when it involved the debate of Justice and Mercy, had long been presented in the form and vocabulary of English law (Stokes; McCune). During the sixteenth century, as the dramatic focus moved from the salvation of the soul to the punishment of vice, trial scenes in the plays were more fully realized in terms familiar to contemporary audiences. *Liberality and Prodigality* finishes with a lengthy and detailed trial, and similar scenes conclude *Like Will to Like, Tide Tarrieth No Man, The Most Virtuous and Godly Susanna,* and *Nice Wanton.*[6]

Abstract debates about divine justice were displaced in the move to a secular context by the language and personnel of English courts and, most strikingly, by their punishments. Although straightforward hanging is the most common fate of vice figures, there are also instances of mitigation. Sedition begs for but is not allowed to seek sanctuary in *King Johan* (lines 2474-75). Claudius is exiled instead of executed in *Appius and Virginia* (43), and in *Good Order* Gluttony is sentenced to abjure the kingdom, and the process is described (490). Severus, in *The Glasse of Governement,* condemns the evildoers to public whipping, the cucking stool, and banishment from the city (87). Judge Nemo, in *The Three Ladies of London* (1581), condemns those brought before him to whipping and prison. Few among the governing estates would argue with this judge's desire to "devise such punishment for the malefactors, as may be a terror hereafter to all parasites how they abuse the name of an officer, or entyse the children of any burghers."[7]

On the surface it may seem that these moral interludes illustrate only a shift in the locus of moral judgment from the next world to this one. However, common to these works is an emphasis on discipline and governance, whatever the setting. The majority of morality plays from this period represent the effort to reestablish or impose order, whether on an individual or national basis, through the administration of justice. In many of the plays, what in the past would have been a soul torn between vices and virtues became a ruler—or the kingdom under the aegis of a neglectful ruler—torn between good and evil factions in the political community. So we find Magnyfycence, King Darius, Cambises, and King Johan in the plays which bear their names, as well as Principality in *Albion, Knight,* Rex Humanitas in *Ane Satire of Thrie Estaitis,* and Assuerus in *Godly Queen Hester.* The medieval personifications of vice and virtue were transformed into specific good and evil counselors and characters representing the various estates in the English body politic. From the elaborate religious pageantry of *Wisdom* through the comic debate over generosity presented for Elizabeth in *Liberality and Prodigality,* moral interludes voiced condemnation of that which threatened the body politic and recommendation of the proper roles for each estate.

This discourse on governance is best embodied in works that treat the social problems infecting the kingdom due to the influence of corrupt advisers, such as *Magnyfycence, King Johan, Godly Queen Hester, Ane Satire of Thrie Estaitis, Albion, Knight,* and *Respublica.* In each the action turns on how the ruler responds to the efforts of counselors and the estates to exert influence. The young ruler, Magnyfycence, is corrupted by a host of false courtiers and rejects the advice of Measure. King Assuerus is nearly undone by his depraved adviser, Hamon, only to be saved by the Jewish community in the form of Hester and Mardocheus. In *Albion, Knight* the Vices discuss their plot to foment strife among the Lords Temporal, Lords Spiritual, the Commons, and Principality, the king. At the same time they plan to separate Albion Knight, the figure for England, from Dame Plenty, Rest, and Peace. In *King Johan* the widow England and her son Communality are abused by the clergy. Sedition and his relatives persuade Clergy, Nobility, and Civil Order to rebel against the king. *Ane Satire of Thrie Estaitis* in many ways epitomizes these plays about disorder and governance. The king, Rex Humanitas, is rid of his false counselors, Flattery and Deceit among others, through the aid of the justice figure, Divine Correction. The evils of the realm are corrected through the forum of a parliament, where the king is aided in his reform by John the Commonweal. John brings charges of injustice against those forces corrupting the polity, and later joins the king and other estates in parliament. Although he is atypical in terms of his extensive role in government, a figure representing the people of England or the Commons is not unusual in these interludes.[8]

Punishment Personified and Pardon Eclipsed

Clearly, English writers and audiences in this period conceived of authority in terms of their real-life experience. The degree of this paradigmatic shift is most obvious in the characters establishing order and in the associated iconography. That justice and mercy were no longer seen predominantly as theological abstracts is powerfully evident in the gender of their personifications.[9] Though typically virtues were personified as women in allegories, there was a medieval tradition of Mercy acting as a father confessor.[10] So it is not all that strange that the mercy figure is a man in some of the morality plays: Good Hope in *Magnyfycence,* Mercy in *Mankind,* Pity in *Hickscorner,* and Charity in *Youth* are all male. However, there is no such tradition for Justice, and so it is very striking that justice figures in drama after 1500 are usually male; Justice and Nemesis in *Respublica* are notable exceptions. Sometimes even Justice's relatives become male. In *Albion, Knight* Peace is Justice's brother, and in *King Darius* Justice is the exiled brother of Equity. Needless to say, judges, magistrates, court officials, and jurors are always men. In the classical tradition the Cardinal Virtues were personified as women, as were the advocates in the ancient Parliament of Heaven. However, the producers and consumers of English morality plays were thinking in terms of secular courts, not of virtues familiar from the Ciceronian or Macrobian inheritance.

This change in gender certainly is related to Protestant objections to images and allegory. The iconoclastic impulse that made artists and printers reluctant to produce images which might be misconstrued may well have dissuaded writers from using customary mimetic forms on the stage. The substitution of a male figure would not offend zealous reformers but still could convey divine authority. The female figure of Justice continued to appear in other representational forms, especially painting and prints. However, this female personification appears in contexts in which the artist could obviously allude to the humanist tradition. That the justice characters in these plays are male probably stems from Protestant anxiety over the meaning of a woman with a sword. Thought it is true that monarchs were ordinarily identified through the attributes of scepter, orb, and crown, swords also had a close association with royal justice (King; Billington). This is indicated by the swords used in English coronation ceremonies. One sword, known as the curtana, had its point broken off and symbolized royal mercy. The remaining swords symbolized royal justice—a sharp one

for the laity, and a dull one for the clergy. These swords were representative
of one of the clauses in the coronation oath in which the monarch was
asked to swear that both justice and mercy would be used in rendering
judgment (Legg xix-xxxi; Richardson). Henry VIII and Edward VI used
the icon of the sword to great effect, yet there are very few pictures of
Mary or Elizabeth which include a sword. Artists shied away from Justicia
with the dual heritage—a woman with a sword symbolized justice in both
the classical and Catholic traditions. Elizabeth went to lengths to present
herself as Astrae and not as one of the Daughters of God.

Accompanying this inversion in the engenderment of justice is a change
in its dominant symbol. Well into the fourteenth century, the iconographic
identification of Justice was through her possession of the balance, though
this sometimes was supplemented with a sword. The balance was used to
represent the psychostasis, or weighing of souls, on Doomsday. However,
in the fifteenth century the sword is added with increasing frequency to
artistic depictions of Justice, and by the sixteenth century it has nearly
eclipsed the balance as the symbol of judgment.[11] Fortunately, reference
to such iconographic detail is not absent altogether, although it is unusual
in these plays. For example, in *Appius and Virginia*, there is an explicit
description of Justice pointing his sword at Appius's chest. God's Judgment
strikes Moros with a sword in William Wager's *The Longer Thou Livest, The
More Fool Thou Art* (1560-68). Divine Correction mentions the sword he
uses against Iniquity in *Ane Satire of Thrie Estaitis;* there is also reference
to his wings.[12] The vice, Nicholas Newfangle, in *Like Will to Like* makes
three references to the sword carried by Severity, and Sisamnes is executed,
and then flayed, with the Executioner's sword in *Cambises.*[13]

Just as representations of mercy were crowded off the stage by the
increased roles for justice, there was little place for objects symbolizing
the possibility of forgiveness in judgment. Visually as well as verbally,
in early Tudor drama justice was meant to be understood primarily as
retribution. The iconic attributes of dramatic characters responsible for the
restoration of order served to legitimate the real figures asserting authority
through the auspices of secular justice. In England men wrote the laws,
administered justice, and executed punishment. These plays show that
concern about the immediate uses of justice in secular courts had displaced
more abstract debate about theological issues. The abuse of justice and
mercy in governance gave rise to festering social ills; there was no time for
feminine aspects of the godhead when the commonwealth was threatened.

Pardon for those on trial is hard to come by in these plays. Mercy and Peace always triumph in the medieval tradition of the Parliament of Heaven, but the balance of the scales had tipped decisively for Justice and Truth under the Tudors. Of the fourteen plays of judgment listed above, only four feature the pardon of any of the vice figures, and those grants of mercy are given grudgingly on specific grounds. The evil counselor, Claudius, is pardoned only at the insistence of the wronged Virginia in *Appius and Virginia,* with the substitution of exile for hanging (43). The final scene in *Liberality and Prodigality* concerns Prodigality's claims of repentance and pleas for the Prince's mercy; the Judge admits to being moved by his sincerity and agrees at least to submit the petition for a pardon to the Crown (lines 1280-1312). In *King Johan* Imperial Majesty pardons the three estates, Nobility, Clergy, and Civil Order, upon their promises to punish the evil counselors who led them to betray King Johan. Imperial Majesty also promises the chief Vice, Sedition, a pardon in return for his confession of treason, only to dispatch him to Tyburn to be drawn, hanged, and quartered, and his head set on London Bridge (lines 2318-592). Divine Correction pardons the king in *Ane Satire of Thrie Estaitis,* and the Vices of lust that led him astray, but three other Vices are hanged near the end of the play (lines 1703-1860, 3998-4271). Nemesis pardons Adulation in *Respublica* after he promises to advance the gain of the commonwealth over his own. However, she delivers Avarice to an officer of the court to give judgment, and tells Justice to judge Insolence and Oppression (lines 1880-83, 1908-09, 1911-19) Not infrequently morality plays showed the detrimental effects on the kingdom when royal generosity becomes profligacy, and the pardon seems to be perilously close in this ideology of justice to the abuse of other forms of royal largesse.

The relatively private act of pardon, when selectively used, could factor nicely into the royal authority used to promote order. But it could never compare for drama with the theatrical ceremony of public punishment. As part of the ritual of execution for capital crimes, felons were expected to demonstrate penitence and contrition publicly, acknowledging the justness of their execution from the gallows before those assembled for the display (Carlton; Sharpe; Smith).[14] The general pattern in these speeches was for the condemned to admit he or she rightly had been judged by law, and to accept the penalty. The speakers emphasized that their fate was representative of that in store for others who would sin against God and England. Of course, there were those who refused to comply with this expectation of seeking forgiveness, and this, too, is preserved by the unrepentant in drama.[15] Three morality plays include scaffold speeches, a practice emblematic of the value placed on exemplary justice. In *Like Will to Like, Ane Satire of Thrie Estaitis,* and *The Most Virtuous and Godly Susanna,* just before the malefactors are executed, they admit their guilt and beg those watching to learn from their wretched mistakes. Punishment purged the body politic of corrupt elements and restored health. The felon's last words secured his or her reincorporation in the community through acceptance of the dominant ideology, the admission of guilt, and so the possibility of forgiveness—in the next life. Pardon again had been displaced.

Parallel Changes in Legal Practice

The complaints of abuse in the plays clearly reflect contemporary practices in England. Let's begin with accusations of the abuses of forgiveness. There was good reason to claim that irresponsible use of the traditional forms of mercy available in the legal process featured largely in the failure of courts to administer justice. Exploiting ready means to mitigate the capital sanction for felony was common among all those caught up in crime and its sanctioning. Many managed to avoid punishment altogether. For example, some felons escaped trial through the privilege of ecclesiastical sanctuary. There were also places that enjoyed the right of permanent sanctuary through royal grant. This secular and jurisdictional privilege kept criminals out of the ambit of royal justice.[16] Because the system relied to a great extent on lay participation, there were many ways to frustrate prosecution and punishment. For example, neighbors could fail to raise the hue and cry, or the presentment jury could decide there was not enough evidence to justify a charge. Not all criminal charges were brought on behalf of the Crown. Victims of surviving kin could bring private suits, known as appeals, against a suspect. These often resulted in private arbitrations and settlements (Whittick; Powell, "Arbitration").

Those who were tried potentially could profit from actions available to them and to those sitting in judgment. Many of the men and women tried by jury benefited from jury nullification of the law. This occurred when jurors favored a defendant whom they thought had committed the crime charged. Juries regularly adjusted the law and the facts to ensure that the defendant would not be executed (Green). Judges, too, had a variety of means to ensure that not all the condemned were executed. The bench played a decisive role in the application of a privilege meant in theory only for the clergy. In practice, benefit of clergy was granted to many laymen. By the end of the fourteenth century it frequently was allowed to anyone who could pass a literacy test or even feign literacy (Gabel). Judges also could override a jury's guilty verdict, and sentence the accused to lesser forms of punishment such as outlawry, imprisonment, and fines (Bellamy, *Crime*).

Finally, there was the king's pardon, the constant object of public outcry about corrupt administration of the law. Royal pardons were granted in a variety of ways, and for many different purposes. Pardons of course *(de cursu)* were available to those charged with excusable homicide. By the fourteenth century they were issued by Chancery on judges' recommendations. Pardons of grace *(de gratia)* were granted as the king's prerogative to felons not technically entitled to escape punishment. In actuality, the king's pardon was available to almost anyone before trial if he or she could pay for it in Chancery. During the fourteenth and fifteenth centuries pardons were offered on a large scale on condition of a term of military service. Sovereigns also offered general pardons through Parliament on such occasions as coronations or after subduing revolts. Although they often contained exclusions, pardons were used by the Crown as a political tool, to reward supporters, raise funds, and control enemies. There were efforts in Parliament throughout the late Middle Ages to limit and control pardons of grace by statute, yet these were never sufficiently enforced.[17]

The ideology of justice given voice in these morality plays mirrored contemporaneous changes in the administration of the law. The Tudor era is notable for repeated joint efforts by the Crown and Parliament to eradicate the worst abuses of the justice system through innovations in its administration and through statutes (Milsom; Baker, "Refinement"). The evolution of the conciliar courts, particularly Chancery and Star Chamber, provides a clear example of the Crown's manipulation of the law to bolster its authority. Prerogative courts did not take business away from the older courts; rather, they attracted the suitors unwilling to tolerate the expense and delay of common-law procedure. Chancery's distinctiveness lay in its administrative powers. It was a forum similar to many other informal ones for arbitration and mediation that sought equitable judgments; its appeal was in the force of central bureaucracy, not in a special kind of justice. The Council in Star Chamber also used procedures not available in common-law courts. Among other matters, it had jurisdiction over cases of corruption in offices and institutions. This meant that it investigated and punished those thought to interfere with the administration of justice. In the common-law courts, a number of practices gradually developed during the later Middle Ages which contributed to an active and independent prosecution by the Crown in the sixteenth century (Cockburn, "Trial"; Baker, "Criminal Courts"; Langbein). Generally speaking, there was a tendency to relieve individuals in the community of the responsibilities of accusation, investigation, and trial, and to rely instead on bureaucrats. This enabled judicial control of courtroom procedure and directed the outcome of the trial.

At the same time definitions of felonies were refined as the category of capital felony repeatedly was expanded to include more crimes. The process of mitigation also necessitated that distinctions be made in the seriousness of acts. Crown and Parliament apparently sought to achieve greater order by executing the worst offenders and making certain that most others received some form of punishment. The final judicial assault on the privilege of permanent sanctuary began in 1516, and sanctuary rights were whittled away under the Reformation Parliament though not completely abolished until 1623 (Ives). Benefit of clergy rapidly came under the control of the Crown through legislative efforts. Both bench and Parliament were eager to reduce ecclesiastical authority and refine the use of this privilege to the government's ends (Bellamy, "Benefit"). Restrictions on its use began in 1489; other conditions were added over the next fifty years, which further limited its availability. In 1576 an act gave lay authorities complete control over benefit of clergy. Such changes also ensured that lesser sanctions were available. Imprisonment, fines, and corporal punishment were ordered with increasing frequency. And new methods of sanctioning wrongdoers were introduced: transportation and forced labor could be the sentence for those who had been reprieved from execution (Jenkins).

The royal prerogative to pardon was employed throughout the sixteenth century, often just as it had been in the past, for political ends. Parliament, however, continued in the attempt to bar the worst offenders from qualifying. Public complaints of the Crown's abuse of the general pardon prompted Parliament in continuing efforts to impose restrictive terms on that pardon's availability and to legislate the restoration of capital punishment for the most offensive felonies by specifically listing them as crimes that were barred from mitigation. By the end of the century Parliament did manage to exert closer control over the availability and qualifications for pardons, but the Tudor sovereigns never stopped issuing general pardons to commemorate events, such as their coronations, in order to increase popular support (Blatcher).

Order and the Common Weal

Writers and their patrons exploited the traditional representation of authority and legitimate foci of concern in drama in order to persuade their fellows of the validity of their ideology. By the mid-sixteenth century morality plays were an acknowledged public format allowing these estates to claim a share in, and also to criticize, the authority of the Crown. Under Tudor rule the age-old struggle between vices and virtues for the soul, which is resolved only by divine forgiveness, had been turned inside out. English audiences in the sixteenth century instead were shown that the struggle between corrupt and righteous forces within the body politic could be resolved through secular judgment and punishment. Early Tudor drama forcefully articulates contemporary fears of disorder and the belief that peace can be maintained through royal justice. Yet the frequent appearance of rulers and their counselors should not overshadow the fact that these morality plays explore the respective roles of each estate in governing the kingdom. These plays are about the preservation of the commonwealth, and about the obligations of each estate necessary to that goal.

Audiences are told of royal obligation as well as prerogative: the need to secure the common good required the execution of justice, in the form of punishment if need be. When John the Commonweal is given a place in Parliament, Correction claims, "Blist is that realme that hes ane prudent King, / Quhilk dois delyte to heir the veritie, / Punisching thame that plainlie dois maling / Contrair the Common-weill and equitie" (*Ane Satire of Thrie Estaitis,* lines 3810–13). Albion is told by the Vice Injury, "Sir, ye ought to be contented best of all / Where justice is treated with due equity; / And where no favour nor meed should be; / And, when reason hath tried there every deal, / That such an act were good for the common weal" (*Albion, Knight* 121). Severus expresses similar beliefs in *The Glasse of Governement:* "It is a happy common wealth where Justice may be ministered with severitie, and where no mediacions or sutes may wrest the sentence of the Lawe" (86). Just as the inclusion of reference to the common weal indicates the kingdom was no longer seen as a private interest, so the inclusion of personifications of other estates emphasizes the cooperative nature of national reform.

Morality plays preserve a debate over the role of counsel in a monarchy, and the responsibility of all in the kingdom to maintain the common good. In sixteenth-century England justice was presented as the icon of governmental authority, an authority that could flourish only with the participation of each estate and the submission of all in the body politic to the ultimate sovereignty of the monarch. But this authority was not embodied solely in the monarch.[18] Studies of Tudor political iconography tend to emphasize a nascent "absolutist" tendency in the public displays, rituals, and entertainments promoted by these rulers. But each of the Tudors, for differing reasons, needed the endorsement and support of as many governing factions as possible. Beginning with Henry VII, they manipulated drama to promote the emerging ideology of justice, which privileged retribution over reconciliation, and royal over local jurisdiction. Yet those who wrote, patronized, and enjoyed these plays were calling out not only for reform of national interests through the courts, but also for a hand in the administration of that justice. Under the aegis of royal justice Parliaments were called, kings chastened, counselors exiled or executed, and criminals controlled.

The structure of morality plays and the crucial role of patronage in the century before the opening of public theaters allowed drama to function as a vehicle for the demands of those who also wished to rule, albeit under the ultimate authority of the monarch. These plays reveal the manipulation of literary and ludic traditions that occurred as those involved in governance attempted both to appease and cajole other members of the polity. A common thread running through many of these plays, however faintly, is the recognition that the kingdom was a commonwealth. The ideal of order secured by the sword of royal justice was accepted at some cost to the autonomy of local and regional lordship. At the same time, those lords in the ruling estates sought to define their place in the body politic and to describe how that sword would be wielded. The reform of governance through justice for the good of the commonwealth was the subject of a discourse that shaped both the representation and reality of English polity.

Notes

1. I am grateful to Mac Nelson and Tom Green for their comments on this article in previous versions. The dates provided for the plays are taken from Houle.

2. The issues involved in this debate increasingly are presented in terms of contemporary notions of good lordship and the forms taken by the obligations it engendered. In general, the concept of "bastard feudalism" is being displaced by studies of the forms taken by political patronage. The following indicate the range of these studies of lordship and kingship. For the late Middle Ages, see Lander; Bellamy, *Bastard Feudalism;* Bean; Horrox; and Powell, *Kingship*. For the sixteenth century, see Elton; Starkey.

3. This is an important element in the work of Green, Bellamy, and Powell among others working on the medieval period. Influential interpretations for the early modern period include Herrup; Hay et al.; Cockburn, *History;* and Langbein.

4. The multifaceted nature of mercy for medieval culture is evident in her associated icons; she might be holding balm, an alms box, an olive branch, a lily, or she might be baring her breast.

5. Justice and Mercy also appear in numerous other plays which fall outside the compass of this essay. A glance at the index in Lancashire will show the popularity of the Four Daughters in a wide variety of public entertainments.

6. For other plays involving acts of judgment, see *Good Order, King Johan, Ane Satire of Thrie Estaitis, Weather,* and *All for Money.*

7. There are similar statements about the need for such redress in *Appius* 43; *Cambises* 178-79; *Wealth and Health* 304-08.

8. Already mentioned are the characters in *King Johan, Albion, Knight,* and *Respublica;* others are Commons Cry and Commons Complaint in *Cambises* and Commons in *Horestes.*

9. The medieval iconography of mercy and justice has received significant attention (Mâle; Tuve; Norman; O'Reilly), but there is comparatively little for the early modern period (King; Fleischer).

10. For an example of Mercy as a father confessor, see Bazire; for another study of male and female roles for virtues, see Spivack.

11. Michael the Archangel, another figure commonly used throughout Europe in representations of the Last Judgment, experiences this same iconic change. This is discussed at length by Mâle. O'Reilly and Norman similarly point out the reciprocal influences among literary, dramatic, and visual portrayal, and the tendency during the late Middle Ages for both vices and virtues to be represented with greater individuality and more concrete attributes. For related discussions, see Egerton; Harbison.

12. This probably is an indication of the conflation of Justice with St. Michael. Traditionally associated with Doomsday, this archangel was represented with sword and balance: the balance for psychostasis, and the sword to threaten eternal punishment to those weighed in the balance and found lacking. For the complex interrelationships in theater and art during the late Middle Ages, see Mâle; Muir; Potter.

13. Nemesis in *Respublica* is said to be recognized by her wheel and wings, which show the extent of her rule, as well as by the rudder she carries.

14. For a comparative view of late medieval French public rituals of punishment, see Cohen.

15. So, for example, in *The Most Virtuous and Godly Susanna*, the Elders confess while their hands are tied to the stake, but the Vice, Ill Report, refuses to repent or pray and is hanged.

16. If a criminal could reach a church or churchyard before being seized, he or she had forty days either to surrender for trial or to abjure the realm and leave by the nearest port (Thornley).

17. The standard work for the period up to the fourteenth century is Hurnard. There is no single work on the king's pardon in the later Middle Ages, but see Green chs. 1-4; Bellamy, *Crime* ch. 6.

18. "The paradox is that the more the king is characterised as kingly, self-complete, royal *in himself*, the more he covers up the ulterior source of his royalty in the body of the realm. Conversely, it is precisely through the monarch's natural frailties, as if through the holes in a tattered robe, that one sees his politic body, the true object of patriotic loyalty, the *corpus mysticum* of the nation" (Womack 125).

Works Cited

Albion, Knight. Six Anonymous Plays. 2nd ser. Ed. John S. Farmer. 1906. New York: Barnes & Noble, 1966. 117-32.

Anglo, Sydney. *Spectacle, Pageantry, and Early Tudor Policy.* Oxford: Claredon, 1969.

Appius and Virginia. Five Anonymous Plays. 4th ser. Ed. John S. Farmer. 1908. Guildford: Traylen, 1966. 1-46.

Baker, J. H. "Criminal Courts and Procedure at Common Law 1550-1800." *Crime in England, 1550-1800.* Ed. J. S. Cockburn. Princeton: Princeton UP, 1977. 15-48.

———. "The Refinement of English Criminal Jurisprudence, 1500-1848." *Crime and Criminal Justice in Europe and Canada.* Ed. Louis A. Knafla. Calgary: Wilfrid Laurier UP, 1981. 17-42.

Bale, John. *King Johan. Four Morality Plays.* Ed. Peter Happé. Harmondsworth: Penguin, 1979.

Bazire, Joyce. " 'Mercy and Justice.' " *Neuphilologische Mitteilungen* 83 (1982): 178-91.

Bean, J. M. W. *From Lord to Patron: Lordship in Late Medieval England.* Philadelphia: U Pennsylvania P, 1989.

Bellamy, J. G. *Bastard Feudalism and the Law.* London: Routledge, 1989.

———. "Benefit of Clergy in the Fifteenth and Sixteenth Centuries." *Criminal Law and Society in Late Medieval and Tudor England.* New York: St. Martin's, 1984.

———. *Crime and Public Order in England in the Later Middle Ages.* Toronto: U of Toronto P, 1973.

Bevington, David. *Tudor Drama and Politics: A Critical Approach to Topical Meaning.* Cambridge: Harvard UP, 1968.

Billington, Sandra. *Mock Kings in Medieval Society and Renaissance Drama.* Oxford: Clarendon, 1991.

Blatcher, Marjorie. *The Court of King's Bench, 1450-1550: A Study in Self-Help.* London: Athlone, 1978.

Bushnell, Rebecca W. *Tragedies of Tyrants: Political Thought and Theater in the English Renaissance.* Ithaca: Cornell UP, 1990.

Carlton, Charles. "The Rhetoric of Death: Scaffold Confessions in Early Modern England." *Southern Speech Communication Journal* 49 (1983): 66-79.

The Castle of Perseverance. The Macro Plays. Ed. Mark Eccles. EETS os 262. London: Oxford UP, 1969. 1-111.

Cockburn, J. S. *A History of English Assizes, 1558-1714.* Cambridge: Cambridge UP, 1972.

———. "Trial by the Book?: Fact and Theory in the Criminal Process, 1558-1625." *Legal Records and the Historian.* Ed. J. H. Baker. London: Royal Historical Soc., 1978.

Cohen, Esther. *The Crossroads of Justice: Law and Culture in Late Medieval France.* Leiden: Brill, 1993.

Coleman, Janet. *Medieval Readers and Writers, 1350-1400.* London: Hutchinson, 1981.

Collinson, Patrick. *From Iconoclasm to Iconophobia: The Cultural Impact of the Second English Reformation.* Reading: U of Reading, 1986.

The Contention between Liberality and Prodigality. Ed. John S. Farmer. London: Oxford UP, 1913.

Edgerton, Samuel Y., Jr. "Icons of Justice." *Past & Present* 89 (1980): 23-38.

Elton, G. R. *Policy and Police: The Enforcement of the Reformation in the Age of Thomas Cromwell.* Cambridge: Cambridge UP, 1972.

Everyman, and Medieval Miracle Plays. Ed. A. C. Cawley. New York: Dutton, 1959.

Ferguson, Arthur B. *The Articulate Citizen and the English Renaissance.* Durham: Duke UP, 1965.

Fleischer, Martha Hester. *The Iconography of the English History Play.* Salzburg: Institut für Englische Sprache und Literatur, 1974.

Fox, Alistair. *Politics and Literature in the Reigns of Henry VII and Henry VIII.* Oxford: Blackwell, 1989.

Frost, George L., and Ray Nash. "*Good Order*: A Morality Fragment." *Studies in Philology* 41 (1944): 483-91.

Fulwell, Ulpian. *Like Will to Like. The Dramatic Writings of Ulpian Fulwell.* Ed. John S. Farmer. 1906. New York: Barnes & Noble, 1966.

Gabel, Leona C. *Benefit of Clergy in England in the Later Middle Ages.* Northampton, MA: Smith College, 1929.

Gascoigne, George. *The Glasse of Governement. The Complete Works of George Gascoigne.* 2 vols. Ed. John W. Cunliffe. 1907-10. New York: Greenwood, 1969. 2: 1-90.

Given-Wilson, C. "The King and the Gentry in Fourteenth-Century England." *Transactions of the Royal Historical Society* 5th ser. 37 (1987): 87-102.

Godly Queen Hester. Six Anonymous Plays. 2nd ser. Ed. John S. Farmer. 1906. New York: Barnes & Noble, 1966. 245-87.

Green, Thomas Andrew. *Verdict According to Conscience: Perspectives on the English Criminal Trial Jury, 1200-1800.* Chicago: U of Chicago P, 1985.

Griffiths, R. A. "Public and Private Bureaucracies in England and Wales in the Fifteenth Century." *Transactions of the Royal Historical Society* 5th ser. 30 (1980): 109-30.

Gunn, S. J. "The Courtiers of Henry VII." *English Historical Review* 108 (1993): 23-49.

Harbison, Craig. *The Last Judgment in Sixteenth-Century Northern Europe: A Study of the Relation between Art and the Reformation.* New York: Garland, 1976.

Hay, Douglas, et al., eds. *Albion's Fatal Tree: Crime and Society in Eighteenth-Century England.* New York: Pantheon, 1975.

Herrup, Cynthia B. *The Common Peace: Participation and the Criminal Law in Seventeenth-Century England.* Cambridge: Cambridge UP, 1987.

Heywood, John. *Weather. Dramatic Writings of John Heywood.* Ed. John S. Farmer. 1905. New York: Barnes & Noble, 1966. 91–135.

Hickscorner. Six Anonymous Plays. Ed. John S. Farmer. 1905. New York: Barnes & Noble, 1966. 123–60.

Horestes. Quellen des weltlichen Dramas in England vor Shakespeare. Ed. Alois Brandl. Quellen und Forschungen zur Sprach- und Kulturgeschichte der germanischen Volker 80. Strassburg: Trubner, 1898.

Horrox, Rosemary. *Richard III: A Study of Service.* Cambridge: Cambridge UP, 1989.

Houle, Peter. *The English Morality and Related Drama.* Hamden, CT: Archon, 1972.

Hurnard, Naomi D. *The King's Pardon for Homicide before A.D. 1307.* Oxford: Clarendon, 1969.

Impatient Poverty. Recently Recovered "Lost" Tudor Plays, with Some Others. Ed. John S. Farmer. 1907. Guildford: Traylen, 1966. 311–48.

Ives, E. W. "Crime, Sanctuary, and Royal Authority under Henry VIII: The Exemplary Sufferings of the Savage Family." *On the Laws and Customs of England.* Ed. Morris Arnold et al. Chapel Hill: U of North Carolina P, 1981. 296–320.

Jenkins, Philip. "From Gallows to Prison? The Execution Rate in Early Modern England." *Criminal Justice History* 7 (1986): 51–71.

King, John N. *Tudor Royal Iconography: Literature and Art in an Age of Religious Crisis.* Princeton: Princeton UP, 1989.

King Darius. Anonymous Plays. 3rd ser. Ed. John S. Farmer. 1906. Guildford: Traylen, 1966. 41–92.

Lancashire, Ian. *Dramatic Texts and Records of Britain: A Chronological Topography to 1558.* Toronto: U of Toronto P, 1984.

Lander, J. R. *Government and Community: England, 1450–1509.* London: Arnold, 1980.

Langbein, John H. *Prosecuting Crime in the Renaissance: England, Germany, France.* Cambridge: Harvard UP, 1974.

Legg, Leopold G. Wickham. *English Coronation Records.* Westminister: Constable, 1901.

Lindsey, David. *Ane Satire of Thrie Estaitis. Four Morality Plays.* Ed. Peter Happé. Harmondsworth: Penguin, 1979.

Lupton, Thomas. *All for Money. The Literature of the Sixteenth and Seventeenth Centuries.* Ed. J. O. Halliwell. London, 1851.

Lusty Juventus. The Dramatic Writings of Richard Wever and Thomas Ingelend. Ed. John S. Farmer. 1905. New York: Barnes & Noble, 1966. 1–42.

McCune, Patricia. "The Ideology of Mercy in English Literature and Law." Diss. U of Michigan, 1989.

Mâle, Emile. *Religious Art in France: The Late Middle Ages. A Study of Medieval Iconography and Its Sources.* Ed. Harry Bober. Trans. Marthiel Matthews. Princeton: Princeton UP, 1986.

Mankind. The Macro Plays. Ed. Mark Eccles. EETS os 262. London: Oxford UP, 1969. 153–84.

Milsom, S. F. C. *Historical Foundations of the Common Law.* 2nd ed. London: Butterworths, 1981.

The Most Virtuous and Godly Susanna. Ed. John S. Farmer. London: Malone Soc., 1937.

Muir, Lynette. "Medieval English Drama: The French Connection." *Contexts for Early English Drama.* Ed. Marianne G. Briscoe and John C. Coldewey. Bloomington: Indiana UP, 1989. 56–76.

Mundus et Infans. Six Anonymous Plays. Ed. John S. Farmer. 1905. New York: Barnes & Noble, 1966. 161–92.

Nice Wanton. English Moral Interludes. Ed. Glynne Wickham. London: Dent, 1976. 146–62.

Norman, Joanne S. *Metamorphoses of an Allegory: The Iconography of the Psychomachia in Medieval Art.* New York: Lang, 1988.

O'Reilly, Jennifer. *Studies in the Iconography of the Virtues and Vices in the Middle Ages.* New York: Garland, 1988.

Potter, Robert. *The English Morality Play: Origins, History, and Influence of a Dramatic Tradition.* London: Routledge, 1975.

Powell, Edward. "Arbitration and the Law in England in the Late Middle Ages." *Transactions of the Royal Historical Society* 5th ser. 33 (1983): 49–67.

———. *Kingship, Law, and Society: Criminal Justice in the Reign of Henry V.* Oxford: Clarendon, 1989.

Preston, Thomas. *Cambises. Specimens of the Pre-Shaksperean Drama.* 2 vols. Ed. John Matthews Manly. Boston: Ginn, 1897. 2: 159–210.

Pride of Life. The Non-Cycle Mystery Plays. Ed. Osborn Waterhouse. EETS extra ser. 104. London: Kegan Paul, 1909.

Rawcliffe, Carole, and Susan Flower. "English Noblemen and Their Advisers: Consultation and Collaboration in the Later Middle Ages." *Journal of British Studies* 25 (1986): 157–77.

The Revels History of Drama in English. Ed. Clifford Leech and T. W. Craik. 8 vols. 1976–83. Vol. 2. Ed. Norman Sanders et al. London: Meuthen, 1980.

Richardson, H. G. "The Coronation in Medieval England." *Traditio* 16 (1960): 111–202.

Scattergood, V. J. *Politics and Poetry in the Fifteenth Century.* London: Blanford, 1971.

Sharpe, J. A. " 'Last Dying Speeches': Religion, Ideology and Public Execution in Seventeenth-Century England." *Past & Present* 107 (1985): 144–67.

Skelton, John. *Magnyfycence. Four Morality Plays.* Ed. Peter Happé. Harmondsworth: Penguin, 1979.

Smith, Lacey Baldwin. "English Treason Trials and Confessions in the Sixteenth Century." *Journal of the History of Ideas* 15 (1954): 471–98.

Spivack, Charlotte. "Feminine vs. Masculine in English Morality Drama." *Fifteenth-Century Studies* 3 (1988): 137–44.

Starkey, David. "Which Age of Reform?" *Revolution Reassessed: Revisions in the History of Tudor Government and Administration.* Ed. Christopher Coleman and David Starkey. Oxford: Clarendon, 1986. 13–27.

Stokes, Myra. *Justice and Mercy in Piers Plowman.* London: Croom Helm, 1984.

Thornley, Isobel D. "The Destruction of Sanctuary." *Tudor Studies.* Ed. R. W. Seton-Watson. London: Longmans, 1924. 182–207.

The Three Ladies of London. Ed. John S. Farmer. 1911. New York: AMS, 1970.

Tuve, Rosemond. *Allegorical Imagery: Some Medieval Books and Their Posterity.* Princeton: Princeton UP, 1966.

Udall, Nicholas. *Respublica.* Ed. W. W. Greg. EETS os 226. London: Oxford UP, 1969.

Wager, William. *The Longer Thou Livest, and Enough Is as Good as a Feast.* Ed. R. Mark Benbow. Lincoln: U of Nebraska P, 1967.

Walker, Greg. *Plays of Persuasion: Drama and Politics at the Court of Henry VIII.* Cambridge: Cambridge UP, 1991.

Wapull, George. *The Tide Tarrieth No Man.* Ed. John S. Farmer. 1910. New York: AMS, 1970.

Wealth and Health. Recently Recovered "Lost" Tudor Plays. Ed. John S. Farmer. 1907. New York: Barnes & Noble, 1966. 273-309.

Westfall, Suzanne R. *Patrons and Performance: Early Tudor Household Revels.* Oxford: Clarendon, 1990.

Whittick, Christopher. "The Role of the Criminal Appeal in the Fifteenth Century." *Law and Social Change in British History.* Ed. J. A. Guy and H. G. Beale. London: Royal Historical Soc., 1984. 55-85.

Wickham, Glynne. *Shakespeare's Dramatic Heritage: Collected Studies in Medieval, Tudor and Shakespearean Drama.* London: Routledge, 1969.

Wisdom. The Macro Plays. Ed. Mark Eccles. EETS os 262. London: Oxford UP, 1969. 113-52.

Womack, Peter. "Imagining Communities: Theatres and the English Nation in the Sixteenth Century." *Culture and History, 1350-1600: Essays on English Communities, Identities, and Writing.* Ed. David Aers. Detroit: Wayne State UP, 1992. 91-145.

Youth. Six Anonymous Plays. 2nd ser. Ed. John S. Farmer. 1906. New York: Barnes & Noble, 1966. 91-116.

Lawful Symmetry: The Politics of Treason in 2 Henry VI

NINA LEVINE

COMPARISONS between the scaffold and the stage have been important in directing attention to the politics of punishment and playing in early modern England. But as recent scholarship reminds us, to align the scaffold too closely with the stage is to locate power almost exclusively in the Crown and to reduce the judicial process to a blunt instrument of state control.[1] To be sure, accounts of trials and executions in the period offer ample evidence of the Crown's role in producing a powerful "theatre of punishment," as J. A. Sharpe has described it, in which even the condemned participated, "helping to assert the legitimacy of the power which had brought them to their sad end" (156). But there is also evidence that the state's carefully scripted spectacles of power did not always go according to plan: a bungled execution, a recalcitrant criminal, or a riotous crowd could easily undermine the solemnity of state power.[2] The response of the populace, in particular, caused concern for the authorities, as witnessed by the numerous pamphlets circulated in defense of the state's prosecution of traitors in the late sixteenth century.

Studies of the politics of playing during this period also caution against aligning the stage too closely with the scaffold. Much has been written, for example, about the capacity of the Elizabethan and Jacobean stage to expose the theatricality of state punishment and power and thereby undermine its coercive domination.[3] But even as this argument has invited consideration of a subversive stage, its attention to the state's role in producing spectacles of power has frequently left unexamined the potentially disruptive roles played by the other participants. As a way of understanding the complex and unstable politics of both the scaffold and the stage during this period, we may do well, then, to follow the direction suggested by the authorities who presided over trials and executions and look not only to the Crown but also to those who stood as audience to these performances.

Accordingly, this essay examines three representations of treason trials in late Elizabethan England for what they can tell us about relations between the Crown and its subjects in judicial performances. The case of William Parry, tried and executed for treason in 1585, and the cases brought by the Lancastrian Crown against the armorer Horner and the duke of Gloucester in *2 Henry VI* all point to the Crown's powerful role in staging judicial dramas. At the same time, however, all three cases also expose the limits of that power by representing justice less as a stable spectacle than as a complex drama played out between the Crown and its subjects, a drama whose conclusion is shaped in part by the participation of the populace. Significantly, in all three cases this drama turns on questions about the law.

Because of the prominent place Jack Cade's rebellion has come to occupy in discussions about Shakespeare's politics, *2 Henry VI* may seem an unlikely choice for considering either the subversive potential of playing or the populace's involvement in the process of justice. With its horrific scenes of artisan riot, it has been argued, *2 Henry VI* offers persuasive evidence for Thomas Nashe's claim that the stage participated in the spectacle of the scaffold and that, rather than encouraging "tumults or rebellion," it laid before its audience "the halter and the gallowes" (89).[4] But the play also provides a provocative alternative to this warning, I argue, with scenes in which the Crown's unjust prosecution of treason ends up involving and, finally, authorizing the populace's participation in the judicial process. With the Crown's case against the armorer Horner and again with the prosecution of Gloucester, *2 Henry VI* moves toward a dialectical relation between the Crown and its subjects, a relation that is mediated by the law and, in this case, perhaps by the stage as well.

I

"My case is rare and strange" (Holinshed 4: 571), William Parry wrote on 18 February 1585, in an eleventh-hour appeal to Leicester for clemency in his treason case. Parry's troubles seem to have begun the previous December when, as a newcomer to Parliament, he spoke out against a bill inspired by the Bond of Association, the notorious "lynch-law" devised by the Privy Council to protect the queen and the nation against the looming Catholic threat. Objecting specifically to a proposed treason statute against Jesuits and Catholic priests (27 Eliz. c. 2), Parry declared that it was "full of blood, danger, despair and terror to the English subjects of this realm" (qtd. in Neale 39). The House responded with immediate censure: Parry was placed in custody for the remainder of the discussion, although not without an objection from one member who "thought it not agreeable to the liberties and freedom of the House that any Member thereof, for showing his opinion in a bill read among themselves, should be taken from his seat and sequestered from the society" (qtd. in Neale 40). Two months later, when Parliament reconvened after the holidays, its members were greeted by the news that Parry, one of their own, had been arrested for plotting to kill the queen. In a matter of weeks, Parry was brought to trial, found guilty, and "on the second daie of March being tuesdaie . . . was drawne from the Tower thorough the citie of London to Westminster, and there in the palace court, hanged, boweled, and quartered" (Holinshed 4: 560).[5]

The story of Parry's treason first circulated in an anonymous pamphlet, *A true and plaine declaration of the horrible Treasons practised by W. Parry, the Traitor, Against the Queenes Majestie* (1585), but received its fullest coverage in the 1587 edition of Holinshed's *Chronicles*, where it appeared alongside accounts of the trials and bloody executions of Edmund Campion, Sir Francis Throckmorton, and the Babington conspirators. There is no mention here, however, of Parry's outburst in Parliament nor of the Bond of Association. Instead, the chronicler painstakingly reproduces an array of textual evidence for Parry's guilt—statements by Edmund Neville, his accuser, Parry's own confession, corroborating letters, an account of the trial itself, a brief tale of his sordid life and treasonous plot, even a taunting ballad of his rise "From the alehouse / To the gallows" (4: 586). By rehearsing, and controlling, the "facts" of Parry's crime and punishment for its readers, the account reiterates the orthodox Tudor position on disobedience and rebellion as it reinforces the dissymmetry between subject and sovereign that Michel Foucault has described as essential to the "spectacle of the scaffold" (49). The point of such spectacle in late sixteenth-century England, as George Whetstone explained in his account of the execution of the Babington conspirators, was to provide "necessarie instruction for all subjects, especially the common multitude to learne, whoe are manye times tempted to rebellion" (B3v).

It is not surprising, therefore, that the Holinshed account clearly provides such "necessarie instruction" for its readers, inviting them to follow the example of those onlookers at Parry's trial who, "striken as it were at heart with the horror of his intended enterprise, ceased not, but pursued him with out cries, as; Awaie with the traitor, awaie with him, and such like" (4: 579). What is surprising, however, is the extent to which the account also betrays anxieties about controlling this multitude. It is Parry himself who first draws attention to the populace. In his appeal to Leicester, Parry admits that "to leave so great a treason unpunished were strange," but he also warns that his trial and execution might be harmful to the realm: "to drawe it by death in example were dangerous; . . . to indict him, arreigne him, bring him to the scaffold, and to publish his offense, can doo no good" (4: 571). Although the chronicler's marginal note dismisses this remark as "glosing rhetorike," Parry's words nonetheless speak to the Crown's fears about controlling reactions to public displays of justice.

Similar fears are expressed at the trial itself, this time by representatives of the Crown. Christopher Hatton, the chief prosecutor, insists on following legal procedure exactly. The confession must be read publicly and follow the form and manner of the indictment, Hatton declares, in order to avoid trouble from the "great multitude":

Wherefore I praie you *for the satisfaction of this great multitude* let the whole matter appeere, that everie one may see that the matter of it selfe is as bad as the indictment purporteth, and as he hath confessed.

Whereto in respect that the justice of the realme hath beene of late verie impudentlie slandered, all yeelded as *a thing necessarie to satisfie the world* in particular, . . . though in the law, his confession served sufficientlie to have proceeded thereupon unto judgement. (4: 575; emphasis added)[6]

What is "necessary" in Hatton's thinking about the multitude is not "instruction" but "satisfaction." The shift in language is significant in revising the model of dissymmetry between monarch and subject typically set forth in Elizabethan representations of treason and admitting instead to a more reciprocal relation, one that rests on, and is mediated by, a shared sense of justice associated with the nation's laws.

The history of treason law in the late Middle Ages and in Tudor England, as John Bellamy tells it, charts the conflicts and compromises between the king in his efforts to extend the scope of treason, frequently as a means of both discouraging insurrection and broadening royal prerogatives, and the Parliament in attempting to narrow it, in part to maintain their own powers and liberties (*Law* 297). The powerful Tudor monarchs succeeded, however, not only in effecting more restrictive treason legislation; they also worked to influence the trial itself by means of interrogation and torture, or in some cases by punishing the jury for an unsatisfactory verdict.[7] Controlled by the Crown, treason trials and executions tended to follow a familiar script in which all involved played their parts in the "performance" of justice, even on the gallows. As Lacey Baldwin Smith has documented, condemned traitors usually followed "the prescribed formula for scaffold addresses, admitting the worthiness of their death, denying the righteousness of their cause, and holding themselves up as fearful examples of the just fate reserved for traitors" ("English" 481).

Yet as the Holinshed account of Parry's trial indicates, no matter how carefully the Crown worked to script treason's performance, it was not always successful in controlling the players. In the end Parry refused to play his part, "raging" that his confession was extorted under torture and that the queen would "answer for his bloud before God" (4: 579). Hatton's concern about satisfying the "multitude" points to other problems as well: cast as audience, the multitude was encouraged to see their subjection, as well as their safety, in the fate of the condemned; at the same time, these witnesses also served as a reminder to the Crown that it too was subject to a higher authority—that inscribed in the law. The Parry trial offers persuasive evidence, then, that the "great multitude" was not only critical of "the justice of the realm" but that it also possessed an understanding of due process and was able to discern, to some degree at least, the uses and abuses of law. Most importantly, perhaps, the trial suggests that the necessity of satisfying the "great multitude" may in the end have helped to shape the Crown's performance of justice.

Although it is difficult to determine the degree to which spectators were able to follow the often confusing details of Elizabethan treason legislation, that they were concerned with matters of justice and due process is well documented. In 1581, for example, when the Catholic Edmund Campion declared from the scaffold that his only treason was his religion, his protestations moving "some there present to teares" (Holinshed 4: 456), the authorities went out of their way to defend the legality of the proceedings. Reading aloud from a pamphlet prepared in anticipation of Campion's charge, the authorities reminded both the condemned on the scaffold and the crowd before him of the "manie good proofes and witnesses produced and sworne before their faces" and insisted that his treasons were "against the ancient lawes and statutes of this realme, which manie hundred yeres past were in force against like traitors, and not for facts of doctrine or religion, nor yet for offenses against anie late or new statutes" (4: 458). The trial of Sir Francis Throckmorton in 1584 likewise necessitated the publication of a pamphlet to counter reports circulating abroad that the Crown had treated him with "crueltie and injustice" (4: 536) by extracting his confession under torture. More than twenty years later, Sir Walter Ralegh would win the sympathy of the populace at his trial by pointing out the prosecution's violation of legal procedure: "by this means," he declared, "you may have any man's life in a week" (qtd. in Greenblatt, *Sir* 118).

If these cases tell us something about the difficulties of prosecuting treason in the public space of the courtroom and the scaffold, what can they tell us about the performance of treason on the public stage? If the trials and executions produced by the Crown were potentially unstable, was there an even greater potential for danger in the performances over which the Crown had admittedly less control? The Holinshed account of Parry's treason suggests that audiences in the public theaters, not unlike those following a trial, might be incited as well as instructed by a staging of treason. But Hatton's picture of a critical and skeptical multitude sitting in judgment on the Crown's prosecution of justice is also important in allowing for a range of responses among the populace between the extremes of docile obedience, on the one hand, and open rebellion, on the other.

Not unlike the Parry trial, *2 Henry VI* speaks to the struggles and negotiations between the Crown and its subjects played out in treason legislation and litigation as it too invites its audience to sit in judgment on scenes of state justice. Charting the nation's approach to bloody internecine conflict in the fifteenth century, the play reverberates with treason accusations: Eleanor, duchess of Gloucester, the armorer Horner, the duke of Gloucester, Suffolk, the clerk Emmanuel, Lord Say, Cade and his followers, Somerset, and York and his sons—all are accused of being traitors. But the play warrants particular attention in the way that it, more than any of Shakespeare's other histories, links treason with fears about rebellion among the common people as well as the nobles. First performed in the early 1590s, a period in which outbreaks of disorder were not uncommon in London, *2 Henry*

VI foregrounds the intersection of treason and popular revolt with the figure of Jack Cade, the rebellious clothier, who is both pawn and player in treason's performance.

The Cade scenes have long provided a point of entry into considerations about Shakespeare's politics. To many, the play's emphasis on the anarchic lawlessness of Cade's rebellion offers proof that the young playwright's sympathies lay with the educated ruling elite and not the "*vox-populi* and the stinking breath he insists goes with it" (Wilson 168).[8] In these readings of the play, the rebelling artisans, that "fourth sort or classe" Sir Thomas Smith described as having "no voice nor authoritie in our common wealth" (76), are seen as being incapable of participating in rule.[9] Shakespeare is saying, M. M. Reese writes, "that this is the sort of thing that happens when power falls into the hands of those who have not been trained to bear it" (126). More recently, Richard Wilson has made the case for a conservative Shakespeare by proposing a connection between *2 Henry VI* and the midsummer Southwark riot of 1592, where carnival appeared to turn dangerous when feltmakers clashed with guards at the Marshalsea prison. Response from the Privy Council was immediate: festivities, including plays, were forbidden, while householders and masters were to enforce a curfew for their apprentices. Shakespeare's company was able to earn an exemption from the ban that summer, Wilson speculates, with a law and order staging of artisan-rebellion (173–76).

But if *2 Henry VI* comes down hard on the revolting populace with the scenes of Cade's revolt, it also criticizes the Crown's ability to administer justice. Representing treason as a political construction, "a matter made" (3: 707), as John Foxe aptly described it in a pointed defense of Eleanor Cobham some years earlier, the play offers case after case in which evidence is either fabricated or manipulated by those competing for power within the Lancastrian state. The case against Eleanor establishes the model: in order to entrap the duchess, the conspirators literally stage a scene of necromancy and so produce the evidence—"the devil's writ" (1.4.57), as York refers to the scribbled prophecies about the king's death—that results in her exile and her husband's dismissal as lord protector. The manipulation of treason on the part of the nobles is, of course, parodied at the lower end of the social scale by Cade: stirred to rebellion by the treasonous York, Cade quickly adopts the strategies of his "betters," tyrannically extending the scope of treason and thereby executing his enemies with outrageous indiscrimination—and without due process. As both oppressor and oppressed, the overdetermined Cade provocatively collapses the distinctions essential to Elizabethan treason law: a grotesque parody of the absolutist concept of royal prerogative—"Away, burn all the records of the realm, my mouth shall be the parliament of England" (4.7.14-15)—he is also a nightmarish caricature of a revolting populace who turns the law against the lawgiver.

As the Holinshed account of Parry's trial suggests, the part played by the common multitude is crucial in shaping the outcome of treason's performance, but when we let Cade's voice speak for all the commons, as Annabel Patterson has rightly reminded us, we fail to hear the other popular voices that are also raised in this play (*Shakespeare* 47).[10] The armorer's case is important in this regard not only because both the accuser and the accused are that "fourth sort of men which doe not rule" (Thomas Smith 76), but also because the trial itself takes place before an audience in which nobles mix with neighbors and prentices. The common people are heard from again in conjunction with Gloucester's treason "trial" and murder when they speak their demands through Salisbury. By bringing the Crown together with the people in these two cases, Shakespeare suggests a way out of the opposing but related choices represented by the corrupt nobles, on the one hand, and the rebellious weavers and butchers, on the other. In both cases the play invites its audience to measure the Crown's performance of treason against the authority of the law, and in the case of Gloucester it shows them the success with which popular pressure may be brought to bear on the monarchy. The play thus offers its audience a glimpse—however fragmentary—of the ways in which a legal system that is typically exploited by those in power can also work to authorize the voices of the common people, even in the face of opposition from the Crown. And so while it may be argued, as Richard Helgerson does, that the play is involved in "staging exclusion," in eliminating "commoner participation in the political nation" (214), it is also worth considering the extent to which the play includes the populace in the political process, an inclusion, I would argue, that is enabled, even as it is hindered, by the law. At the same time, by encouraging the "great multitude" that comprises its audience to sit in judgment on the Crown's as well as Cade's mockery of the law, the performance of the play itself could be said to enact a version of communal justice within the theater similar to the one it represents onstage.

II

As Shakespeare presents it, the case against Thomas Horner, the armorer, at first appears to be fairly straightforward: an apprentice by the name of Peter Thump accuses his master of speaking treasonous words, of "saying that the Duke of York was rightful heir to the crown" (1.3.26–27) as the two of them sat together polishing the duke's armor. Acting on the apprentice's charge, the court arranges for a trial by combat with the result that the apprentice defeats his master, who then confesses his treason and dies. In order to clarify the political and legal issues at stake in Shakespeare's version of the incident, it may be helpful to turn to some of the earlier accounts, starting with a brief report in the late fifteenth-century *Chronicle of the Grey Friars*: "Thys yere was a fyghtynge in Smythfelde betwene ane armerar of fletstret and his servant for worddes ayenst the kynge wherof hys servant apelyd hym; and the servant slew the master in the felde" (18). Although this Yorkist chronicle was not a source for *2 Henry VI*, Shakespeare's handling of the servant's victory has more in common with this unembellished report than with his Tudor sources, which significantly reinterpret the outcome. The problem with a servant slaying his master, from a Tudor perspective at any rate, lies with the unsettling contradiction it opens up in a sociopolitical hierarchy in which apprentices are subject to masters and both are subject to the king.[11] An apprentice was required by the terms of his indenture to serve his master well, "his secrets keep close, his commandments lawful and honest everywhere he shall willingly do: hurt nor damage to his said master he shall none do" (qtd. in Steven Smith 220). And while it was high treason for a subject to "compass or imagine" his monarch's death, for a servant to slay his master was petty treason, punishable by hanging (Bacon 4: 294).

As might be expected, the Tudor chronicles revise the narrative in ways that correct or minimize the inversion of a servant's victory over his master. Robert Fabyan's chronicle, for example, insists on the armorer's innocence: his defeat is attributed to his drinking whereas the servant's treachery is soon proven when he commits another crime for which he is brought to justice, "hanged for felony at Tyborne" (618). Following Fabyan, Edward Hall's chronicle, the principal source for *2 Henry VI*, likewise vindicates the drunken armorer and condemns the "false" servant:

he [the armorer] beyng a tall and a hardye personage, overladed with hote drynkes, was vanqueshed of his servaunte, beyng but a cowarde and a wretche, whose body was drawen to Tiborne, & there hanged and behedded. (207-08)

In Hall's radical compression of the events, no mention is made of the servant's subsequent felony, so that his hanging now appears to be a direct, and just, punishment for his wrongful slaying of his master. The Tudor revisions work, then, to serve orthodox thinking, transforming a potentially subversive incident into a tidy *exemplum* of social and political order.

Yet these accounts do not speak with one voice, and the fact that they sometimes include references to due process and subjects' rights may also indicate the necessity of justifying or at least explaining legal procedures for sixteenth-century readers even while holding to the orthodox line. The Holinshed chronicler, for example, repeats the standard Tudor version of the incident, but he also exhibits a concern for due process absent from his sources when he explains that the "false servant" was hanged after being "convict[ed] of felonie *in court of assise*" (3: 210).[12] Significantly, the injustice of the combat is here corrected by the courts, not by a kind of divine lynching as in Hall.

In contrast to the Tudor chronicles, however, Shakespeare's version complicates the legal framework of the case in ways that raise rather than answer questions about justice and due process. To begin with, the play invests what had been a relatively isolated incident in the sources—one confined to nameless commoners—with political import by linking it with the dynastic struggle that gives shape to the *Henry VI* plays. As a result, the servant's victory over his master is also a victory for the Lancastrian court over the Yorkist opposition. Complicating the politics even further, Shakespeare introduces the element of political protest into the servant's accusation by linking Thump's complaint with those of the petitioners who have come together "in the quill" (1.3.3), or "in a body" as the *Oxford English Dictionary* defines it, in hopes of strengthening their individual grievances. Although intended for the "good Duke Humphrey" (1.1.162), their petitions are unfortunately intercepted by the duke of Suffolk and the queen, with predictable results: the complaint against Suffolk "for enclosing the commons" (1.3.21) is destroyed whereas Thump's accusation against his master is heard because it serves the interests of Suffolk and Margaret. Helping to frame the accusation—at one point putting words in Peter Thump's mouth—Suffolk and Margaret succeed in bringing the case before the court as proof that York should not be appointed regent of France. In the trial by combat that follows, Shakespeare's servant slays his master; but in direct contrast to the Tudor chronicles, here the victory is hailed as just: "And God in justice hath reveal'd to us / The truth and innocence of this poor fellow" (2.3.102-03), the king concludes with typically unreflective piety. Shakespeare thus turns the orthodoxy of his principal source on its head, revising Hall's account so as to expose the crass manipulation of treason charges by the ruling elite and, at the same time, to celebrate justice in the unlikely figure of Peter Thump.

But how are we to understand the politics of Shakespeare's revisions and inventions on the Elizabethan stage? For one, the play shifts the blame away from the apprentice and redirects it toward Margaret and Suffolk in a critique of corrupt rulers who would exploit the law in order to control their opposition. But in rewriting the brief incident so that it resonates with many of the same questions about due process debated in Elizabethan treason legislation, Shakespeare produces more than yet another mirror for magistrates who abuse their power. The play's staging of the armorer's case speaks, in fact, to what had become a highly contested issue in Elizabethan treason legislation and prosecution—treason based on words. The apprentice's charge against Horner, "for saying that the Duke of York was rightful heir to the crown," raises many of the same legal problems as a number of prominent cases during the period, including those of William Parry and Sir Nicholas Throckmorton. The status of spoken words had become one of the most politically volatile issues around which relations between the Crown and its subjects were negotiated.

Until the fifteenth century, treason had been defined primarily as an overt act in accordance with the great treason statute of 1352 (25 Edw. III st. 5 c. 2). Although this act defined treason as "imagining and compassing the king's death," "imagining" tended to be construed in terms of actions rather than spoken words or "secret" thoughts.[13] With the Tudors, however, the scope of treason was legally expanded to include words. The statute of 1534 (26 Hen. VIII c. 13), prompted by Henry VIII's need to suppress opposition to his policies, deemed it treasonous to express "maliciously" in words or writing the desire to harm the monarch or to call the king a heretic or usurper (Elton 286-87). In 1571 Elizabeth reinstituted the repressive measures of the 1534 statute in response to the Northern Rebellion and the papal bull: the scope of treason was again extended to include "Pryntinge Wrytinge Cyphryng Speache Wordes or Sayinges" (*Statutes* 4: 526), and it was under this statute (13 Eliz. c. 1) that William Parry was indicted (Bellamy, *Tudor* 76).

But if expanding the scope of treason gave more authority to the Crown, it also prompted concerns about protecting the rights of individuals against false accusations. Without witnesses, accusations based on spoken words typically came down to one man's word against another's; as Parry himself pointed out in his initial response to Neville's charge, "his no, was as good as Nevills yea" (Holinshed 4: 563). *2 Henry VI* also points to the problem with accusations based solely on words when master Horner explains to the court: "My accuser is my prentice, and when I did correct him for his fault the other day, he did vow upon his knees he would be even with me. I have good witness of this; therefore I beseech your Majesty, do not cast away an honest man for a villain's accusation" (1.3.198–202). Horner's argument here is notable in anticipating that of Edward Coke, who, writing in the reign of the Stuarts, offered this critical perspective on Tudor legislation:

Divers latter acts of parliament have ordained, that compassing by bare words or sayings should be high treason; but all they are either repealed or expired. And it is commonly said, that bare words may make an heretick, but not a traytor without an overt act. And the wisdom of the makers of this law would not make words only to be treason, seeing such variety amongst the witnesses are about the same, as few of them agree together. . . . not only the ignorant and rude unlearned people, but also learned and expert people minding honesty, are oftentimes trapped and snared, yea, many times for words only, without other fact or deed done or perpetrated: therefore this act of 25 E. 3. doth provide, that there must be an overt deed. (14)[14]

Significantly, Coke bases his argument against the Tudor statutes about spoken words by upholding the precedent established in the treason act of 1352.

With the repressive treason statutes in place during Elizabeth's reign, the struggle between the Crown's authority and the rights of the individual was typically fought over the issue of witnesses. And the fact that Elizabethan statutes (13 Eliz. c. 1 and 23 Eliz. c. 2) stipulated at least two accuser-witnesses, and strictly limited the conditions under which accusations based on treasonous words could be made, offers some measure of how pressure to guarantee justice was brought to bear on legislation (Bellamy, *Tudor* 155). But with the 1585 statute against Jesuits and seminary priests (27 Eliz. c. 2), the very bill Parry had opposed, the requirement for two witnesses was waived for indictments against Catholics. At the same time, the Elizabethan courts also began to practice what Bellamy has called a "deceitful subterfuge" (*Tudor* 81), basing a single indictment on a number of statutes, including the 1352 statute which did not mention witnesses, as a way of avoiding procedural constraints and the specific requirement for witnesses.[15]

By exposing the abuses and manipulations that can ensue when treason is based on evidence as tenuous as a servant's report of his master's words, Shakespeare's staging of the armorer's treason invites a critique of repressive legislation that would increase the Crown's power at the expense of due process for its subjects. In this regard, the armorer's case also lends validity to the more general critique of legal procedure voiced later in the play by Cade:

> Thou hast appointed justices of peace, to call poor men before them about matters they were not able to answer. Moreover, thou hast put them in prison, and because they could not read, thou hast hang'd them, when, indeed, only for that cause they have been most worthy to live. (4.7.41–46)

According to Coke, who as England's attorney general in the 1590s would have been in a position to know, it was "the ignorant and rude unlearned people," as well as the "learned and expert," who were "oftentimes trapped and snared . . . for words only" (14).

If the apprentice's evidence raised questions about legislation and due process for an Elizabethan audience, then what response would the trial itself have provoked? For while it was not unusual for accusations involving one man's word against another's to be submitted to trial by battle in the fifteenth century, such procedures would certainly have appeared antiquated, at the very least, at the end of the sixteenth century, when the last official judicial battle had been fought nearly a hundred years before (Elton 264). In a period characterized by a decline in violence and a growth in litigation, would a London audience have immediately recognized this battle between master and servant as a travesty of justice?[16] Or would some have applauded the apprentice's victory along with Henry VI?

Recent discussions of this scene suggest that the trial may have generated a number of responses. Fought by drunken clowns wielding sandbags tied to staves, the combat is clearly a carnivalesque version of justice, the mock-heroics exposing the trial as spectacle, staged by Margaret and Suffolk to enlarge their power within the court. As one recent editor has remarked, justice in this instance "becomes propaganda, and the process of the trial is reduced to sickening show as a sober man beats a drunken man to death" (Hattaway, Introduction 15). But it is also possible to see the apprentice's victory as just in spite of the nobles' role in exploiting his foolish simplicity. Craig Bernthal, in a consideration of the scene's social and political contradictions, points out that "the play seems to affirm . . . that God *is* in charge and that traitors will be punished" (53). The play itself voices a range of interpretations: Horner's confession, Peter's self-affirmation—"O Peter, thou hast prevail'd in right!"(2.3.98-99)—and the king's praise all point to a just conclusion, although for members of Shakespeare's audience seasoned in the rituals of the scaffold, Horner's dying confession may have been less persuasive. York's more pointed comment—"Fellow, thank God, and the good wine in thy master's way"(95-96)—may be closer to the truth.

But whether some in Shakespeare's audience condemned the servant's victory as an outrageous display of injustice and others applauded it as a miraculous triumph, the final result is to give a certain power to the common people. For although Margaret and Suffolk set up the spectacle, and although it is in their interest for Thump to win, in encouraging the apprentice's victory, they end up licensing and authorizing the common voices that will later turn against them. Rather than laying "the halter and the gallowes" before "the ruder handicrafts servants" (89) as a way of discouraging them from rebellion, as Nashe would have it, this performance— whatever we think of Peter Thump's victory—encourages apprentices to speak out against their masters and to take political action. Surrounded by the cheering apprentices, Peter's fight against his master becomes a "fight for credit of the prentices" (2.3.71). And if his victory thus provides a mirror for his fellows on the stage, as witnessed by the play's subsequent artisan-rebellion, it also provides a mirror for his fellows in the audience, some of whom might still bear bruises from the clash with the guards of Marshalsea prison.

For those members of the audience concerned about questions of law and due process, however, the apprentice's victory over his master may have occasioned less celebration. From their perspective, the unsettling conclusion only reinforces the play's critique of tyrannical rulers who would cast their subjects in a deadly play of justice. At the same time, however, the topsy-turvy figure of the triumphant apprentice might also point a way out of this tyranny. In *2 Henry VI*, as in Hatton's court, the "great multitude" must be satisfied, and if it is not, the play suggests, it looks for a means of redress. One means, of course, is figured by Cade's revolt, which is fueled in part by the people's rage against a corrupt and oppressive legal system that denies them a voice. But another, more effective means is illustrated by the popular outcry following the murder of Gloucester, the "good Duke" whom "the common people favor" (1.1.158–59).

III

With the trial of Gloucester in act 3, the play again exposes the Crown's staging of a judicial drama, but here the abuse of legal procedure provokes a call for justice on the part of the populace that results in a direct confrontation between subjects and their monarch. Once again, Suffolk and Margaret exploit the law as a means of eliminating their opposition within the court, arresting Gloucester for "high treason" (3.1.97) under the pretense of protecting the king from "treason's secret knife" (174). The staging of treason is now openly equated with policy, but as the cardinal cynically reminds the court, it is still important to offer a show of justice:

> That he should die is worthy policy,
> But yet we want a color for his death.
> 'Tis meet he be condemn'd by course of law.
> (3.1.235–37)

Not unlike Hatton at Parry's trial, Suffolk expresses concerns about satisfying the multitude: "The commons haply rise, to save his life; / And yet we have but trivial argument, / More than mistrust, that shows him worthy death" (3.1.240–42). Hoping to strengthen their case and so avoid objections from the people, the conspiring nobles base the indictment not on Gloucester's overt acts but on "his purpose" (3.1.256). The commons are not satisfied, however; and when they hear of Gloucester's sudden death, they rise up "like an angry hive of bees" (3.2.125), threatening the king that unless Suffolk is either executed or banished, "They will by violence tear him from your palace, / And torture him with grievous ling'ring death" (3.2.246–47). Heeding their demands, the king banishes Suffolk.

In recording the part played by the common multitude in the judicial drama, the play offers a way out of the tyranny of the scaffold: justice is now unequivocally associated with the people, who for once are able to use the law to their advantage. Turning the accusation of treason back upon the oppressor, they frame their complaint against Suffolk by pointing to their care of the king's "most royal person" (3.2.254). Significantly, the play's staging of Gloucester's "treason" not only validates their cry for justice but, in demonstrating their success in issuing ultimatums to the monarch, it also appears to endorse such political action. By allowing the common people to triumph in their demands, Shakespeare has again revised the "facts" of his chronicle sources in ways that alter the politics of the case.

Historically, the action against Suffolk provided an important precedent for Parliament's use of law against royal prerogative. In a bill of articles initiated by the Commons in 1450, Suffolk was accused of a number of crimes, among them "ymagyning and purposyng falsely and traitorously to distroy youre moost Roiall persone and this youre said Reame" (Bellamy, *Law* 124). In this instance, however, Suffolk benefited greatly from the king's support: he was allowed time to review the charges against him and to prepare a response. "There can be little doubt," Bellamy writes, "that the procedure of the trial was fashioned to Suffolk's benefit and that the king's lawyers applied themselves not to his prosecution but to secure an acquittal or the next best thing" (*Law* 170). By throwing himself on the mercy of the king, and not the peerage, Suffolk was able to escape with a sentence of five years in exile. In 1451, following Suffolk's death at the hands of pirates, the Commons again brought charges against the duke in Parliament, hoping this time to declare him a traitor and so to assure the forfeiture of his lands. This time, they met with defeat. According to Bellamy, "[t]his was virtually the end of accusations by the commons or lords of parliament against the king's ministers for over 170 years" (*Law* 211).

If historical precedent invited Shakespeare to explore questions about royal prerogative and common law, Hall and Holinshed provided him with a ready-made approach to these issues in their condemnation of Suffolk and, in this instance, their generally sympathetic treatment of the populace. For the most part Shakespeare follows his sources, but when he does choose to revise them, the changes tend to heighten support for the commoners. In the chronicle accounts, for example, two years pass between the murder of Gloucester and the charges against Suffolk. In *2 Henry VI* the charges follow immediately upon the discovery of Gloucester's body, the compression working to justify the populace's outrage. Shakespeare also goes beyond his sources by inventing widespread support for the protest among the nobles. With the blood "settled in his face"(3.2.160) providing evidence of Gloucester's murder, Salisbury and Warwick join with the noisy crowd, acting as their spokesmen in negotiations with the king. The "rude multitude" (3.2.135) thus comes to provide a moral touchstone in this scene, and Suffolk's abuse of power is now tellingly signaled by his elitist contempt for the men of Bury St. Edmunds: " 'Tis like the commons, rude unpolish'd hinds, / Could send such message to their sovereign" (3.2.271-72).

The play also departs from the chronicles by simplifying the legal issues at stake in this conflict. As a result, the sentence of exile is seen as a victory for the common people rather than a compromise. The king agrees to their demands and even thanks "them for their tender loving care" (3.2.280). Like Peter, the commoners have "prevail'd in the right," but here the justice of their victory is unequivocal. The revision is significant: Shakespeare has overturned the outcome of an important confrontation in English legal history between the monarch and Parliament; in the process, he has established a precedent for the successful participation in state justice on the part of the populace.

We may measure the extent to which *2 Henry VI* endorses this victory by returning once more to the chronicles. The Tudor accounts, while opposing Suffolk, at the same time record a degree of anxiety about popular protest. Hall, for example, warns of the potential for widespread revolt in the uprising against Suffolk:

Of these wordes sprang dedes, and of this talkyng, rose displeasure, whiche had grown to greate mischiefe, if pollitique provision had not, with all celeritie resisted the fyrst fury: for the commons in sundry places of the realme assembled together, gathered great companyes, and elected a Capitayn, whome they called, blew berd: but or they had attempted any enterpryse, their headdes were apprehended and so the membres sodainly were dispersed, without any hurte committed, or perpetrated. (218-19)

In Fabyan, these same rebels are "layd for & taken, & put to death" (622). Shakespeare, by contrast, controls anxiety about the commoners' outrage in a number of ways. Significantly, the noisy crowd never appears in this scene; instead its complaints are voiced through Salisbury's act of "ventriloquism," as Patterson has demonstrated, in keeping with an established tradition of popular protest (*Shakespeare* 48). The play thus encourages its audience to hear the justice of the protest by placing it in the mouth of a noble and by keeping the threatening spectacle of a demanding populace at bay—but at the same time not silencing them completely. For while Salisbury delivers their demands to the king, the outraged men of Bury punctuate his decorously balanced cadences with threats of violence as they cry from within: "An answer from the King, or we will all break in!" (3.2.278).

Shakespeare's handling of this sequence is significant not only in giving the populace a victory and thereby rewriting legal precedent, but also in locating the means to such a victory in the tension between petitioning and riot, the primary forms of political action that were available to the populace during this period. The play thus anticipates, and endorses, what Patterson has described as the "more assertive concept of petitioning" that was emerging at the beginning of the seventeenth century, "one in which physical force in the background was represented or preempted . . . by legal-constitutional reasoning" (*Reading* 61). We might understand the sequence, then, not so much as a successful alternative to the unsuccessful petitioning on the part of the commoners near the start of the play or to the lawless riot near its close, but rather as a means of political intervention that gains its strength by drawing on both petitioning and riot.

As nobles come together with the men of Bury to redress the injustice of Gloucester's murder, *2 Henry VI* makes a persuasive case for including the populace in the judicial process. And in marking out a space for their participation, it also affords a provocative glimpse of political relations not unlike those put forth by some of the century's more radical legal and political theorists, by those who argued that Parliament and the law constituted the highest authority in the land.[17] In *De Republica Anglorum*, for example, Smith describes Parliament as a place where "everie Englishman is entended to bee there present, either in person or by procuration and attornies . . . from the Prince (be he King or Queene) to the lowest person of Englande" (79). Smith then concludes: "That which is doone by this consent is called firme, stable, and *sanctum*, and is taken for lawe" (78). The Crown, as both Smith and Shakespeare suggest, is certainly not all-powerful; instead, its authority rests on its relation to its subjects, a relation that is negotiated by the nation's laws. This is not to say that the play holds up the law as an absolute authority to which all are subject or as an ideal code that insures justice for all. In *2 Henry VI*, as in England's own history, the law is imperfect and easily abused, as Gloucester, the play's most ardent supporter of the law's authority, tragically discovers. But the solution is not to "kill all the lawyers" (4.2.76), nor is it to lay "the halter and the gallowes" before the audience. Condemning both the corrupt rulers and the lawless rebels, the play looks instead to the audience that stands as witness to the drama of justice, reminding them that they too have a role to play in the dialectic of power negotiated in the nation's laws.

Notes

1. See Laqueur and Linebaugh for recent discussions of early modern punishment that challenge the earlier emphasis on state power in studies by Foucault and Hay, for example.

2. Peter Linebaugh, for example, documents the resistance produced by "the hanged men and women whose views and actions continually challenged both law and their own class" (xxii), whereas Thomas Laqueur focuses on the "carnival crowds" for whom "executions were a species of festive comedy or light entertainment" (323).

3. For discussions of the stage's capacity to expose the theatricality of punishment and power, see Greenblatt "Invisible"; Mullaney 116-34; Cunningham; Breight; and Shapiro.

4. For recent assertions of this view of the politics of *2 Henry VI*, see Wilson and Dutton 84-85.

5. For another account of Parry's trial, see Howell 1095-1111. It is not clear what motivated the case against Parry: some suspect that he was either a spy who knew too much or a double agent, others that the charges against him were constructed by the queen's advisers as proof of a widespread Catholic conspiracy, and still others that he was a bit mad (Neale 40-41; Smith, *Treason* 18-19).

6. The authorities' concern about the appearance of justice is commonplace in treason trials and would be echoed by the queen herself before the execution of Mary Queen of Scots: "we Princes, I tell you, are set on stages, in the sight and view of all the world duly observed. The eyes of many behold our actions. . . . *It behoveth us, therefore, to be careful that our proceedings be just and honourable*" (qtd. in Neale 119; emphasis added).

7. As Sir Thomas Smith notes with some criticism: "Yet I have seene in my time (not in the raigne of the Queene nowe) that an enquest for pronouncing one not guiltie of treason contrarie to such evidence as was brought in, were not onely imprisoned for a space, but an houge fine set upon their heads, which they were faine to pay: An other enquest for acquiting an other, beside paying a fine of money, put to open ignominie and shame. But those doinges were even then of many accounted verie violent, and tyrannical, and contrarie to the libertie and custome of the realme of England" (121). For a discussion of torture, see Langbein.

8. See also Tillyard, Reese, Bullough, and Dutton. For alternate views of the politics of rebellion and protest in this play, see Hattaway, "Rebellion"; Patterson, *Shakespeare* 32-51; and Cartelli.

9. It needs to be emphasized, however, that Smith's subsequent qualification provides evidence that these men did have some voice and authority: "For in cities and corporate townes for default of yeomen, they are faine to make their enquests of such manner of people. And in villages they be commonly made Churchwardens, alecunners, and manie times Constables, which office toucheth more the common wealth, and at the first was not imployed upon such lowe and base persons" (76-77).

10. In exploring relations between the Crown and the populace, my own argument is indebted to Patterson's work on the politics of popular protest in this play.

11. For a discussion of the social and political contradictions generated by the servant's slaying of his master, see Bernthal.

12. Hall's account also displays a concern for justice and the rights of the commons in the account of the "great insurrection" at Norwich that follows directly, and without transition, from the armorer's case. In this popular revolt, the citizens defiantly shut the city gates against the Prior in protest for his taking away "their auncient fredomes and usages." Hall's response to this injustice is curiously ambivalent. On the one hand, he admits that their cause was just—the king, after all, "restored the citezens to their auncient liberties"—but on the other, he justifies the execution of the leaders: "this was not the dewe meane to come to their right and purpose, and therefore because they erred and went out of the pathe, they were by punishemente brought again to a very straight trade and the right waie" (208).

13. Bellamy notes an increasing tendency on the part of the king's lawyers during the late fifteenth century, however, to widen the interpretation of the statute to include words (*Tudor* 11). There has been a good deal of debate about whether the scope of the 1352 statute included treasonous words; for a review of the controversy, see Bellamy, *Law* 122.

14. Coke's understanding of treason law was no doubt informed by the double perspective of his career: as Elizabeth's attorney general in the 1590s, he earned a reputation for being unusually brutal in prosecuting cases of treason and sedition, but during the reign of James I, he became an outspoken advocate of upholding common law over royal prerogative and ended up being dismissed from his position as chief justice in 1616 and briefly imprisoned for treason in 1621. For discussions of Coke's career, see Levy 229-65 and Helgerson 65-104.

15. "When there was some doubt about the scope of the law," Bellamy writes, "the professional judges were pressured to interpret in the manner most beneficial to the prince, and usually their conferences ended with their doing just that. They may have misunderstood the history of the treason law, or they may have misconstrued it deliberately" (*Tudor* 81-82).

16. Lawrence Stone emphasizes the Crown's role in discouraging aristocratic violence in the sixteenth century (240); for a discussion of objections raised by the Christian humanists, see Bornstein.

17. For a discussion of late sixteenth-century theories on sovereignty, see Allen 247-70.

Works Cited

Allen, J. W. *A History of Political Thought in the Sixteenth Century*. London: Methuen, 1928.

Bacon, Francis. *The Works of Francis Bacon*. 16 vols. 1825-34. Vol. 4. London, 1826.

Bellamy, John. *The Law of Treason in England in the Later Middle Ages*. Cambridge: Cambridge UP, 1970.

———. *The Tudor Law of Treason*. London: Routledge, 1979.

Bernthal, Craig A. "Treason in the Family: The Trial of Thumpe v. Horner." *Shakespeare Quarterly* 42 (1991): 44-54.

Bornstein, Diane. "Trial by Combat and Official Irresponsibility in *Richard II*." *Shakespeare Studies* 8 (1975): 131-41.

Breight, Curt. " 'Treason doth never prosper': *The Tempest* and the Discourse of Treason." *Shakespeare Quarterly* 41 (1990): 1-28.

Bullough, Geoffrey. *Narrative and Dramatic Sources of Shakespeare*. 8 vols. 1957-75. Vol. 3. London: Routledge, 1960.

Cartelli, Thomas. "Jack Cade in the Garden: Class Consciousness and Class Conflict in *2 Henry VI*." *Enclosure Acts: Sexuality, Property, and Culture in Early Modern England*. Ed. Richard Burt and John Michael Archer. Ithaca: Cornell UP, 1994. 48-67.

Chronicle of Grey Friars. Ed. J. G. Nichols. London: Camden Soc., 1852.

Coke, Edward. *The Third Part of the Institutes of the Laws of England*. 1797. Buffalo: Hein, 1986.

Cunningham, Karen. "Renaissance Execution and Marlovian Elocution: The Drama of Death." *PMLA* 105 (1990): 209-22.

Dutton, Richard. *Mastering the Revels: The Regulation and Censorship of English Renaissance Drama*. Iowa City: U of Iowa P, 1991.

Elton, G. R. *Policy and Police: The Enforcement of the Reformation in the Age of Thomas Crowell*. Cambridge: Cambridge UP, 1972.

Fabyan, Robert. *The New Chronicles of England and France*. Ed. Henry Ellis. London: Rivington, 1811.

Foucault, Michel. *Discipline and Punish: The Birth of the Prison*. Trans. Alan Sheridan. New York: Vintage, 1979.

Foxe, John. *Actes and Monuments*. 8 vols. New York: AMS, 1965. Vol. 3.

Greenblatt, Stephen. "Invisible Bullets: Renaissance Authority and Its Subversion, *Henry IV* and *Henry V*." *Political Shakespeare: New Essays in Cultural Materialism*. Ed. Jonathan Dollimore and Alan Sinfield. Ithaca: Cornell UP, 1985. 18-47.

———. *Sir Walter Ralegh: The Renaissance Man and His Roles*. New Haven: Yale UP, 1973.

Hall, Edward. *The Union of the Two Noble and Illustre Famelies of Lancastre and Yorke*. 1548. Ed. Henry Ellis. London, 1809.

Hattaway, Michael. Introduction. *The Second Part of King Henry VI*. Cambridge: Cambridge UP, 1991.

———. "Rebellion, Class Consciousness, and Shakespeare's *2 Henry VI*." *Cahiers Elisabethains* 33 (1988): 13-22.

Hay, Douglas, et al., eds. *Albion's Fatal Tree: Crime and Society in Eighteenth-Century England*. New York: Pantheon, 1975.

Helgerson, Richard. *Forms of Nationhood: The Elizabethan Writing of England*. Chicago: U of Chicago P, 1992.

Holinshed, Raphael. *Holinshed's Chronicles of England, Scotland, and Ireland*. 6 vols. Ed. Henry Ellis. 1807-08. Vols. 3-4. New York: AMS, 1965.

Howell, T. B. *A Complete Collection of State Trials*. Vol. 1. London, 1816.

Langbein, John H. *Torture and the Law of Proof: Europe and England in the Ancien Regime*. Chicago: U of Chicago P, 1976.

Laqueur, Thomas W. "Crowds, Carnival and the State in English Executions, 1604-1868." *The First Modern Society: Essays in English History in Honour of Lawrence Stone*. Ed. A. L. Beier, David Cannadine, and James M. Rosenheim. Cambridge: Cambridge UP, 1989. 305-55.

Levy, Leonard W. *Origins of the Fifth Amendment: The Right against Self-Incrimination.* New York: Oxford UP, 1968.

Linebaugh, Peter. *The London Hanged: Crime and Civil Society in the Eighteenth Century.* Cambridge: Cambridge UP, 1992.

Mullaney, Steven. *The Place of the Stage: License, Play, and Power in Renaissance England.* Chicago: U of Chicago P, 1988.

Nashe, Thomas. *Pierce Penilesse, His Supplication to the Divell.* 1592. Ed. G. B. Harrison. New York: Barnes & Noble, 1966.

Neale, J. E. *Elizabeth I and Her Parliaments, 1584–1601.* New York: St. Martin's, 1957.

Patterson, Annabel. *Reading between the Lines.* Madison: U of Wisconsin P, 1993.

———. *Shakespeare and the Popular Voice.* Cambridge: Blackwell, 1989.

Reese, M. M. *The Cease of Majesty: A Study of Shakespeare's History Plays.* New York: St. Martin's, 1961.

Shakespeare, William. *The Riverside Shakespeare.* Ed. G. Blakemore Evans. Boston: Houghton, 1974.

Shapiro, James. " 'Tragedies naturally performed': Kyd's Representation of Violence." *Staging the Renaissance: Reinterpretations of Elizabethan and Jacobean Drama.* Ed. David Scott Kastan and Peter Stallybrass. New York: Routledge, 1991. 99–113.

Sharpe, J. A. " 'Last Dying Speeches': Religion, Ideology and Public Execution in Seventeenth-Century England." *Past & Present* 107 (1985): 144–67.

Smith, Lacey Baldwin. "English Treason Trials and Confessions in the Sixteenth Century." *Journal of the History of Ideas* 15 (1954): 471–98.

———. *Treason in Tudor England: Politics and Paranoia.* Princeton: Princeton UP, 1986.

Smith, Steven R. "The London Apprentices as Seventeenth-Century Adolescents." *Rebellion, Popular Protest and the Social Order in Early Modern England.* Ed. Paul Slack. Cambridge: Cambridge UP, 1984. 219–31.

Smith, Thomas, Sir. *De Republica Anglorum.* Ed. Mary Dewar. Cambridge: Cambridge UP, 1982.

Statutes of the Realm. Vol. 4. Record Commission, 1831.

Stone, Lawrence. *The Crisis of the Aristocracy, 1558–1641.* Oxford: Clarendon, 1965.

Tillyard, E. M. W. *Shakespeare's History Plays.* 1944. New York: Collier, 1962.

Whetstone, George. *Censure Upon Notable Traitors.* 1587. Amsterdam: Da Capo, 1973.

Wilson, Richard. " 'A Mingled Yarn': Shakespeare and the Cloth Workers." *Literature and History* 12 (1986): 164–80.

Framing (the) Woman: The White Devil and the Deployment of Law

KATHRYN R. FININ-FARBER

THE SPECTACLES enacted on the early modern stage often reflect the highly litigious society from which they emerge: the drama of this period is full of legal representations, frequently written by men who were themselves trained at the Inns of Court.[1] John Webster is one such figure, and critics have seen parallels between his representation of Vittoria's arraignment in *The White Devil* and the contemporary trials of such diverse figures as Sir Walter Ralegh and Lady Penelope Rich.[2] Yet as Jean Howard has so persuasively argued, the stage does not merely reflect contemporary issues but itself enacts ideological contestation (34). Vittoria's arraignment, which is both the structural and thematic center of *The White Devil*, functions in just such a contestatory manner. While the murder of Vittoria's husband catalyzes legal intervention, Camillo's death is clearly not the focus of this criminal investigation. Vittoria's appearance before an ecclesiastical court demonstrates that the force of law, the authorized agent of state power, is brought to bear on Vittoria's flagrant violation of the chaste, silent, and obedient code for female behavior.[3] Such church courts had jurisdiction over moral values, "prosecut[ing] sexual and matrimonial offences," and Monticelso, the ecclesiastical representative in this play, indicts Vittoria in order to reinsert the promiscuous female body into her proper chaste place (Laurence 255). Vittoria not only rejects Monticelso's equation of unchastity with guilt, however, but engages in a transgressive mode of questioning which undermines our confidence in the very process whereby guilt is discovered.

This essay traces the way in which Vittoria calls into question the predetermined frames of reference which, to a large extent, determine the outcome of legal proceedings. She repeatedly works to undercut the stability of legal discourse, attacking the very oppositions that underlie and give this discourse meaning: such oppositions as "truth/untruth, guilty/innocent, consent/non-consent" (Smart 33).[4] Thus, *The White Devil* displays a gendered version of the "inequalities and corruptions of the legal system" which were the focus of so much public debate in this period (Goldberg 48).[5] That the promiscuous female body gives voice to some of the contemporary concerns about the propriety of the Jacobean legal system itself accounts for the oft-noted confusion about audience response to Vittoria. Charles Lamb, for example, described this phenomenon as Vittoria's "innocence-resembling boldness," which leads us to expect "when she has done her pleadings, that her very judges, her accusers, the grave ambassadors who sit as spectators, and all the court, will rise and make proffer to defend her in spite of the utmost conviction of her guilt" (qtd. in Moore 51).[6]

Lamb's unwavering belief in Vittoria's guilt rests upon her very real violation of the code of conduct for chaste women. I will argue, however, that Vittoria's suggestion of coerced consent in act 1 complicates the issue of her guilt. Critics have traditionally written this suggestion off as a specious line of defense, but Vittoria's claim appears less improbable when one looks at the emerging histories of crime in early modern England. In his study on illicit sexual activity, for example, G. R. Quaife asserts that "fear played a substantial yet often indirect role" in the eventual submission of single women, wives, and widows (66). This fear ranges from the threat of increased physical violence to the more pernicious spreading of rumors detailing a woman's supposed infidelity. The suggestion of coercion in act 1, of course, remains just that, but it provides both the basis of Vittoria's defense and a ground from which to judge her response to Monticelso's sentence: her piercing cry of rape. This charge of forced penetration articulates the complexly gendered relationship among Vittoria, the law, and the cultural assumptions law enforces; what it portends for the possibility of justice is a question we must take up if we are to avoid becoming complicit in the systems of domination deployed against Vittoria.[7]

I

Figuring (Out) the Female

Vittoria's "criminal" behavior is established early in this play, as are the ambiguities which will form the ground of her defense. Vittoria signals her rejection of the early modern code for proper female behavior both by welcoming Brachiano's sexual advances and then establishing the terms for her submission. She operates more like a shrewd businesswoman than an impassioned lover or a passive victim, telling Brachiano of her "foolish, idle dream," which involves a graveyard, a "goodly yew-tree," and their respective spouses, who "vow'd / To bury me alive" (1.2.221-23, 233-34). The would-be agents of her death, however, are intercepted:

> When to my rescue there arose methought
> A whirlwind, which let fall a massy arm
> From that strong plant,
> And both were struck dead by that sacred yew
> In that base shallow grave that was their due.
> (1.2.240-44)

In effect, Vittoria barters her chastity, exchanging her body for the death of her husband and Brachiano's wife. The figurative nature of this dream-story provides a gloss for the businesslike nature of her submission and simultaneously obscures her responsibility for generating these two murders.

The confusion that frequently accompanies dreams, where signs and their referents break apart, is markedly absent in this scene. Despite the imagery of castration within the dream itself, Vittoria's dream does not undermine the ability of words to function as reliable conveyors of meaning. Indeed, Brachiano signals his understanding of the doubled nature of Vittoria's "sacred yew" saying, "Sweetly shall I interpret this your dream: / You are lodged within his arms who shall protect you" (1.2.248-49). Flamineo also underscores the clarity of his sister's "dream" while simultaneously marking Vittoria's active participation in her own seduction: "Excellent devil," he observes, "She hath taught him in a dream / To make away his Duchess and her husband" (1.2.245-47). In the end, the confusion associated with dreams becomes displaced in this play and enters the stage during Vittoria's arraignment: that is, *The White Devil* locates confusion exactly where we would expect to find clarity—at the home of justice.

Thus, this text rejects the idealized view of law, preferring instead to stage the complex and messy reality of legal practice.

Vittoria's errancy, we should emphasize, is figured both sexually and linguistically in this seduction scene. Because she draws on the obfuscating power of language to convey her message, Vittoria breaches *rhetorical* as well as social decorum.[8] As Patricia Parker obsrves, the many handbooks of rhetoric and poetry in this period link order in language to social order. The double meaning of Vittoria's phrase "sacred yew," for example, violates the "proper discipline" of words advocated by someone like Thomas Wilson, author of *Arte of Rhetorique* and *The Rule of Reason,* because "the 'doubtfulnesse' of words—their capability of being 'twoo waies taken'— not only undermines reason's 'rule' but may lead to specious and *politically dangerous 'consequentes'* based on the transport of words outside an acceptable range of regulated meaning" (Parker 100; emphasis added). That Vittoria poses a danger to this particular political system is clear in the way her behavior is criminalized and brought under control in the arraignment scene.

Moreover, Vittoria's linguistic improprieties extend beyond the use of figurative language. She displays a disturbing propensity to reject the ideologically motivated frames of reference that allow us to judge behavior as proper or improper. Vittoria's sexual willingness in this scene, for example, is accompanied by a suggestion of coercion that confuses our traditional reading of these conditions as mutually exclusive. Explaining her behavior to Cornelia, Vittoria exclaims, "I do protest if any chaste denial, / If anything but blood could have allayed / His long suit to me" (1.2.280–82). Vittoria suggests that women may seem willing when, if fact, their "complicity" is a means of avoiding a more deadly solution. The work done by social historians provides a context in which to judge Vittoria's claim. Quaife, for example, finds that "[a] large number of matrons claimed that they had been forced" and cites numerous cases where "fear, violence and blackmail . . . played a significant role" in a woman's eventual submission (134). These fears are borne out in the cases where women reject a man's advances: the retribution such a woman faced ranges from death threats, to "smear[ing] her washing and front door with human excrement," to circulating rumors of the woman's infidelity (141). The threat of such rumors was a particularly potent form of coercion in this period—and not only because of the high value placed on a woman's sexual reputation. Ecclesiastical courts found the very "existence of such rumour, of such common fame was a fact in itself that the accused must be able to explain" (39). Of course, explaining such a rumor in an environment that naturalizes aggressive male sexuality and supposes a voracious sexuality in women is no easy task.

While Vittoria's status as a noble affords her a certain measure of protection unavailable to servant women or women of the middling sort, she is not immune to these cultural forces, as her own brother demonstrates. Prior to the liaison between Vittoria and Brachiano, Flamineo reassures the duke, who wants to "pursue [his] noble wishes" with "the fair Vittoria," but doubts her interest (1.2.4, 6):

what is't you doubt? her coyness? That's but the superficies of lust most women have . . . O they are politic! They know our desire is increas'd by the difficulty of enjoying; whereas satiety is a blunt, weary and drowsy passion. . . . (1.2.17-23)

Flamineo never considers the possibility of Vittoria refusing in any genuine way, only of *appearing* to refuse the duke.[9] Violence inevitably accompanies such an attitude because refusal is perceived as a game of deferral on the woman's part to be followed by the man's more forceful "persuasion."[10] Thus, while Vittoria's willingness would seem to render force unnecessary, we need to situate her submission within a cultural context that legitimizes aggressive male sexuality as a means to pierce a woman's always already feigned resistance.

This notion of force as a necessary and legitimate precursor to gaining a woman's consent pervades sexual politics throughout the ages, even while the particular forms of persuasion and violence shift. Andreas Capellanus, for example, in his treatise on courtly love, suggests a man "ought not to seek the love of a woman who you know will grant easily what you seek" (149), and as regards peasant women, he states:

do not hesitate to take what you seek and to embrace them by force. For you can hardly soften their outward inflexibility so far that they will grant you their embraces quietly or permit you to have the solaces you desire unless first you use a little compulsion as a convenient cure for their shyness. (150)

The gruesome reality of this medieval "cure" is obscured in Capellanus's text as well as in Flamineo's explanation of female "coyness." The violence that underlies such attitudes toward female resistance only becomes explicit much later, in the official discourse of nineteenth-century medical jurisprudence. As Anna Clark observes, these texts consistently confuse consent with surrender to violence: "In such works, men wrote 'contusions on various parts of the extremities and body . . . are compatible with final consent on the part of the female,' or 'it is to be recollected that many women will not consent without some force' . . . [and] asserted that it was impossible for one man to violate a conscious, healthy woman" (17). The issue of consent, which is so crucial to nineteenth- and twentieth-century definitions of rape, we should note, was a non-issue in medieval law, which viewed rape as a property crime, not a crime against the person. That this redefinition of rape occurs in the mid- to late sixteenth century, combined as it is with the potentially contradictory expectations for women to be chaste and obedient, marks the early modern period as a particularly complex moment in the long-lived story whereby men use "a little compulsion" to ensure their desire overrides any female resistance.

The references to aggressive male sexuality that frame Vittoria's submission lend support to her assertion that "no chaste denial" would have sufficed. Nevertheless, Vittoria suggests a victimization without allowing herself to become a victim. As a result, her mother, along with many critics, refuses to accept the violent undercurrent of Vittoria's "seduction" as a legitimate explanation for her behavior.[11] The ideology of this period requires a woman in Vittoria's situation to "submit to enforced sex, tell all afterwards, and kill herself" (Jardine 191). Vittoria's rejection of this equation is precisely what activates the law's intervention. Despite the inability of the postmodern period, let alone the early modern, to represent this complicated notion of coerced consent as anything but consent itself, Vittoria will base her defense on this very notion.

Initially, however, Monticelso pursues a series of non-legal actions in order to stop the illicit relationship between Brachiano and Vittoria. One such example is the "emblem" that Monticelso and Brachiano's brother-in-law, Francisco, present to Camillo in an attempt to convince him that he has been cuckolded. Camillo responds to this emblem with a reference to Ovid's story of Narcissus: "Here is a stag my lord hath shed his horns, / And for the loss of them the poor beast weeps. / The word *Inopem me copia fecit*" (2.1.322–24). Monticelso provides an "official" interpretation of the phrase: "That is, / Plenty of horns hath made him poor of horns" (2.1.324–25). Yet the Cardinal's clarification is oxymoronic and prompts Camillo to ask, "What should this mean?" (2.1.326). Monticelso then states his point as directly as possible, " 'tis given out / You are a cuckold" (2.1.326–27), but critics have long differed over how to read this Ovidian tag.[12]

Rather than try to resolve the confusion with yet another interpretation, it seems to me that this textual borrowing *introduces* confusion. We can see Webster's introduction of Ovid's Narcissus as the introduction of the other which so problematizes the Narcissus story and which proves so fundamental in Vittoria's arraignment. Ovid's Narcissus, as Claire Nouvet notes, is a story of a "criminal unresponsiveness" justly punished, "a narrative about responsibility . . . which it understands as it were etymologically (since responsibility comes from *respondere,* to respond), as the duty of responding to the call of the other" (104). She suggests that Narcissus's failure to respond to Echo is an inability to accept the otherness of the self, that is, the possibility of the self as a figural object rather than a stable subject:

> the fear of the other, the rejection of the other, the killing of the other, are all accomplished because a human subject tries to assure himself of both his selfhood and his humanity; they result from a proud self-assertion which, unwilling to confront the hypothesis that the self might be a mere figure, is therefore all too willing to reassure itself by *projecting this figural status onto the 'other,' and the other alone.* . . . the self can assert itself as a human subject only by positing an other [which] it deprives of both humanity and subjectivity. . . . [This] allows the self to ignore its own figural predicament and to believe in the possibility of a world cleansed of the threat of figurality. (131; emphasis added)

The figural threatens because in it meaning slips, the signifier becomes unanchored and the endless drift "prevents language from ever fulfilling itself in the determination of one, true, final meaning" (Nouvet 129). Historically, of course, woman has been associated with the figural, while the literal becomes the privileged (male) discourse precisely because of its apparent stability.[13] The introduction of Ovid's Narcissus, then, begins an assault on the (male) subject and the kind of "transparent" language this subject uses to reassure itself of its stability.

Ironically, Francisco responds to this emasculating presence of the figural by drawing on yet another mythical story that reenacts the very process Nouvet describes so well in her reading of Narcissus. Francisco tells Camillo a tale concerning "Phoebus the god of light, / Or him we call the sun, would need be married" (2.1.332–33). Responding to the pleas of all the various trade workers:

> [Jupiter] entreats of Jove
> That Phoebus might be *gelded,* for
> .   .   .   .
> What should they do if he were married
> And should beget more, and those children
> Make fireworks like their father?
> (2.1.343–49; emphasis added)

Francisco then shifts the subject of castration from the male god of light to Camillo's promiscuous wife, whose "issue, should not providence prevent it, / Would make both nature, time, and man repent it" (2.1.351–52). How are we to read this linking of the promiscuous female body to a story of castration? Traditionally, the female body functions as other precisely because it is already understood to be castrated: that is, "as a failed male body . . . as the pathetic obverse of the male, as a voracious mouth" (Newman 6). By connecting the story of castration to Vittoria, Francisco reasserts that which marks the female *as* different: a difference which is read hierarchically to reaffirm the male position of wholeness and centrality.

Despite Francisco's attempt to reassert the difference between male and female, his fear of the procreating promiscuous female displays the process through which woman is presented as "the dangerous, supplemental, figural term" who threatens the stable male subject (Waller 160). That is, his attempt to circumscribe the dangerous potential of the promiscuous female unwittingly conjures the disruptive potential of this "castrated" body: the specter of a castrated position that is originary, not secondary, a position that threatens the substantiality of the (male) subject.[14] Maintaining the otherness of this "castrated" female body who calls into question his status as a stable and dominating subject has everything to do with Monticelso's criminal unresponsiveness throughout Vittoria's arraignment. In order for his subject status to be secure, this woman must be forced to take up her proper role in the signifying system, which Judith Butler describes as the need to "everywhere reassure . . . [masculine] power of the reality of its illusory autonomy" (45). Rather than functioning as a "reassuring sign," however, a " 'being for' a masculine subject who seeks to reconfirm and augment his identity" (45), the promiscuous female body in this play repeatedly calls into question the authority and stability of the masculine subject.

II
Resisting Rhetoric

Like many legal proceedings, Vittoria's arraignment attempts to reestablish the boundary between what the dominant group defines as proper and
improper behavior. Monticelso focuses on proving what he calls Vittoria's
"black lust," which "shall make her infamous / To all our neighbouring
kingdoms" (3.1.7-8). Such an indictment will enable Monticelso to circumscribe the danger of the promiscuous female body whose unleashed
sexuality "is seen as able to destroy all control, undermining the institutions
of society by threatening their continuity" (Belsey 165).[15] That all this
punitive attention is focused on Vittoria while Brachiano is reprimanded
privately points to the very public arena in which female sexuality is situated.[16] It is finally on the grounds of Vittoria's "public fault," the "corrupted
trial" she has made of her life, that the Cardinal sentences her (3.2.255,
258). Vittoria's relentless and transgressive mode of questioning, however,
illuminates how this entire proceeding is constructed around a male point
of view, focusing our gaze on the profoundly gendered nature of law.

Vittoria participates as actively in her trial as she did in her "seduction."
Her participation, however, is anything but cooperative as she repeatedly
attacks the trial's very mode of operation. Vittoria goes on the offensive
right from the start, rejecting the lawyer's use of Latin: "Pray my lord, let
him speak his usual tongue. / I'll make no answer else" (3.2.13-14). The
issue is not whether Vittoria understands Latin, for she does, but rather
Vittoria refuses to "have my accusation clouded / In a strange tongue: all
this assembly / Shall hear what you can charge me with" (3.2.18-20). As
Vittoria observes, the use of Latin divides the audience, both on stage and
off, along class lines, into those who can or cannot understand it. She seems
to be "working the crowd," insisting that the audience be included in the
entertainment such a public trial provided. Given that "it was desirable for
the Crown to gain approval of its judicial acts, particularly in cases involving
public figures, a defendant's ability to play to the gallery was not an entirely
negligible weapon" (Goldberg 45). More important, Vittoria signals her
refusal of male authority by calling into question the legitimacy of using
Latin in this context. As Joan Kelly points out, the learning of Latin is an
indicator of the decline in women's power during the Renaissance: "Latin
literacy . . . placed [a woman] as well as her brothers under male cultural
authority . . . male educators who, as humanists, suppressed romance and

chivalry to further classical culture, with all its patriarchal and misogynous bias" (35). Vittoria's rejection of Latin, then, is an attempt to shift the predetermined frame of reference which in and of itself disempowers her.

We should note that if Vittoria's sexual activity renders her criminal, her active participation in the courtroom only indicts her further, given the Renaissance commonplace that connects women's speech with wanton sexuality. Vittoria seems to typify the wife without virtue who is "lusty, headstrong and talkative. . . . Woman's moist humours, which make her lascivious, also loosen her tongue" (Jardine 104). Given this context, any defense Vittoria provides against charges of loose living will be considered an example of loose language, which the dominant ideology links tauto-logically back to promiscuous behavior.[17] Vittoria signals her awareness of this dilemma by asking Monticelso, "What is my just defense / By him that is my judge call'd impudence?" (3.2.125-26). While Vittoria will claim the right to "personate masculine virtue" (3.2.135), that is, to speak publicly in order to defend herself, there is no *proper* way for her to do so given what Parker calls "the complex of misogynist double entendres surrounding the figure of the woman who takes upon herself the traditional male role of the public orator pleading a 'cause' or 'case' in court" (106). Such a woman violates the stricture for women to be "identified with the property of the home . . . with a private rather than a common place" (104). Through a tropological linking, then, a woman's "private places" ipso facto become common when her "case," a term which in this context conflates female genitalia with legal terminology, is "so openly known to the world" (106).

By calling attention to how any verbal defense Vittoria makes in court reinforces the criminal charge, given the rules of the game, this text empha-sizes the gendered nature of legal discourse. Indeed, establishing such rules is one of the fundamental ways that law exercises power and serves the interests of the dominant group. As Carol Smart observes, "how they [the parties legally represented] are allowed to speak, and how their experience is turned into something the law can digest and process, is a demonstration of the power of law to disqualify alternative accounts" (11). Far from displaying the "law's fairness of operation," a necessary component of its effectiveness as J. A. Sharpe notes, this text suggests law is an important tool that shores up men's power to control women's movement and speech (*Early Modern* 12).[18] Such a reading demonstrates how law is deployed against the female body and simultaneously provides a way to understand why Vittoria chooses to fight the very process itself. Thus, despite the illegitimate nature of her stance, Vittoria's active participation enables her to establish an agency within a discourse that would render this woman silent, passive, and guilty by virtue of her very presence in the courtroom.[19]

Vittoria's response to the lawyer's semi-translated plea provides a good example of her disruptive defense and demonstrates her incessant resistance to the language of this legal proceeding. Appealing to the "Most literated judges," he says:

> connive your judgements to the view
> Of this debauch'd and diversivolent woman
> Who such a black concatenation
> Of mischief hath effected, that to extirp
> The memory of't, must by the consummation
> Of her and her projections—.
>
> (3.2.26–32)

Vittoria, however, refuses to allow the "obscurity of [the] charge to imply the assumption of guilt" (Champion 126), and she interrupts the lawyer for a second time:

> Surely my lords this lawyer here hath swallowed
> Some pothecary's bills, or proclamations.
> And now the hard and undigestible words
> Come up like stones we use give hawks for physic.
> Why this is Welsh to Latin.
>
> (3.2.35–39)

Vittoria not only marks the obfuscating nature of the lawyer's language, but her phrase "undigestible words" suggests something inherently alien or foreign in legal discourse. Moreover, Vittoria's comparison of Latin to Welsh infects the former, the language of the learned and the sacred, with the savage and barbarous qualities associated with the latter. Not only does her defense violate decorous feminine behavior, but it takes a particularly subversive form by calling attention to the treacherous potential within language itself: Vittoria's defense is offensive in more than one way.

Vittoria's unremitting focus on the language of this legal proceeding prevents the arraignment from advancing in its usual fashion. Frustrated by Vittoria's interruptions, the lawyer himself finally takes up this attention to language: "My lords, the woman / Knows not her tropes nor figures, nor

is perfect / In the academic derivation / Of grammatical elocution" (3.2.39–
42). Despite the fact that Vittoria's quasi-legal elocution is obviously more
lucid than the lawyer's, he accuses her of improper *grammatical* relations
so that, as in the seduction scene, her trespass doubles, moving from the
social to the rhetorical.[20] As a result, the opening of this legal proceeding displays an intersection between "unruly women and unruly tropes"
(Parker 98): it displays an unsettling lack of linguistic and social control in
the very arena constructed to enforce social order.

We need to shift the focus away from Vittoria's transgressions for a
moment, however, and ask what the lawyer's "tropes" and "figures" are
doing here in the first place. The *Oxford English Dictionary* defines the
word "trope" as "a figure of speech which consists in the use of a word or
phrase in a sense other than that which is proper to it," whereas the word
"figural" is defined as "any of the various 'forms' of expression deviating
from the normal arrangement or use of words which are adopted in order
to give beauty, variety or force to a composition." While the two terms
overlap, particularly because the literal and proper are so often linked
in rhetorical and philosophical discourse, the figural is understood to
be a kind of ornamental supplement to "normal," that is, plain or literal,
language.[21] This very association of figurative language with the improper
and ornamental has traditionally rendered it suspect and caused it to be
banned from "rational" discourse.[22] That the lawyer's complaint situates
figural language at the heart of law calls into question law's own ideology.
After all, the ostensible aim of law is to discover truth and render justice in
an impartial manner. But because figural language "wanders, dangerously,
from the fixed meanings that can be marshaled into the march of logical
'consequence'" (Parker 101), it undermines and problematizes this very
route to truth. The question of why tropes and figures are so important
in the legal process remains unanswerable given law's own ideology, but
when the veil of ideology is lifted we begin to see that the presence of
such figural language enables the dominant group to write its version of
the "truth," which it subsequently presents to the world as Truth. The
myths of law as impartial and justice as blind efface this nasty suggestion
that law and justice are profoundly interested ideological positions.[23]

As if sensing the danger of the lawyer's comment, Monticelso intervenes
and attempts to bring the unruliness of both the female and the figural
under control. The lawyer is dismissed and Monticelso promises Vittoria,
"I shall be plainer with you, and paint out / Your follies in more natural

red and white / Than that upon your cheek" (3.2.51-53). On one level, Monticelso situates plain language in opposition to the lawyer's figural language, and its difference resides in its obvious, literal, and singular meaning. That is, plain language posits a direct connection from signifier to signified. But the Cardinal's allusion to plain language also relies upon an opposing figure of the female body: Vittoria's supposedly painted and unnatural cheeks. Monticelso asserts this unnatural red as evidence of her guilt, yet Vittoria rejects the Cardinal's (single) interpretation. She defends herself by reintroducing the ambiguity of language: "Oh you mistake. / You raise a blood as noble in this cheek / As ever was your mother's" (3.2.53-55). While Monticelso uses the painted female body to render his promise of plain language meaningful, Vittoria relies upon the "natural-ness" of the maternal body to figure her innocence.[24] Who can determine, finally, whether this red signifies guilt or noble innocence? By presenting an alternative account, Vittoria renders ambiguous Monticelso's clear and obvious connection between signs and their referents. Of course, plain language proves to be an unattainable goal, since Monticelso cannot even purge the figural from his own discourse: the Cardinal's very promise to speak plainly itself relies upon the metaphor of "painting out" Vittoria's promiscuous behavior.[25]

Vittoria's decision to make language a central site of struggle will not change the outcome of this legal proceeding, but her resisting rhetoric does, finally, undermine the process itself by exposing Monticelso's pro-found partiality. The most flagrant example of the Cardinal's interested stance comes in response to Vittoria's challenge to his use of the word "whore." He asks, "Shall I expound whore to you? Sure I shall; / I'll give their perfect character" (3.2.78-79). Monticelso subsequently launches into a vituperative attack against Vittoria: an attack full of metaphors that invoke a powerful litany of the negative stereotypes surrounding women. Initially Monticelso draws on the notion of women as duplicitous temptresses whose fair appearance only masks a murderous reality, defining "whores" as "Sweetmeats which rot the eater" and "Poison'd perfumes" (3.2.80, 81).[26] He alludes to the "unnatural" nature of whores, comparing them to "Shipwrecks in calmest weather" (3.2.82), and claims they are evil, "the true material fire of hell" (3.2.85). The problem with such proliferating metaphors is that while each of his comparisons alludes to the point, Monticelso never finally arrives at his destination, which is to give us the "perfect character" of a whore. Rather than leading to a proper and stable signified, the word "whore" becomes a signifier associated with multiple signifieds: an overdetermined concept whereby a transgressive female body is made responsible for myriad social (and personal?) ills far beyond any reasonable scope.

Two examples from Monticelso's subsequent characterization of "whore" lend support to this notion. First, he expands his comparison and deepens his critique by linking whores to the absence that accompanies language, specifically legal language. He claims that whores are "those brittle evidences of law / Which forfeit all a wretched man's estate / For leaving out one syllable" (3.2.89–91). While Monticelso attempts to make the promiscuous female body responsible for this inability to achieve linguistic plenitude, he nonetheless suggests that no contract can cover all contingencies or master all aspects of its territory. Thus, he inadvertently joins *with* Vittoria in undermining the stability of patriarchal writ. Second, Monticelso claims that whores figure the corruptibility and fragility of the human body: "They are worse, / Worse than dead bodies, which are begg'd at gallows / And wrought upon by surgeons, to teach man / Wherein he is imperfect" (3.2.95–98). How are we to read this doubled "worse" which heightens an already excessively overwrought rhetoric? Women whose sexuality is unleashed and uncontrolled are twice worse than a criminal's corpse because they no longer "reassure [masculine] power of the reality of its illusory autonomy" (Butler 45). That is, a woman like Vittoria who has catalyzed this fury of linguistic excess functions as a *being,* rather than a "being for" who shores up masculine identity. Monticelso, we should note, attempts to reverse this process at the end of his vituperative attack. "What's a whore?" he asks; "She's like the guilty counterfeited coin / Which whosoe'er first stamps it brings in trouble / All that receive it" (3.2.98–101). A whore, it seems, merely reflects the man who first "stamps" her, and this returns woman to her comforting subjected status, while simultaneously effacing the woman herself, who becomes the familiar object of exchange between men. That Monticelso's metaphor "implicitly assigns blame to the guilty man," however, undercuts his presentation of "woman as the cause of social and metaphysical ruin" (Stevenson 162). Monticelso seems to arrive at a place he did not intend to visit and from which he cannot easily extricate himself. Just how this paranoid tirade furthers Monticelso's case is difficult to determine, yet the very excesses which characterize his speech reveal a fundamental anxiety that female promiscuity not only murders patriarchal control of women's sexuality, but may also undermine the very conditions which authorize a male-centered and male-dominated world.

We need to consider Monticelso's metaphoric language within the particular frame of this *legal* proceeding whose purpose is to reinsert the promiscuous female body into its proper chaste place, particularly given metaphor's status as the rhetorical figure most closely associated with a violation of proper place. Since metaphor is defined as "giving the thing a name that belongs to something else" it "usurp[s] the place properly occupied by the original term" and so involves a "transfer which is not quite proper, of a substitution which is also a displacement" (Parker 36–37). It is a transfer that finally seems to involve a trespass. In the end, rather than restoring propriety, Monticelso participates in a linguistic orgy that renders language, like the very woman he indicts, promiscuous.

Vittoria's resistance deepens as Monticelso's case proceeds, and the questions she raises, combined as they are with her refusal to cooperate, lend credence to her eventual claim of rape: in the end Monticelso forces his sentence on an unwilling woman who challenges the very grounds of his case. When, for example, the Cardinal produces his only real evidence, "a letter, / Wherein 'twas plotted he and you should meet" (3.2.190–91), Vittoria points to that which renders this evidence inconclusive, "You read his hot love to me, but you want / My frosty answer" (3.2.199–200). Vittoria's point, we should note, extends beyond this particular letter. Given her unremitting focus on the ambiguity of language, this response raises the specter of an inevitable inconclusiveness that problematizes all such legal evidence. Vittoria then exposes her fundamental opposition to this legal proceeding: she asks, "Condemn you me for that the Duke did love me?" (3.2.201). The implication of Vittoria's question is quite startling. She rejects the entire femme fatale tradition that lends meaning to the Cardinal's case: a tradition that transports male desire to the site of the (seductive) female body and renders her culpable, even criminal. Yet, in the end, male (hetero)sexuality is not the issue—there is no place for it as criminal. While we can shift focus from Vittoria's transgressions in order to examine the role of unruly figures in this arraignment, Vittoria herself is, finally, unable to shift the focus from the female body whose very presence in a legal setting always already renders her promiscuous.

Despite Vittoria's vociferous objections to the Cardinal's assumption of her guilt, Monticelso declares that the "thousand ducats" Brachiano sent to Vittoria "Twas interest for his lust" (3.2.219, 222). In her final and most overt attempt to undermine Monticelso's criminal case, Vittoria exclaims:

> Who says so but yourself? If you be my accuser
> Pray cease to be my judge, come from the bench,
> Give in your evidence 'gainst me, and let these
> Be moderators.
>
> (3.2.223–26)

While not uncommon in early modern courts, this doubled role of prosecutor/judge was increasingly contested by those pressing for legal reforms, precisely because of law's own claim to be the "symbolic embodiment of the impersonal claims of human justice" (Eagleton 47).[27] The English ambassador's description of Monticelso's attitude as "too bitter" only underscores Vittoria's claim of impropriety (3.2.107). More importantly, Vittoria's question, "Who says so but yourself?" makes explicit the problematic nature of the Cardinal's case: he *forces* a connection between what seems true and what is true. Thus Vittoria reveals the way Monticelso leaps from signifier to signified, establishing a metaphorical rather than a logical link between the two.[28] Absolute and unambiguous proof is difficult to come by, however. It can always be challenged since, as Monticelso's attempts to speak plain language show, the figural cannot be purged from language. In the end, plain language is an illusion that veils the enforced nature of singular meaning. This text, then, not only situates metaphor within the discourse of the arraignment, but implies that metaphor may operate as a structuring principle of law. Such a suggestion necessarily demystifies law, which claims its privileged status from its ability to establish the truth of events and therefore dispense justice impartially.

We should note, finally, that Vittoria's ambiguous stance in regard to the law plays a crucial role in her ability to undermine it so effectively. Since she has indeed violated the code of conduct for chaste women, Vittoria is certainly not innocent. But because she focuses on the context of her actions and interrogates the court's procedures, Vittoria has confused the very oppositions that underlie and give meaning to the legal system: such oppositions as "truth/untruth, guilty/innocent, consent/non-consent" (Smart 33). That is, by shifting the focus of the debate and revealing the gendered nature of this legal proceeding, Vittoria puts these terms themselves on trial and undermines our confidence in the very process whereby consent, guilt, and truth are established.

III
Penetrating Law—Forced Entry

Fully authorized by his title and gender, Monticelso brings this criminal proceeding to a close, and he does so by silencing Vittoria: "Nay hear me," he insists, "You shall have time to prate" (3.2.243–44). By defining her speech as a kind of babble, Monticelso not only infantilizes Vittoria, but undermines the legitimacy of the alternative account she presents throughout this arraignment. While such a move allows Monticelso to present the (one) "true" story, it simultaneously displays what Barbara Johnson calls law's "forcible transformation of ambiguity into decidability" (107). In a piercing refusal of this very process, however, Vittoria charges Monticelso with rape. That is, she describes the *normal* operation of masculine power as an illegitimate act of violence, suggesting law is a forced penetration rather than a penetrating force that discerns truth.

That the force of law has a deeply gendered thrust is borne out by the Cardinal's sentencing, a term that conflates linguistic and judicial closure. He releases Flamineo and Marcello, since "The court hath nothing now to charge you with" (3.2.251). Vittoria, by contrast, is condemned for her "public fault" (3.2.255). Monticelso declares: "Such a corrupted trial have you made / Both of your life and beauty . . . here's your sentence: you are confin'd / Unto a house of convertites" (3.2.258–62). The term "confin'd," which functions as a cultural substitute for childbirth, evokes linguistic evidence of Vittoria's (criminally) exercised sexuality even as it describes her punishment. While this particular mode of punishment, aimed at reform, was increasingly popular in the seventeenth century, it remains atypical for sexual offenses, especially those that had not produced a bastard child. The more likely scenario would have involved shaming the offender through public penance, "which normally involved the guilty party standing before the congregation in service time, dressed in a white sheet, carrying a white wand, and confessing the fault that had incurred punishment" (Sharpe, *Seventeenth-Century* 27). Vittoria's refusal to accept the equation of her unchastity with guilt, however, clearly renders this form of penitent punishment untenable.

Vittoria's reaction to this imposition of masculine authority signifies her complexly gendered relationship to the law and the cultural assumptions law enforces. "A rape, a rape!" she cries, "Yes, you have ravish'd justice, / Forc'd her to do your pleasure" (3.2.272–73). That Vittoria *figures* her treatment in this legal setting as a rape provides the culmination of her offensive challenge to masculine authority and the kind of language it wields. Unlike many of her counterparts in early modern drama, Vittoria uses the term "rape" metaphorically. On one level, then, Vittoria reintroduces the figural at the very point Monticelso seeks to circumscribe the destructive potential of the female body, undermining his attempt to bring the intersecting unruliness of the feminine and the figural under control. That she chooses this particular term of masculine sexual aggression, however, also signifies the *material* violence wreaked by such a gendered legal proceeding. Vittoria posits a modern notion of rape here, specifying the centrality of the female body in an act of rape, even while culturally it still signals a social emasculation for the men of the raped woman's family.[29]

Two sixteenth-century statues redefining rape as a legal category enable Vittoria to make her claim. As Nazife Bashar notes, "Statutes of 1555 and 1597 treated abduction separately from rape," and caused rape "to be seen as a crime against the person, not as a crime against property" (41). While such a change theoretically allows women to control their own bodies, the privileges accorded to masculine points of view throughout early modern culture, and particularly in the legal setting, prevent this legal redefinition of rape from empowering women in their day-to-day lives. Indeed, despite the seriousness with which rape was regarded by legal authorities and statutory law, Bashar details the way in which "law's *practical* application" marks a decided unwillingness among "[m]ale judges and juries . . . to punish in any way other males for any *sexual* offence against females" (33, 40; emphasis added). The archival evidence demonstrates that it was nearly impossible for an adult woman to prove rape: a crime that constituted less that one percent of all felony indictments in this period during which the legal definition of rape shifts from male property to the female body. Of the few cases successfully indicted, almost all involved the rape of girls under ten.[30] The usual outcome in cases involving adult women was a finding of "ignoramus," meaning "the case was rejected before trial due to lack of evidence," and this kind of acquittal occurred more than twice as often for rape than for other crimes (34). While this kind of hostile environment itself deters women from pursuing a rape prosecution, other cultural factors insured that many cases never even got to court. Consider, for example, women who became pregnant as a result of rape. Legal authorities such as William Lambarde and Sir Henry Finch agreed that "[r]ape is the forcible ravishment of a woman, but if she conceive it is not rape, for she cannot conceive unless she consent" (qtd. in Bashar 36).

This kind of historical evidence shows the "congruence between law and what might be called a 'masculine culture' " (Smart 2): a congruence Vittoria articulates with her use of the word "rape." Ironically, then, she appropriates this term, which historically expresses *male* victimization as a result of women's sexual vulnerability, in order to claim a legitimate subject position from which to attack the (predetermined) outcome of this legal proceeding.[31] While Vittoria is unable to prevent the imposition of masculine authority, her refusal to submit to this process—her resistance—calls into question the assumptions upon which this authority is based. It should come as no surprise, then, that Monticelso responds to Vittoria's rape charge by claiming she is "mad" (3.2.273). Monticelso must discredit her challenge to the dominating reality by portraying Vittoria as someone who has lost contact with reality. That Monticelso's version of the story counts as "truth" while Vittoria's is dismissed records the fate of those who, despite the obstacles, publicly challenge masculine prerogatives.

IV
Criminal Unresponsiveness: "What harms it justice?"

Vittoria's charge of rape, we should note, extends beyond her own experience. She aligns herself with "justice," frequently gendered feminine, and claims both have been "forced to do your [Monticelso's] pleasure" (3.2.273). While Monticelso dismisses her charge, the cultural context surrounding rape, that its victim is irreparably compromised, proves to be an accurate representation of justice in this play. Indeed what follows Vittoria's arraignment is Francisco's revenge plot. This kind of "wild justice," to use Francis Bacon's phrase, exists in the margin between crime and justice and confuses the difference between these two categories (Belsey 115). Despite Vittoria's confinement, then, the destabilization of fixed categories continues to proliferate, and the excesses wreaked by revenge finally render "justice" a meaningless word rather than a framing concept around which a civilized society organizes itself. That the word "justice" conveys no legitimate authority, despite the many references to it in act 5, is seen in an exchange between Lodovico and Francisco.[32] Upon learning how Isabella was killed, Lodovico says, "Why now our action's justified" (5.3.265). Francisco, however, indicates the irrelevance of such justification: "Tush for justice. / What harms it justice?" (5.3.265-66). Francisco's question, as stated, is a rhetorical one and goes unanswered. Yet this question informs the entire play: justice does considerable harm when its textual counterpart, law, is shown to operate as a rape. If law is a forced penetration rather than a penetrating force that discerns truth, what *distinguishes* it from revenge, whose excessive violence undermines meaningful social intercourse?

In the end, this text sabotages the plot to deploy justice against the female body by launching an assault on that which makes justice possible. When Giovanni finally enters the scene as the heir apparent to legitimate authority, he unwittingly addresses the central issue: "You bloody villains," he asks, "By what authority have you committed / This massacre" (5.6.280-82). Masculine authority is itself on trial in this play because to undermine stable categories and the notion of proper place is to render everyone's place unauthorized: everyone becomes (a) suspect. That *The White Devil* stages such a criminal dilemma subverts Giovanni's comforting pronouncement, "All that have hands in this, shall taste our justice" (5.6.289). Justice itself needs to be revived.[33] As Vittoria's rape charge suggests, any such attempt must consider both language and gender. That is, we need to find a way of establishing social order without doing violence to the other, for there can be no legitimate revival of justice without responding to the voice of the other, the figural, in this case, the promiscuous female body.

Notes

1. For more on the overlapping of legal and theatrical settings, see Axton.

2. See Waage and Freedman, respectively.

3. While I use the singular form "law" throughout this essay, I follow Carol Smart's view that the unity of this term masks the way in which law "operates with conflicting principles and contradictory effects" (4). Smart claims that this power of law to define itself as "unified in intent, theory, and practice" is one of the major ways law exercises power (4). Maintaining law's own view of itself is important for my argument, which juxtaposes Vittoria's alternative view of law to this traditional one.

4. Thus, while Robert Ornstein suggests that this play suffers from "the lack of moral discriminations" (130), it seems to me that Vittoria launches an investigation into what constitutes "moral" or "ethical" behavior, showing that such terms are ideologically motivated by the dominant discourses, one of which is the law. Irving Ribner calls Webster's plays "an agonized search for moral order" and recognizes the plays' "moral confusion," but nevertheless accepts the very kind of traditional categories like good and evil which Vittoria problematizes (97, 99). In contrast, Dympna Callaghan argues that female transgression in

Renaissance tragedy "throw[s] moral order into confusion" (63). T. F. Wharton views this play as a "moral experiment" in which Webster "make[s] his audience extend their *ethical* tolerance into unheard-of areas" (59). Rupin Desai's phenomenological reading of the play, which suggests readers "invest it with meaning in keeping with our moral/ethical/cultural/social backgrounds" functions as an interesting frame for the widely divergent interpretations of this text (187).

5. Dena Goldberg, who provides a good discussion of Jacobean views of law, terms this a "pre-revolutionary" period "when legal philosophy and the structure of the legal system were alike characterized by . . . flux and turmoil" (48). See also *Renaissance Feminism* by Constance Jordan, especially her chapter on "Woman and Natural Law;" and Jonathan Dollimore's *Radical Tragedy,* which examines how this play "demystif[ies] state power and ideology" through a "process of displacement which shifts attention from individuals to their context and above all to a dominating power structure which constructs them as either agents or victims of power, or both" (231).

6. That Vittoria's defense confuses our traditional notions of guilt versus innocence has been noted by many critics. Travis Bogard, for example, observes that Webster created "a woman in whom good and evil combine to baffle ordinary moral judgment" (60). Lee Bliss argues that Webster "complicates any secure, unambivalent relation to [the play's] opposed characters," and notes, "[s]uch complications threaten conventional moral and emotional alignments" (97).

7. My point here is informed by Francis Barker's exploration of the complicity between "culture" and violence in *The Culture of Violence.*

8. Simon Shepherd notes that this kind of "[c]orrect speech has the ideological function of subsuming the individual subject within a social unit" (4). For more on the Renaissance notion of decorum, see Doran.

9. Peter Stallybrass situates Flamineo in the tradition of the malcontent and notes "how frequently the malcontent's analysis of power and corruption reverts to a withering contempt for the artifices of the powerless" despite the fact that "he himself is the most notable practitioner of the artifices of the powerless" (134).

10. Barker comments on this connection between persuasion and violence in his reading of Marvell's "To His Coy Mistress" (*Tremulous;* see esp. 92).

11. Ralph Berry, for example, calls Vittoria's explanation a "strange and unconvincing denial of personal responsibility" (102), while A. L. and M. K. Kistner write: "Vittoria, in defiance of the facts, places the blame on Brachiano's hot pursuit of her. . . . Like Lodovico, she refuses to accept responsibility for her part in the assignation although it is quite clear that she and Flamineo have schemed to invite Brachiano to her home and have dispatched her husband in preparation for the meeting" (14).

12. For example, F. L. Lucas notes that "the phrase *would* be intelligible, if taken to mean 'having so fair a wife has left me worse off than with no wife at all,' yet the translation in the next line—'Plenty of hornes hath made him poore of hornes'—remains obscure" (221). Lucas posits two possible interpretations but concludes "[p]robably the phrase as a whole applies only to the stag in the picture; and Camillo's only point of resemblance consists in being also a horned beast" (221). Waage writes, "the motto . . . seems to be introduced by the plotters to make Camillo's condition so obvious . . . that he will be strongly driven to accept the

commission to escape shame. It is an ironic emblem, in being predictive, not descriptive" (37). John Russell Brown "paraphrases Monticelso's comment as 'the plentiful sexual satisfaction others have received has meant that he has received none at all,' " while R. W. Dent "thinks that Brachiano is the stag, behaving traditionally after satisfying his lust; his loss of horns signifies the consequences of his hours with Vittoria" (Webster, ed. Brennan 145).

13. For more on this gendered division within language, see Ann Rosalind Jones's "Inscribing Femininity"; she examines how language is "a means through which men have shored up their claim to a unified identity and relegated women to the negative pole of binary oppositions that justify masculine supremacy: subject/object, culture/nature, law/chaos, man/woman" (80). See also Paul de Man's article on metaphor, in which he traces the historical connections between the figural and the female, and notes that both are perceived as having the power to seduce and mislead. He observes that figural language, "[l]ike a woman, which it resembles, . . . is a fine thing as long as it is kept in its proper place. Out of place, among the serious affairs of men, . . . it is a disruptive scandal—like the appearance of a real woman in a gentlemen's club where it would only be tolerated as a picture, preferably naked (like the image of Truth), framed and hung on the wall" (13-14).

14. Nouvet suggests that recognition of the "figural status of the self . . . 'dissolves' the assumed substantiality of the human figure defining it as precisely nothing more [than] a figure floating on the watery, nonhuman, nonsubjective Otherness of language. The notion of a substantial self 'dissolves' in its emergence as a mere figure of Speech" (127).

15. See also Callaghan 75-77 and Haselkorn.

16. For related discussions of how women's honor was constructed in terms of their sexuality, see Eaton and Greene.

17. See also "Patriarchal Territories" by Stallybrass, who looks at "definitions of woman as a male property category controlled or disciplined by codes that required of women a closed mouth (silence), a closed body (chastity), and an enclosed life in the home" (Ferguson, Quilligan, and Vickers xxxvi). For more on the code for proper female behavior in early modern England, see Hull; Henderson and McManus; and Hannay.

18. For more on the gendered nature of law, see Sachs and Wilson; Edwards; O'Donovan; and MacKinnon.

19. Catherine Belsey makes a similar point in regard to "[d]omestic absolutism [which] requires that women be able to speak in order to acquiesce, but it withholds the right to use that ability to protest or to make demands. To speak from a place of independence, from an autonomous position, to be, in other words, a subject, is to personate masculine virtue" (180-81).

20. H. Bruce Franklin also examines the rhetorical aspects of this scene and observes that the "ridiculous lawyer . . . focuses attention on the various characters' rhetorical styles, puts the audience on its rhetorical guard, and gives it a rhetorical yardstick. The audience will be able to measure ensuing rhetoric partially by comparing it to the lawyer's rhetoric" (39). See also Dallby, esp. 73-101.

21. This view accounts for works such as *An Index to the Figurative Language of John Webster's Tragedies* by Louis Charles Stagg, who excerpts "a key term from each image" and lists them alphabetically in order to provide an "additional tool" for comparative dramatic studies (iii).

22. For more on the problems figural language causes for all "discursive uses of language," see de Man.

23. Some of the most persuasive arguments for the interested nature of law and justice come from the colonized "third" world. See, for example, Ngugi wa Thiong'o's *The Trial of Dedan Kimathi,* which takes place in neocolonial Kenya and presents law as a tool of British oppression; see also *The Wine of Astonishment* by Earl Lovelace, who examines the oppressive nature of British law from a Caribbean perspective.

24. Frances Dolan's essay on art, nature, and face-painting in early modern England provides a rich and detailed historical context for the way in which Monticelso uses the discourse of face-painting to discredit Vittoria's self-fashioned agency while simultaneously drawing on "nature" to legitimize his attempt to reassert control over her; see esp. 229-32.

25. Franklin looks at the rhetoric of this scene and contrasts the Cardinal's "extravagant" and "highly mannered" language to the "extreme brevity" of Vittoria's language, which he characterizes as an example of Cicero's Attic style: that is, the very "plain language" Monticelso claims to use (43).

26. For more on misogynistic discourse as "a dramatic agent of violence and a vital instrument of gender differentiation," see Callaghan 123-30. For more on the duplicitous identity of women, see Loomba, esp. 73-74 and 79-80.

27. Goldberg points to three aspects of the Jacobean legal system that undermine this ideal of law: the "vendetta law," which promotes a "tendency to think of law as a form of vengeance"; the penal code, which resulted in approximately eight hundred hangings each year; and the "combative nature of the trial procedure," in which there was "no clear distinction between the functions of the judge and the prosecuting attorney" (34-35). It remains unclear, however, how the kind of partiality this text represents affected popular support for the ecclesiastical courts. J. A. Sharpe, for example, believes the unpopularity of the church courts has been overemphasized, and observes that these courts "could not have operated without a wide degree of popular support and co-operation" (*Early Modern* 26).

28. Larry Champion comments on this determination to "impose judgment whatever the legal consequences," even though Monticelso's "evidence is at best circumstantial" (126). "Despite Vittoria's guilt," he writes, "Webster forces the spectators to see Monticelso's actions, not as the ultimate endurance of moral values, but as the brute use of position and power to achieve familial vengeance" (127).

29. As Coppélia Kahn observes, such emasculation occurs in cultures that locate male honor in an exclusive right to the female body: his "manhood is tarnished" when this exclusivity is violated (132). See also Stimpson; Cunningham; and Vickers.

30. Sharpe and Quaife provide similar statistics concerning rape indictments, and all three historians agree that the number of actual rapes was underreported.

31. For more on men as victims of rape, see Deborah G. Burks's essay on *The Changeling,* which examines early modern cultural anxieties surrounding women's complicity with their rapists. For more on the importance of "restoring rape to the literal, to the body: restoring, that is, the violence—the physical, sexual violation" (4), see Higgins and Silver.

32. Jacqueline Pearson makes a similar point, although she attributes the meaninglessness of language to the imminence of death; see 81-83.

33. For more on how the discontinuities within the text problematize any easy route to

justice, see Dollimore's chapter on *The White Devil;* Belsey, especially her chapter "Autonomy"; and Loomba. For contrasting views that focus on this final scene as an example of
justice being served, see Berry and Kistner.

Works Cited

Axton, Marie. *The Queen's Two Bodies: Drama and the Elizabethan Succession.* London:
    Royal Historical Soc., 1977.
Bacon, Francis. "Of Revenge." *The Essays.* Ed. John Pitcher. Harmondsworth: Penguin, 1985.
    72-73.
Barker, Francis. *The Culture of Violence: Tragedy and History.* Chicago: U of Chicago P, 1993.
———. *The Tremulous Private Body: Essays on Subjection.* London: Methuen, 1984.
Bashar, Nazife. "Rape in England between 1550 and 1700." *The Sexual Dynamics of History:
    Men's Power, Women's Resistance.* Ed. London Feminist History Group. London: Pluto,
    1983. 28-42.
Belsey, Catherine. *The Subject of Tragedy: Identity and Difference in Renaissance Drama.*
    London: Methuen, 1985.
Berry, Ralph. *The Art of John Webster.* Oxford: Clarendon, 1972.
Bliss, Lee. *The World's Perspective: John Webster and the Jacobean Drama.* New Brunswick,
    NJ: Rutgers UP, 1983.
Bogard, Travis. *The Tragic Satire of John Webster.* Berkeley: U of California P, 1955.
Burks, Deborah G. " 'I'll Want My Will Else': *The Changling* and Women's Complicity with
    Their Rapists." *ELH* 62 (1995): 759-90.
Butler, Judith. *Gender Trouble: Feminism and the Subversion of Identity.* New York: Rout-
    ledge, 1990.
Callaghan, Dympna. *Woman and Gender in Renaissance Tragedy: A Study of* King Lear,
    Othello, The Duchess of Malfi *and* The White Devil. Atlantic Highlands, NJ: Humanities
    Press International, 1989.
Capellanus, Andreas. *The Art of Courtly Love.* Trans. John Jay Parry. Ed. Fredrick W. Locke.
    New York: Ungar, 1957.
Champion, Larry S. *Tragic Patterns in Jacobean and Caroline Drama.* Knoxville: U of
    Tennessee P, 1977.
Clark, Anna K. "Rape or Seduction? A Controversy over Sexual Violence in the Nineteenth
    Century." *The Sexual Dynamics of History: Men's Power, Women's Resistance.* Ed. London
    Feminist History Group. London: Pluto, 1983. 13-27.
Cunningham, Karen. " 'Scars Can Witness': Trials by Ordeal and Lavinia's Body in *Titus
    Andronicus.*" *Women and Violence in Literature.* Ed. Katherine Anne Ackley. New York:
    Garland, 1990. 139-62.
Dallby, Anders. *The Anatomy of Evil: A Study of John Webster's* The White Devil. Lund:
    Gleerup, 1974.
de Man, Paul. "The Epistemology of Metaphor." *On Metaphor.* Ed. Sheldon Sacks. Chicago: U
    of Chicago P, 1979. 11-28.
Desai, Rupin W. " 'Spectacles fashioned with such perspective art': A Phenomenological

Reading of Webster's *The White Devil.*" *Medieval & Renaissance Drama in England* 1 (1984): 187-98.

Dolan, Frances E. "Taking the Pencil out of God's Hand: Art, Nature, and the Face-Painting Debate in Early Modern England." *PMLA* 108 (1993): 224-39.

Dollimore, Jonathan. *Radical Tragedy: Religion, Ideology and Power in the Drama of Shakespeare and his Contemporaries.* Chicago: U of Chicago P, 1984.

Doran, Madeleine. *Endeavors of Art: A Study of Form in Elizabethan Drama.* Madison: U of Wisconsin P, 1954.

Eagleton, Terry. *William Shakespeare.* Oxford: Blackwell, 1986.

Eaton, Sara. "Defacing the Feminine in Renaissance Tragedy." *The Matter of Difference: Materialist Feminist Criticism of Shakespeare.* Ed. Valerie Wayne. Ithaca: Cornell UP, 1991. 181-98.

Edwards, Susan S. M. *Female Sexuality and the Law: A Study of Constructs of Female Sexuality as They Inform Statute and Legal Procedure.* Oxford: Robertson, 1981.

Ferguson, Margaret W., with Maureen Quilligan and Nancy J. Vickers. Introduction. *Rewriting the Renaissance: The Discourses of Sexual Difference in Early Modern Europe.* Ed. Ferguson, Quilligan, and Vickers. Chicago: U of Chicago P, 1986. xv-xxxi.

Franklin, H. Bruce. "The Trial Scene of Webster's *The White Devil* Examined in Terms of Renaissance Rhetoric." *Studies in English Literature* 1.2 (1961): 35-51.

Freedman, Sylvia. "*The White Devil* and the Fair Woman with a Black Soul." *Jacobean Poetry and Prose: Rhetoric, Representation, and the Popular Imagination.* Ed. Clive Bloom. New York: St. Martin's, 1988. 151-63.

Goldberg, Dena. *Between Worlds: A Study of the Plays of John Webster.* Waterloo, ON: Wilfrid Laurier UP, 1987.

Greene, Gayle. "Women on Trial in Shakespeare and Webster: 'The Mettle of [their] Sex.'" *Topic: A Journal of the Liberal Arts* 36 (1982): 5-19.

Hannay, Margaret Patterson, ed. *Silent But for the Word: Tudor Women as Patrons, Translators, and Writers of Religious Works.* Kent, OH: Kent State UP, 1985.

Haselkorn, Anne M. "Sin and the Politics of Penitence: Three Jacobean Adulteresses." *The Renaissance Englishwoman in Print: Counterbalancing the Canon.* Ed. Haselkorn and Betty S. Travitsky. Amherst: U of Massachusetts P, 1990. 119-36.

Henderson, Katherine Usher, and Barbara F. McManus, eds. *Half Humankind: Contexts and Texts of the Controversy about Women in England, 1540-1640.* Urbana: U of Illinois P, 1985.

Higgins, Lynn A., and Brenda R. Silver. Introduction. *Rape and Representation.* Ed. Higgins and Silver. New York: Columbia UP, 1991. 1-11.

Howard, Jean E. *The Stage and Social Struggle in Early Modern England.* New York: Routledge, 1994.

Hull, Suzanne W. *Chaste, Silent & Obedient: English Books for Women, 1475-1640.* San Marino, CA: Huntington Library, 1982.

Jardine, Lisa. *Still Harping on Daughters: Women and Drama in the Age of Shakespeare.* New York: Columbia UP, 1983.

Johnson, Barbara. *The Critical Difference: Essays in the Contemporary Rhetoric of Reading.* Baltimore: Johns Hopkins UP, 1980.

Jones, Ann Rosalind. "Inscribing Femininity: French Theories of the Feminine." *Making a Difference: Feminist Literary Criticism*. Ed. Gayle Greene and Coppélia Kahn. London: Routledge, 1985. 80–112.

———. "Surprising Fame: Renaissance Gender Ideologies and Women's Lyric." *The Poetics of Gender*. Ed. Nancy K. Miller. New York: Columbia UP, 1986. 74–95.

Jordan, Constance. *Renaissance Feminism: Literary Texts and Political Models*. Ithaca: Cornell UP, 1990.

Kahn, Coppélia. *Man's Estate: Masculine Identity in Shakespeare*. Berkeley: U of California P, 1981.

Kelly, Joan. *Women, History, and Theory*. Chicago: U of Chicago P, 1984.

Kistner, A. L., and M. K. Kistner. "*The White Devil* and John Webster." *Studia Neophilologica* 61 (1989): 13–21.

Laurence, Anne. *Women in England, 1500–1760: A Social History*. New York: St. Martin's, 1994.

Loomba, Ania. *Gender, Race, Renaissance Drama*. Manchester: Manchester UP, 1989.

Lovelace, Earl. *The Wine of Astonishment*. Oxford: Heinemann, 1982.

Lucas, F. L., ed. *The Complete Works of John Webster*. 4 vols. Boston: Houghton, 1928. Vol. 1.

MacKinnon, Catharine A. *Feminism Unmodified: Discourses on Life and Law*. Cambridge: Harvard UP, 1987.

Moore, Don D., ed. *Webster: The Critical Heritage*. London: Routledge, 1981.

Newman, Karen. *Fashioning Femininity and English Renaissance Drama*. Chicago: U of Chicago P, 1991.

Nouvet, Claire. "An Impossible Response: The Disaster of Narcissus." *Yale French Studies* 79 (1991): 103–34.

O'Donovan, Katherine. *Sexual Divisions in Law*. London: Weidenfeld & Nicolson, 1985.

Ornstein, Robert. *The Moral Vision of Jacobean Tragedy*. Madison: U of Wisconsin P, 1960.

Parker, Patricia. *Literary Fat Ladies: Rhetoric, Gender, Property*. London: Methuen, 1987.

Pearson, Jacqueline. *Tragedy and Tragicomedy in the Plays of John Webster*. Manchester: Manchester UP, 1980.

Quaife, G. R. *Wanton Wenches and Wayward Wives: Peasants and Illicit Sex in Early Seventeenth Century England*. New Brunswick, NJ: Rutgers UP, 1979.

Ribner, Irving, *Jacobean Tragedy: The Quest for Moral Order*. New York: Barnes & Noble, 1962.

Sachs, Albie, and Joan Hoff Wilson. *Sexism and the Law: A Study of Male Beliefs and Legal Bias in Britain and the United States*. Oxford: Robertson, 1978.

Sharpe, J. A. *Crime in Early Modern England, 1550–1750*. London: Longman, 1984.

———. *Crime in Seventeenth-Century England: A County Study*. London: Cambridge UP, 1983.

Shepherd, Simon. *Amazons and Warrior Women: Varieties in Feminism in Seventeenth-Century Drama*. Brighton: Harvester, 1981.

Smart, Carol. *Feminism and the Power of Law*. London: Routledge, 1989.

Stagg, Louis Charles. *An Index to the Figurative Language of John Webster's Tragedies*. Charlottesville: UP of Virginia, 1967.

Stallybrass, Peter. "Patriarchal Territories: The Body Enclosed." *Rewriting the Renaissance:*

The Discourses of Sexual Difference in Early Modern Europe. Ed. Margaret W. Ferguson, Maureen Quilligan, and Nancy J. Vickers. Chicago: U of Chicago P, 1986. 123–42.

Stevenson, Sheryl A. " 'As Differing as Two Adamants': Sexual Difference in *The White Devil.*" *Sexuality and Politics in Renaissance Drama.* Ed. Carole Levin and Karen Robertson. Lewiston, NY: Mellen, 1991. 159–74.

Stimpson, Catherine R. "Shakespeare and the Soil of Rape." *The Woman's Part: Feminist Criticism of Shakespeare.* Ed. Carolyn Ruth Swift Lenz, Gayle Greene, and Carol Thomas Neely. Urbana: U of Illinois P, 1980. 56–64.

Vickers, Nancy. " 'The blazon of sweet beauty's best': Shakespeare's *Lucrece.*" *Shakespeare and the Question of Theory.* Ed. Patricia Parker and Geoffrey Hartman. New York: Methuen, 1985. 95–115.

wa Thiong'o, Ngugi. Excerpt from *The Trial of Dedan Kimathi. Barrel of a Pen: Resistance to Repression in Neo-Colonial Kenya.* Trenton: Africa World P, 1983. 5–6.

Waage, Frederick O. *The White Devil Discover'd: Backgrounds and Foregrounds to Webster's Tragedy.* New York: Lang, 1984.

Waller, Marguerite. "Usurpation, Seduction, and the Problematics of the Proper: A 'Deconstructive,' 'Feminist' Rereading of the Seductions of Richard and Anne in Shakespeare's *Richard III.*" *Rewriting the Renaissance: The Discourses of Sexual Difference in Early Modern Europe.* Ed. Margaret W. Ferguson, Maureen Quilligan, and Nancy J. Vickers. Chicago: U of Chicago P, 1986. 159–74.

Webster, John. *The White Devil.* Ed. Elizabeth M. Brennan. New Mermaids Series. London: Benn, [1966] 1978.

Wharton, T. F. *Moral Experiment in Jacobean Drama.* New York: St. Martin's, 1988.

Notes on Contributors

KAREN CUNNINGHAM is associate professor of English at The Florida State University in Tallahassee, where she teaches Shakespeare, Renaissance drama, and gender studies. Her articles on early modern literature, law, and pedagogy have appeared in such journals as *PMLA, Journal of Medieval and Renaissance Studies*, and *Exemplaria*. She is currently working on a book, *"Desperate Imaginings": Early Modern Treason and Drama*, from which the present essay is drawn.

CONSTANCE JORDAN is the author of *Renaissance Feminism: Literary Texts and Political Models* (Cornell, 1990). She is currently at work on a book about Shakespeare's romances.

LUKE WILSON is assistant professor of English at Ohio State University. He has published articles on Renaissance literature in *Representations, Studies in the Literary Imagination, ELH,* and *Cardozo Studies in Law and Literature*, and is currently completing a book on human agency in early modern English legal and theatrical discourse.

M. LINDSAY KAPLAN is assistant professor of English at Georgetown University. She has published several essays on slander and early modern women's legal concerns. She is co-editor of and a contributor to *Feminist Approaches to Early Modern Culture: Emerging Subjects and Subjectivities* (Cambridge, 1996). She is currently completing a book on the culture of slander in early modern England.

KATHERINE EGGERT is assistant professor of English at the University of Colorado, Boulder. She has published essays on *Henry V* and *The Faerie Queene*, and is completing a book entitled *Showing Like a Queen: Female Authority and Literary Experiment in Spenser, Shakespeare, and Milton*.

JODI MIKALACHKI, assistant professor of English at Wellesley College, has written on female vagrants, feminist Milton criticism, and most recently on *Cymbeline* and early modern English nationalism. She is completing a book on the recovery of native origins in early modern England.

CHARLES STANLEY ROSS is professor of English and comparative literature at Purdue University. His translation of Boiardo's *Orlando Innamorato* has been reprinted by Oxford in the World's Classics series. His new book, *The Custom of the Castle from Malory to Macbeth*, will be published this year (California, 1996).

PAT MCCUNE is assistant director of the Program in British Studies at the University of Michigan. She is currently writing about the female personification of justice in late medieval British and Netherlandish manuscripts.

NINA LEVINE, assistant professor of English at the University of South Carolina, has published articles on Shakespeare and is currently completing a book about the politics of gender in Shakespeare's history plays.

KATHRYN R. FININ-FARBER is a Ph.D. student in the Department of English at the State University of New York at Binghamton. She is currently completing her dissertation, "Justice, Language, and the Female Body in Early Modern Drama."